WEGO LIBRARY FOUNDATION

TOP 16 SECRETS OF WEALTH CREATION BY PATENT

"This book serves as a comprehensive guide for aspiring innovators, offering a step-by-step roadmap to transform their ideas into patented products. It covers everything from patent filing and commercialization strategies to patent valuation methods. GI, Design, copyright & Trademark"

Top 16 Secrets of Wealth creation by Patent

Author

WeGo Library Foundation

Co-authors & Contributors

Dr. Raosaheb Ghegade
Dr. Mohini Suryawanshi
Dr. Datta Gujarathi
Dr. S G More
Dr. Prakhar singh
Dr. Nilesh Pawaskar
Parag Khedkar
Shrikant Joshi
Ninad Kulkarni
Anand Jadhav
Ravi Thatte
Unmesh Deshmukh
Sanjay Khanzode
Uday Wad
Mahendra Pangarkar
Milind Tare
Ravi Bedekar
Dr Asmita Hawaldar
Dr Nikhil Pathak
Advocate Mayuri Pawar
Umesh Jadhav
Girish Kuber
Nikhil Tapadia
CA Prakash Pathak
CA Vivek Garud
Omprakash Rawat
MG Kulkarni
M M Patil
Yogmaya Verma
Nilesh Kapdne
Ujwala Jagtap
Satish Jagtap
Anant Gosavi
Akshay Jadhav
Nisha Wable - Jadhav
Jayant Thomre
Smita Shinde

"This book serves as a comprehensive guide for aspiring innovators, offering a step-by-step roadmap to transform their ideas into patented products. It covers everything from patent filing and commercialization strategies to patent valuation methods. GI, Design, copyright & Trademark"

The True Path to Becoming a Superpower: Research, Patents, and Commercialisation

Desire without determination achieves nothing. For years, India has aspired to become a global superpower—but for a long time, those aspirations lacked the conviction, planning, and execution required to make them a reality. Today, however, the landscape is shifting. What was once dismissed as wishful thinking is now transforming into a national mission driven by commitment, planning, and action.
A nation's strength lies in its economy. Economic independence means producing what we need, exporting what others need, and reducing reliance on imports. But it goes beyond just production and trade—strong economies are built on innovation, security, and adaptability. Complacency is not an option in a world that rewards growth and punishes stagnation.

The Missing Link: A Culture of Research
India has long underutilised one of its most valuable resources—its youth. Instead of cultivating curiosity and creativity, our education system has focused narrowly on grades and job security. Parents push children toward safe careers, and institutions churn out degree-holders. In the process, imagination and innovation are stifled.

To become a surplus economy—one that not only meets its own needs but also supports others—we must groom our youth for research, innovation, and entrepreneurship. The goal must shift from merely getting a job to creating opportunities, businesses, and solutions.

A Systemic Shift Needed
While a few educational institutions promote research, most are designed to produce employable graduates, not inventors. A glance at newspapers shows a growing number of Ph.D. recipients, yet India's global contribution to innovation remains modest. Why? Because much of this research is done for academic qualifications, not real-world impact. It's aimed at promotions, not patents.

Patents hold economic power. They bring international credibility, open markets, attract foreign exchange, generate employment, and stimulate industrial growth. Research must be seen not as an academic formality but as a national economic strategy.

Creating the Right Ecosystem
The talent exists—Indians are leading global corporations and technological advancements abroad. But the country lacked an infrastructure to nurture this talent at home—until now.

The WeGo Library Foundation: A Game-Changer
Dr. Nilesh Pawaskar and a group of like-minded visionaries have launched WeGo Library Foundation, an institution committed to building a complete research ecosystem. From selecting a research topic to filing patents and finally converting them into marketable products, WeGo supports researchers at every stage.

The Foundation collaborates with institutions like Savitribai Phule Pune University, YCMOU, KBCNMU, and the Maharashtra Adivasi Vikas Mandal. With a network of 300 experts, WeGo embodies the belief that one product can employ thousands—and those thousands build the nation through their work and taxes.

But WeGo is more than an institution—it's a movement. Modeled as a modern-day Nalanda, it aims to become a treasure trove of knowledge, offering both physical and digital libraries, expert mentorship, and even Nobel laureates on its advisory panels.

Looking Ahead
India is finally moving in the right direction. With visionary projects like WeGo and growing government support for research and innovation, the dream of becoming a developed nation is no longer a distant goal—it is a work in progress.

Dr. Nilesh Pawaskar
Founder,
WeGo Library Foundation

Table of Content

1-01: BASICS OF PATENT

Introduction: A patent is a legally recognised privilege that the government bestows on the creator of an invention, which can be a process, a product, or simply a novel approach to a problem. In return for full disclosure of the innovation, the country or regional patent office grants this right. The invention is protected by a patent, which means that it cannot be used, sold, distributed, or manufactured commercially without the patent owner's permission. A court, which has the power to prevent patent infringement, is typically where these rights are enforced. In contrast, if a third party successfully challenges a patent, the court may also rule that the patent is invalid. Patent protection is granted for a limited period, generally twenty years.

What a Patent Is?
- **Legal Protection:**
A patent is a form of intellectual property that protects inventions, providing the inventor with the right to exclude others from making, using, selling, or importing the patented invention for a specific period.
- **Exclusivity:**
The core benefit of a patent is the exclusivity it grants to the patent holder, allowing them to control the commercialization of their invention.
- **Incentive for Innovation:**
Patent laws aim to encourage innovation by providing inventors with a financial incentive to develop and disclose their inventions.
- **Public Disclosure:**
In exchange for the exclusive rights granted by a patent, the inventor is required to publicly disclose the invention, making it available for others to build upon.

Need of Patent :
➤ The importance of patents lies in the protection they provide to inventors and their inventions. Patents help to safeguard an inventor's hard work and investment in research and development by preventing others from making, using, selling, or importing the invention without permission. This exclusive right to the invention can be licensed or sold to others, providing inventors with valuable commercialization opportunities and revenue streams.

➤ Patents also promote innovation and economic growth by incentivizing inventors and companies to invest in research and development, as they know that they will have legal protection and a competitive advantage for their ideas. Patents encourage the sharing of ideas and knowledge, as inventors must publicly disclose their inventions in order to obtain a patent. This public disclosure can help to spur further research and development in related fields.

➤ However, there are also potential drawbacks to patents. Some argue that patents can stifle innovation by creating monopolies and preventing competition. Additionally, patents can be expensive and time-consuming to obtain and enforce, making it more difficult for small inventors or startups to compete with larger companies that have more resources to devote to the patent process.

➤ Overall, patents play an important role in protecting inventors, promoting innovation and economic growth, and incentivizing research and development. It is important for inventors and companies to understand the patent process and how it can benefit their businesses and the broader technological landscape.

Rationale Behind IPR:
The primary rationale behind Intellectual Property Rights (IPR) is to encourage innovation and creativity by granting creators and inventors exclusive rights to their work, allowing them to profit from their investments and recoup research and development costs. This incentivizes further investment in research, development, and the creation of new products and services, ultimately benefiting society.

- **Incentivizing Innovation and Creativity:**
IPRs, such as patents, copyrights, and trademarks, provide creators and inventors with exclusive rights to their creations, allowing them to control how their work is used and distributed. This protection encourages individuals and organizations to invest time, effort, and resources into developing new ideas and products.

- **Economic Growth and Development:**
By protecting intellectual property, countries can foster a more competitive and innovative economy, attracting investment and creating jobs. IPRs also facilitate the transfer of technology and knowledge through licensing and other means, contributing to economic growth and development.

- **Protecting the Rights of Creators:**
IPRs recognize the rights of creators and inventors to their intellectual property, ensuring that they can benefit from their work and that their creations are not copied or exploited without their permission.

- **Promoting Fair Competition:**
By providing legal protection for intellectual property, IPRs help ensure that businesses can compete fairly on the basis of the quality and innovation of their products and services.

- **Consumer Protection:**
Trademarks and other IPRs help consumers identify and differentiate products and services, protecting them from imitation or counterfeit goods.

- **Facilitating Trade and Commerce:**
IPRs play a crucial role in international trade, ensuring that businesses can protect their intellectual property in foreign markets and that trade disputes can be resolved fairly.

- **Balancing Public Interest:**
While IPRs provide exclusive rights to creators, they also recognize the importance of the public interest, ensuring that knowledge and innovation are eventually made available to the public.

- **Examples of IPRs:**
- **Patents:** Protect inventions, giving inventors exclusive rights to use, sell, and make their invention for a limited period.
- **Copyright:** Protects original works of authorship, such as books, music, and software.
- **Trademarks:** Protect brand names and logos, helping consumers identify and distinguish products and services.
- **Industrial Designs:** Protect the aesthetic appearance of products.
- **Trade Secrets:** Protect confidential information, such as formulas or processes, that give a business a competitive advantage.

History of Patent:

- In India, the Act VI of 1856 was the first patent-related law. This law was designed to incentivize inventors to reveal the secrets of their creations and to promote the development of new and practical gadgets. The Act was later revoked by Act IX of 1857 since the British Crown had not given its consent for its existence. As Act XV of 1859, new legislation was adopted in 1859 to grant "exclusive privileges." Certain changes to the previous law were included in this one, including the expansion of the priority period from six to twelve months and the exclusive benefits granted to only valuable discoveries. This Act excluded importers from the definition of inventor. With a few exceptions, such as permitting assignees to submit applications in India and requiring prior public use or publishing in India or the UK to determine novelty, this Act was modelled after the United Kingdom Act of 1852.

- The Act of 1859 was consolidated in 1872 to offer design protection. Act XIII of 1872 changed its name to "The Patterns and Designs Protection Act." The Act of 1872 was further modified in 1883 (XVI of 1883) to include a clause protecting the uniqueness of inventions that were revealed at the Indian Exhibition before an application for protection was filed. There was a six-month grace period for submitting these applications following the exhibition's opening date.

- For over 30 years, this Act remained unchanged. However, in 1883, the United Kingdom made several changes to its patent law, and it was thought that the Indian legal system should similarly adopt those changes. To bring the laws pertaining to inventions and designs into line with the changes made to U.K. law, an Act was introduced in 1888.

- The Act II of 1911, which replaced all earlier Acts, was the Indian Patents and Designs Act of 1911. This Act placed the Controller of Patents in charge of managing patent administration for the first time. To establish reciprocal agreements with the UK and other nations to ensure priority, this Act was further modified in 1920. Further revisions were made in 1930 to include, among other things, clauses pertaining to the granting of secret patents, patents of addition, government use of inventions, the Controller's authority to update the patent register, and the extension of the patent's length from 14 to 16 years. An amendment was introduced in 1945 that stipulated that the tentative specification must be filed, and the full specification must be submitted within nine months.

- It was believed that the Indian Patents & Designs Act, 1911, was not accomplishing its goal after independence. Enacting comprehensive patent legislation was deemed necessary due to significant shifts in the nation's political and economic landscape. As a result, in 1949, the Indian government established a committee to evaluate the country's patent laws and make sure they serve the interests of the country. The committee was chaired by Justice (Dr.) Bakshi Tek Chand, a retired judge from the Lahore High Court. Among the terms of reference were—To survey and report on the working of the patent system in India.

  - To review India's current patent laws and offer suggestions for their improvement, especially in relation to the clauses pertaining to the prevention of patent rights misuse.
  - To determine if food and medical patents should be subject to any limitations.

- To make recommendations for actions to guarantee efficient promotion of the patent system and patent literature, especially with reference to patents acquired by Indian innovators.
- To evaluate whether establishing a National Patents Trust is necessary and feasible.
- To evaluate whether it would be beneficial to regulate the patent agent profession.
- To assess the Patent Office's operations and public services and offer appropriate suggestions for enhancement;
- To provide a general report on any enhancements the Committee deems appropriate to suggest in order to make the Indian Patent System more advantageous to the country by promoting innovation and the commercial development and application of inventions.

- On August 4, 1949, the committee turned in its interim report, which included suggestions for preventing the abuse or exploitation of patent rights in India as well as changes to sections 22, 23, and 23A of the Patents & Designs Act, 1911 that were modelled after the UK Acts of 1919 and 1949. The committee also noted that the Patents Act ought to include explicit provisions guaranteeing that food, medications, and surgical and therapeutic equipment are made accessible to the public at the most affordable cost while providing the patent holder with fair recompense.

- • The 1911 Act was modified in 1950 (Act XXXII of 1950) to address the operation of inventions and forced licensing/revocation in accordance with the Committee's proposal. Additional clauses dealt with the Government endorsing the patent with the phrase "licence of right" on an application so that the Controller could issue licenses. Act LXX of 1952 amended the law to require licenses for patents on food and medical products, insecticides, germicides, fungicides, and manufacturing processes, as well as any inventions pertaining to surgical or therapeutic instruments. The Central Government's notice also made mandatory licensing available. Based on the recommendations of the Committee, a bill was introduced in Parliament in 1953 (Bill No.59 of 1953). However, the Government did not press for the consideration of the bill, and it was allowed to lapse.

- The Justice N. Rajagopala Ayyangar Committee was established by the Indian government in 1957 to investigate the possibility of revising the Patent Law and provide the government with recommendations. Both sections of the Committee's report were turned in in September 1959. General aspects of the Patent Law were covered in the first section, while certain clauses of the 1953 acts that had lapsed were covered in depth in the second. The first section also addressed the drawbacks of the patent system and offered legal ideas for a remedy. Despite its flaws, the committee suggested keeping the Patent System in place. This report made significant legal recommendations that served as the foundation for the 1965 Patents Bill. On September 21, 1965, this measure was introduced in the Lok Sabha; unfortunately, it was never passed. The Patents Act of 1970 was passed on the Committee's final recommendation after a revised measure was filed once more in 1967 and sent to a Joint Parliamentary Committee. In terms of patent law, this Act superseded and abolished the 1911 Act. However, designs were still subject to the 1911 Act. With the release of the Patent Rules, 1972 on April 20, 1972, the majority of the 1970 Act's provisions became operative.

- Up to December 1994, this Act stayed in effect for roughly 24 years without any modifications. On December 31, 1994, an ordinance that made some revisions to the

Act was published; however, it was no longer in effect six months later. Another ordinance was then established in 1999. This ordinance was later superseded by the Patents (Amendment) Act, 1999, which went into effect retroactively on January 1, 1995. Applications for product patents in the fields of medications, pharmaceuticals, and agrochemicals might be filed under the modified Act, however these patents were prohibited. Nevertheless, these applications were only to be reviewed after December 31, 2004. In the meanwhile, if certain requirements are met, the applicants may be granted Exclusive Marketing Rights (EMR) to sell or distribute certain goods in India.

- The Patents (Amendment) Act, 2002 (Act 38 0f 2002) made the second amendment to the 1970 Act. This Act became operative on May 20, 2003, when the previous Patents Rules, 1972 were superseded by the new Patent Rules, 2003.

- With effect from January 1, 2005, the Patents (Amendment) Ordinance, 2004 brought the third amendment to the Patents Act 1970. On April 4, 2005, the Patents (Amendment) Act 2005 (Act 15 Of 2005) took the place of this Ordinance and went into effect on January 1, 2005.

Types of Protections:

There are many types of patents, but most inventors need to know about three: utility, design, and plant patents. Each protects a different kind of invention. Savvy inventors can utilize these three main patent applications to secure the rights they need to protect their inventions. They can even use multiple patent filings to mitigate risk, hedge a bet, or expand patent protection.

Design

Protects the design or exterior look of an invention.

Utility

Protects inventions such as machines, processes, or systems.

Plant

Protects the invention of new plant variants.

Each type of patents has own specific eligibility criteria and protects a particular type of invention idea. In addition to this, it is possible for a particular filed of invention idea to have more than one patent.

1.Utility Patents:

Utility patents are patents issued across the world especially in the United States, accounting for more than two-thirds of all issued patents. It is granted for an invention that is new, useful, and non-obvious. It can include any machine, process, manufactured article, composition of matter or any invention that is improvement over previous one.

- There are three types of utility – General utility is based on functionality, Specific utility is how the invention performs the function, and Moral utility makes sure that the invention is not poison or facilitate wrong use.

- To maintain all the patents in force, maintenance fees must be paid, and this came into a rule for the applications filed on or after December 12, 1980.
- This fee is due for six months window after every 3.5, 7.5, and 11.5 years from the grant date of the patent. Post-six months window extra fee amount is charged while paying maintenance fees.

2.Design Patents:

Design patent is a patent issued for designs or structures. It is not limited to and may include specific chairs, shoes, tables, machinery, fonts with novelty, unique computer icons, etc. For a design patent, a design must be aesthetic or ornamental and cannot be functional.

- Just like a normal utility patent, on issuing or granting a design patent, the inventor gets a sole right that stops others from making, using, selling, and importing the design.
- As per USPTO, all design patent applications filed before May 13, 2015, provides a total life of 14 years to a patent from the date of grant as compared to 15 years for design patent applications filed after May 13, 2015. Unlike utility patents, design patents need no maintenance fees.
- As per the latest trends, many companies have filed design patents for inventions involving user interfaces including curved or designed edges or shapes of user display interfaces.
- A design in legal terms is related to the surface ornamentation of an object including the shape or configuration of an object. The inventors need to make sure that the design is inseparable from the object for obtaining design patent protection.
- A design patent only protects the appearance of an object, but a utility patent application must be filed if an inventor wants to protect the functional or structural features of an object.

3.Plant Patents:

- Plant patents may be granted for inventions or discoveries or asexual reproductions of any distinct and new variety of plant. asexual reproduction means the plant is reproduced by grafting or cutting the plant or by using other nonsexual means instead of being reproduced with seed.
- Reproduction of a plant is shown as a discovery of asexual reproduction. This may consist of generation of mutations or hybrid variety including newly found seedlings by cultivating different types of plants.
- The plant patent focuses more on conventional horticulture and protects the inventor rights by keeping others from creating the type of plant or gaining from the plant for around 20 years from the date of filing the patent application. The lifetime of plant patents is 20 years from the date of filing and no maintenance fees apply.

Criteria of Patents:

To obtain a patent, an invention must be novel, non-obvious, and industrially applicable, demonstrating a practical application and a new or inventive solution.

Here's a more detailed explanation of the key criteria:

- **Novelty:**

The invention must be new and not previously disclosed or known to the public anywhere in the world.

- **Non-Obviousness (Inventive Step):**

The invention must not be obvious to someone skilled in the relevant field, meaning it involves an inventive step that is not a mere variation of what already exists.

- **Industrial Applicability:**

The invention must be capable of being made or used in some kind of industry, demonstrating practical utility and commercial potential.

- **Patentable Subject Matter:**

The invention must fall within the category of inventions that can be patented, such as products, processes, or compositions of matter.

- **Enablement:**

    The patent application must provide a clear and complete description of the invention, allowing someone skilled in the field to make and use it without undue experimentation.

Types of Specification:

A patent specification is a techno-legal document that provides detailed disclosures about the invention and the extent of the protection that would be accorded to it to the general public. It gives the applicant the chance to submit technical and scientific details about the innovation in order to be qualified to receive patent protection. There are two types of specification that is submitted as Form 2 along with a patent application (Form 1) including provisional and complete specification.

Provisional specification:

A provisional specification is a broad overview of the invention that discloses the field of invention with broad scope and objective of the invention. The main purpose of submitting a provisional specification is to claim a priority date of patent application. It is useful when the invention is in its conceptual and preliminary level. A patent application can have more than one provisional specification disclosing various aspects of a single invention. If multiple provisional specifications are cognate, the Controller allows the applicant to file a single complete specification. In any case, a complete specification should be filed within 12 months from the earliest date of filing of the provisional specification. If not, the application shall be deemed to be abandoned (Reference Section 9(1) and 9(2),The Patents act, 1970).

Complete specification:

A complete specification includes a complete disclosure of all the technical and scientific details of an invention in the form of embodiments. It should include all the components, features and the best method of performing the invention so that any person skilled in the art can easily understand and recreate the same invention with the information given in the embodiments. A complete specification can be treated as a provisional specification by the Controller, if the applicant requests the Controller within twelve months from the priority date (Refer Section 9(3),The Patents act, 1970).

Content of specification:

The various content of specification as per Section 10 of The Patents act, 1970 is listed below:
(a) Title – The description begins with a title that sufficiently indicates the subject-matter to which the invention relates and should not exceed 15 words.

(b) Name and address of the applicant – The full name and the complete address of the applicant along with the nationality should be disclosed.

(c) Preamble – Preamble is an introductory statement that is different for provisional and complete specification.

In case of provisional specification, the preamble should be "The following Specification describes the invention".

In case of complete specification, the preamble should be "The following complete specification particularly describes the invention and the manner in which it is performed".

(d) Field of the invention – This defines the broad technical area that relates to the invention.

(e) Background of the invention – This includes the existing prior arts and their respective limitations or drawbacks. This should end with one or more problem statements and a corresponding solution statement using the invention. This is useful for the patent examination procedure.

(f) Objective of the invention – An invention can have more than one objective and should be listed in this section. This includes the novel features and/or components that are part of the invention and a simplified process of performing the invention.

(g) Summary of the invention – A summary discloses the scope of the invention and recites the essential features of the invention. This also includes the advantages and application of the invention.

Drawings and Description of drawings:

Drawings are provided for the better understanding of the inventions. In this section, the drawings are listed by Arabic numerals and illustrates the representation of the drawings. The same number is referred in the description wherever applicable. As per rule 15 of The Patent Rules, 2003 the drawings:

- Should be neatly prepared on a A4 size with a clear margin of at least 4 cm on the top and left hand and 3cm at the bottom and right hand of every sheet.
- Scaled sufficiently large to show the inventions and the components/features are numbered sequentially.
- Should not include dimensions and any descriptions except in case of a flow chart.

Detailed description of the invention:

A person with average ability and understanding of the art to which the invention belongs should be able to operate the invention if the section adequately and clearly explains it and the method by which it is to be carried out. To further understand the invention, a detailed drawing can be included with the explanation. In the case of a product invention, a detailed description of the finished product's composition and components is required. When a process invention occurs, the steps involved in the process should be thoroughly described, highlighting each step's unique characteristics. It is essential that the unique component or the step of the invention is characterized to differentiate from the components or steps in the prior art.

If a biological material is used in the invention, it should be included in the description and if such material is not available to the public, the application shall be completed by depositing the material before filing the application to an international depository authority (Refer Section 10, The Patent Act, 1970). All the available characteristics of the material has to be correctly included in the specification including the name, address of the depository institution and the date and number of the deposit of the material at the institution. The source and geographical origin of the biological material should be disclosed in the specification.

Claims:

The claim or claims of a complete specification shall relate to a single invention, or to a group of inventions linked so as to form a single inventive concept. It shall be clear and concise and shall be fairly based on the matter disclosed in the specification. Each claim should contain a single sentence with the proper use of punctuations.

In terms of structure, there are two type of claims namely independent and dependent claims. The first claim is an independent claim, and the subsequent claims are dependent claims. There can be multiple independent claims in an application. Each independent claim defines novel and inventive features of the invention for which the monopoly of the patent is sought. Dependent claims narrow the scope of the independent claims which recites the specific features of a component in the independent claims.

As per The Patent act, 1970 an invention relating either to a product or process that is new, involving inventive step and capable of industrial application can be patented. However, it must not fall into the categories of inventions that are non- patentable under sections 3 and 4 of the Act.

Based on this criterion, either a product or a process can be claimed. The product claim includes apparatus, device, machine and composition of a final product. The process claim recites a series of steps that results in a product.

Abstract:

An abstract commences with a title of the invention and should not exceed 150 words. In the presence of drawings, it should be accompanied with at least one drawing that shall be published. The abstract is a concise summary of the matter contained in the specification that summarizes the technical advancement in the field of the invention, principal use of the invention, a simple process and novel features of the invention which characterize the invention from its prior art. The abstract shall contain the chemical formula or structures depending on the need. This information are particularly useful for the examination process during the prosecution stage to confine the invention to a particular field. (Reference Rule 13,The Patents Rules, 2003).

Patentable Meaning:

Now that you understand what is meant by a patent, and how they work, it's time to see what we mean when we say something is "patentable". In order for any invention to be "patentable", patent law requires the invention to meet **some specific criteria,** such as the ones given below.

1. **Novelty (Newness):** This criterion means that the invention must be something new or original. It must not have been known, used or publicly disclosed before filing for patent rights. In the United States, an exception can be made to this rule, provided that the patent application is filed within one year of disclosure. This is considered a "grace period". Most countries have a grace period. However, some countries do not consider any grace periods.

2. **Useful Requirement:** In order for an invention to be patented, it must have a clearly identifiable "useful" purpose or a practical application.

3. **Non-Obviousness:** If the invention is an improvement of sorts, it must be "non-obvious" to a person having ordinary skill in the art. Obviousness and non-obviousness can be a complex area of patent law. It is recommended to speak with a patent attorney for non-obviousness considerations.

4. **Subject Matter:** The invention must fall under certain categories such as processes, machines, articles of manufacture or composition of matter in order to be eligible for a patent.

It is important to note that just because your invention meets these criteria does not guarantee that it will be granted a patent. Other applicable areas of patent law apply which affect which patents are granted. However, it will help make your application stronger when you file for patent protection by gaining understanding to the above. Additional understanding and shaping of a patent application can be gained through a patent search and analysis and discussions with a patent attorney.

Non-Patentable Inventions: What Cannot Be Patented

Since patentable inventions must be original, usable, *and* ground-breaking, it is important to understand what type of invention cannot be patented. Things like an abstract idea or naturally occurring phenomenon cannot be patented. Below is a more comprehensive list of things that are considered "non-patentable inventions."

1. **Abstract Ideas:** Any kind of concept, formula, theory or algorithm without a specific, demonstrable application cannot be patented.
2. **Laws of Nature:** Discovery of phenomenon or substances that exist naturally are considered non-patentable inventions.
3. **Methods of Doing Business:** Any process or method that is purely financial, organizational or economic are non-patentable unless they contain some type of innovative, novel technological component.
4. **Medical Procedures:** Some medical or surgical processes may not be patented. However, the specific devices used in procedures may be patented.

What qualifies as an abstract idea can be complicated in patent law. What qualifies as a medical procedure may also have complications. If in doubt, it would be best to discuss with a patent attorney.

Difference Between Patentable Search Opinion and Non-Infringement Opinion:

In addition to understanding what can be patentable, inventors should also know the difference between a patentable search opinion and a non-infringement opinion.

A patentable search opinion is when an invention is examined to see if it meets the criteria for a patent. It involves a complex and thorough process of reviewing previous patents, published research, and various other steps to ensure that an invention is eligible for a patent.

On the other hand, a non-infringement opinion is when an invention is evaluated to see if it violates any existing patent rights.

For inventors, understanding the difference between both opinions is crucial. This is because a patentable search opinion helps an inventor understand the likelihood of their invention being granted a patent while a non-infringement opinion evaluates whether that product of the invention is infringing or not infringing on someone else's patent.

Patentee/Patent Holder:

The person who receives patent rights is called a 'Patentee'. The Patentee has the legal ownership of the Patent, making it to be treated like a property. This grants Exclusive rights, which prevent others from making, using or selling the product. Section 48 of Patent Act, 1970 provides the rights of the Patentee. The exclusive rights are provided by the government to promote inventors for creating new and useful things. Although, it's important to note that these rights are conditional and subjected to certain conditions which are given in Section 47 of Patents Act, 1970.

Rights and obligation of the Patentee:
In India, patentees are given specific rights and obligations upon the issuance of the patent. The Patent Act grants the patentee specific rights, so that he can make profit out of his patent.

Rights of patentees:
1. Exclusive right:
The exclusive right to patent is provided by **Section 48** of the Patent Act of 1970. As is well known, a patent can cover either a method or a product. By prohibiting the patent in both cases—whether it involves a product or a process—Section 48 grants exclusive rights.

- If a product is the subject of the patent manufactured by the patentee, the exclusive right to patent prohibits third parties from manufacturing, putting up for sale, selling, importing, or using the product developed by the patentee without his approval.
- If the patentee has obtained a patent for a method, the patentee's exclusive right prohibits third parties from using, selling, or importing the product made using that method without the patentee's permission.

2. Right to Exploit the Patent:
In India, the right to produce, use, market, and distribute the patented goods is granted to the patent holder. If the innovation involves a manufacturing method, the patentee has the right to assign the process to another individual who has been given their permission. The agent of the patent holder may exercise this authority.

3. Right to Assign and License:
The power to assign or give license to third parties for the purpose of producing and distributing the patented goods is provided to the patent holder under Section **69(5) of** the Patent Act of 1970. For a patented product with multiple patent owners, all patent owners must concur to grant the license to a third party collectively. The license is not considered to have been issued until the administrator has correctly authorized the request. Thus, for the assignment or license to be legal and valid, it must be in writing and submitted to the Patent Authority.

4. Rights to surrender:
The patent holder has the right to give up his patent after requesting approval from the controller. After that, in compliance with the Indian Patents Act, the controller advertises this surrender. The controller can then be contacted by those who are eager to own a patent. The controller looks into the parties' claims and gives up ownership if necessary.

5. Right before selling:
A patent is sealed from the date of notification for acceptance until the date of acceptance of the notification, as per **Section 24** of the Indian Patents Act. After the notification of acceptance is presented, the patentee's rights are in effect.

6. Right to Sue for Infringement:
Any violation of the rights of a patent holder is referred to as a patent infringement. In the event that their rights have been violated, patent holders have the option of going before either a district court or a high court. If the defendant is found guilty of infringement, the courts may award both damages and a permanent injunction.

7. Right to Apply for the Patent of Addition:
The Patents Act of 1970, **sections 54 to 56**, contain this clause. The provision allows modifications to the current invention. The patent holder is entitled to the enhanced innovation in these circumstances as soon as the notification of approval is made public. When the notification is presented, the owner is awarded the same rights as those of the earlier patent.

Obligations of patentees:
1. Duty to Disclose the Patent:
It is the patentee's responsibility to provide the controller with all information that is required. The applicant must reveal the innovation to the public, according to **Section 8** of the Patent Act of 1970. At the time of filing a patent application or within six months of applying, the patentee is categorically required to disclose all necessary information regarding the remote application of an identical or nearly identical invention that has been documented, according to **Section 8(1)** of the Patent Act of 1970.
2. Duty to request for examination:
The patent registration process does not provide for any type of scheduled examination for the grant of a patent application, in contrast to other intellectual property rights. According to **section 11(B)** of the Patents Act of 1970, it is the patentee's responsibility to ask the Controller to look at how the patent has developed or grown.
3. Duty to respond to objections:
The Patent Controller sends the inspection request to an analyst, who evaluates the growth before sending the First Examination Report (FER) back to the Patent Controller. In some cases, the First Examination Report will mention some objections. Responding to such reports of objection is required of patentees. They must also communicate within a year after the FER's issuance. The patentee's application will automatically be rejected if this is not done.
4. Duty to clear all objections:
It is the applicant's responsibility to address any and all complaints and oppositions made against his invention, as well as to respond to such objections. If the controller is still unsatisfied, he could also request a meeting. Additionally, it is the applicant's responsibility to attend the consultation and address all objections and oppositions (if any have been lodged) made against the invention.
5. Duty to pay statutory fees:
To be eligible for a patent, patentees must also pay any statutory fees connected to the registration process. If the payment is not made, the patent will not be considered for the grant. **Section 142** of the Patent Act addresses the payment of appropriate fees and the penalties of failing to pay certain costs.

Terms of Patents:
In India, the term of a patent is **20** years from the date of filing the application. However, for applications filed under the Patent Cooperation Treaty (PCT), the term is 20 years from the international filing date.
Here's a more detailed explanation:
- **Standard Patent Term:**
  A patent in India is granted for a period of 20 years from the date of filing the application, regardless of whether it's a provisional or complete specification.
- **PCT Applications:**
  If an application is filed under the Patent Cooperation Treaty (PCT), the 20-year term starts from the international filing date, not the date of filing in India.
- **Maintenance Fees:**
  To maintain the patent in force, annual maintenance fees (annuities) must be paid.
- **Lapse of Patent:**
  If the annual maintenance fees are not paid, the patent will lapse and enter the public domain, meaning anyone can use the invention without the patent holder's permission.

- **Working Statement:**
  It is also mandatory to file a Working Statement once every three years.

Jurisdiction of Patent:
The Indian Patent Office is responsible for administering the Indian law of patents, and its roles include patent administration, patent duration, and patent renewal, among other things. There are four patent offices in India, located in different cities, i.e., Chennai (in southern India), Delhi (in northern India), Kolkata (in eastern India), and Mumbai (in western India). In geographical terms, these four offices cover the length and breadth of the entire country.

Determining territorial jurisdiction for patent applicants:
In India, a patent application needs to be submitted to the Patent Office with the relevant authority. One of the following three factors determines the applicable office's jurisdiction:
• The applicant's (or the first named applicant, in the case of joint applicants) place of residence, domicile, or business.
• The location from which an invention originated; or
• For foreign applicants, the address provided by the applicant for service in India, or the address of the patent agent on file.

The table below illustrates which specific patent office should be approached by patent applicants.

Office	Territorial Jurisdiction
Patent Office Branch, Mumbai	The States of Maharashtra, Gujarat, Madhya Pradesh, Goa and Chhattisgarh and the Union Territories of Daman and Diu & Dadra and Nagar Haveli
Patent Office Branch, Chennai	The States of Andhra Pradesh, Karnataka, Kerala, Tamil Nadu, Telangana and the Union Territories of Pondicherry and Lakshadweep
Patent Office Branch, New Delhi	The States of Haryana, Himachal Pradesh, Punjab, Rajasthan, Uttar Pradesh, Uttarakhand, Delhi and the Union Territory of Chandigarh, Jammu and Kashmir and Ladakh.
Patent Office, Kolkata	The rest of India.

Notably, the courts' authority to enforce a patent (including bringing infringement litigation) differs from the patent office's jurisdiction to handle administrative and prosecution activities related to a patent. Section 20 of the Civil Procedure Code of 1908 and Section 104 of the Indian Patents Act of 1970 establish the requirements for launching an infringement suit. According to Section 20 of the Civil Procedure Code of 1908, the cause of action must occur entirely or in part at the court within the defendant's local jurisdiction, where they live, conduct business, or labour for pay.

After filing:
Selecting the right Patent Office needs to be assessed at the time of filing the application. However, after an application for a patent is filed, it is handed over for examination to one of the four Patent Offices based on a centralized system of allocation. This Patent Office may be different from the one where the application was filed. The applicant has no control over which Patent Office its application will be allotted to for the purpose of examination. However, since

practically all hearings before the Controller are virtual nowadays, the examination of an application by a different patent office will not result in increase in prosecution costs.

It is not possible for an applicant to request to transfer the application for examination to another Patent Office once it is allocated. In other words, there is no scope for the applicant to choose a particular Patent Office for examination, or for an application to be transferred to another Patent Office after filing.

If there is a change in the address of the patent applicant, or its agent, to a location that falls under the jurisdiction of a different Patent Office (i.e., not the office where the application was originally filed) during the pendency of the patent application, there is no requirement to change the Patent Office responsible for handling the application.

Prior Art of Patent in India:

"Prior art" (also known as background art or state of the art) is a term in patent law that is one of the most common reasons of rejection of patent application's claims by the Patent Offices. Thus, it is very important to understand the term "prior art", especially for the applicant of a patent.

Prior art is any proof or evidence in some form (written or oral) that shows that your invention is already known before the effective filing date of a patent application or prior to the date of the invention.

To demonstrate that the invention is original and non-obvious—the two most crucial requirements for obtaining patent rights, the examiner looks into prior works as part of the patent awarding process. According to US patent laws, if an invention is not new or obvious, patent rights cannot be granted.

1. If "the claimed invention was patented, described in a printed publication, or in public use, on sale, or otherwise available to the public prior to the effective filing date of the claimed invention," the applicant is not eligible for patent rights under US law (35 U.S.C. 102).

2. According to 35 U.S.C. 103, if "the differences between the claimed invention and the prior art are such that the claimed invention as a whole would have been obvious before the effective filing date of the claimed invention to a person having ordinary skill in the art to which the claimed invention pertains," the applicant is not entitled to patent rights.

What Qualifies as a Prior Art?

Most of the people think that prior art is restricted to only existing products and granted patents. On the contrary, the prior art is not limited to only products and granted patents, but any document which is in the public domain, be it a granted patent, a patent application or a non-patent reference existing on or before the present day when the search is conducted or the effective filing date that covers the major aspects of the invention is considered as a prior art.

Prior art can include presentation at a public event e.g., conference, use of the invention e.g., demonstration, a previously filed patent application, research papers, thesis, standards, white papers, e-mails, conversations, newsletters, products, articles, videos, blogposts, any internet publications, etc.

Where to Search for a Prior Art?

To identify prior arts (patent/non-patent citations), various paid and/or unpaid databases can be used. Few of those popular databases are Orbit, Derwent, XLSCOUT, Pats nap, Lens.org, Google patents, Google, IEEE, Google scholar, IETF standards, 3GPP standards, ETSI, Espacenet, J-platpat, KIPRIS, CNIPA etc.

Depending on the databases, there are numerous methods to search for prior arts. One method would include an automated search (for example in **XLSCOUT** – AI based module) where either the inventive paragraph or the drafted claim elements/features are entered, and an artificial intelligent module takes over from there to identify all the related/relevant/closest possible prior arts.

Next, we can perform manual searches by making search strings/queries/strategies using all the important/related key words/phrases of the invention. These can further help us in identifying major assignees/inventors and/or important patent classifications related to the invention which can be used in forming further search strategies.

We can also look for more related prior arts present/cited on an identified relevant prior art. Further, all these databases mostly have their own syntax/methods for making search strategies.

Moreover, if client has already some patents/products/papers published on the same technology, then those references/citations can be identified and can help in steering the search accordingly, to find the closest possible prior art.

What does not Qualify as a Prior Art?

- Any information or patent application which is publicly disclosed after your application's filing date doesn't qualify as a relevant prior art.
- For a publication to qualify as a prior art it must offer an "enabling disclosure."
- Some abandoned patent applications may remain confidential, and this cannot be used as prior art. For example, some provisional patent application which are not converted to non-provisional applications are never published and thus not available publicly. Such, applications cannot be used as a prior art.
- Trade secrets are confidential by nature, and they cannot be used as evidence of prior art.
- Confidential disclosures/documents cannot be used as prior art when information is shared under an obligation of confidentiality such as by signing a non-disclosure agreement (NDA).

Territoriality of Patents:

- The territoriality principle is a fundamental concept in intellectual property law, particularly concerning patents. It dictates that intellectual property rights, including patent rights, are only valid and enforceable within the territory of the country or region where they were granted.
- **Why it matters:**
    - **National Sovereignty:** The principle recognizes the sovereignty of nations, allowing them to regulate and protect inventions according to their own standards and laws.
    - **Tailored Protection:** It allows countries to design their intellectual property laws to suit their specific technological and economic development needs.
    - **International Agreements:** While the principle is foundational, international treaties and agreements, like those administered by the World Intellectual Property Organization (WIPO), provide a framework for international patent protection, but they still operate within the confines of the territoriality principle.
- **Implications:**
    - A patent granted in one country has no effect beyond the territorial boundary of that country and cannot be infringed upon in other countries.

- To obtain protection in multiple countries, an inventor must file patent applications in each country or region where they seek protection.
    - This can be a complex and costly process, as each jurisdiction has its own laws, procedures, and requirements.
- **Examples:**
    - A patent granted in the United States for a new medical device does not automatically give the patent holder the right to prevent others from making, using, or selling that device in China.
    - Similarly, a patent granted in India for a new software program does not automatically prevent others from using that software in Brazil.

1-02: PROSECUTION OF PATENT

To file a patent, whether domestically (national) or internationally (PCT), you first prepare a complete patent application with a description, claims, drawings (if any), and an abstract, then file it with the relevant patent office, either your national office or the WIPO for PCT. Here's a more detailed breakdown of the patent filing mechanism, including both domestic and PCT routes:

1. Domestic/National Patent Filing:
- **Preparation:**
    - **Complete Specification:** Prepare a detailed description of your invention, including its background, technical field, problem it solves, and how it works.
    - **Claims:** Define the scope of protection you seek for your invention in clear and concise language.
    - **Drawings (if applicable):** Include visual representations of your invention to aid understanding.
    - **Abstract:** Provide a concise summary of the invention.
    - **Form 1 (Application for grant of patent):** This form is used to file the patent application.
    - **Form 3 (Details of corresponding foreign patent applications):** If you have filed similar applications elsewhere, provide details here.
    - **Form 5 (Declaration of inventorship):** The inventors must sign this form, declaring their inventorship.
    - **Form 26 (Power of Attorney):** Authorize a patent attorney to represent you.
- **Filing:**
    - Submit the application to the national patent office in your country.
    - Pay the required filing fees.
    - You can file online through the patent office's online portal.
- **Post-Filing:**
    - The patent office will assign a date and serial number to your application.
    - The application will be digitized, verified, screened, classified, and uploaded to the internal server.
    - The application is screened for international patent classification, technical field, and abstract (if required).
    - The application will be published 18 months after the filing date or priority date (whichever is earlier).
    - The application will be examined by a patent examiner.
    - If the patent is granted, it will be published in the patent gazette.

2. PCT (Patent Cooperation Treaty) Filing:
- **Purpose:**
  The PCT streamlines the process of seeking patent protection in multiple countries by allowing you to file a single international application.
- **Phases:**
  The PCT process involves two phases:

- **International Phase:**
    - File a single international patent application with the WIPO (World Intellectual Property Organization).
    - This application is processed by the "Receiving Office," which is usually the patent office in the applicant's home country.
    - An international search report (ISR) and a written opinion on patentability are issued by the international searching authority.
    - The PCT application is published in the WIPO global database.
- **National Phase:**
    - After the international phase, you can enter the national phase in one or more countries where you want to seek patent protection.
    - This involves filing national phase applications with the respective national patent offices.
    - The time limit for entering the national phase is generally 30 months from the priority date.

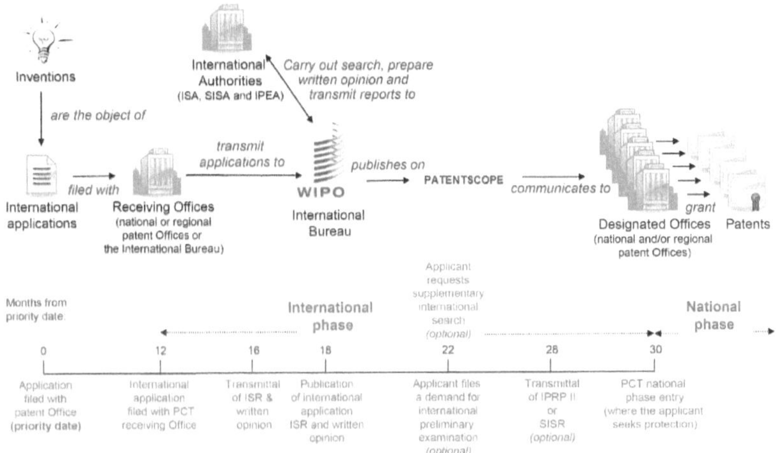

- **Benefits of PCT:**
    - **Simplified Filing:** File a single application instead of multiple national applications.
    - **Deferred Costs:** You can defer the costs of national filings until you have assessed the commercial potential of your invention in different markets.
    - **Early Assessment:** The ISR and written opinion provide preliminary insights into the likelihood of your invention being granted a patent.
    - **Global Coverage:** You can seek patent protection in a large number of countries.

Patent Search:

Patents may be searched using the following resources:

Patent Public Search

The Patent Public Search tool is a new web-based patent search application that replaced internal legacy search tools PubEast and PubWest and external legacy search tools PatFT and

AppFT. Patent Public Search has two user selectable modern interfaces that provide enhanced access to prior art. The new, powerful, and flexible capabilities of the application improve the overall patent searching process.

Global Dossier:

A collection of commercial services called Global Dossier are designed to update the international patent system and provide advantages to all parties involved via a unified portal or user interface. The file histories of linked apps from participating IP Offices—currently include the IP5 Offices—are accessible to users via this secure service. Through this tool, users can view the patent family for a particular application, which includes all related applications filed at participating IP Offices, as well as the applications' dossier, classification, and citation information. Additionally, this service offers users the opportunity to download documents within an application, a Collections View for storing documents and applications for subsequent viewing during the session, and Office Action Indicators to assist users in identifying applications that contain office actions.

Public Search Facility:

The public can access patent and trademark information in a number of formats, such as paper, microfilm, and online, through the United States Patent and Trademark Office's (USPTO) Public Search Facility in Alexandria, Virginia. There is trained personnel on hand to help members of the public.

PTRCs, or Patent and Trademark Resource Centers: on addition to maintaining local search resources, the closest Patent and Trademark Resource Centre (PTRC) might provide instruction on patent search methods.

Patent Official Gazette:

The Electronic Official Gazette allows users to browse through the issued patents for the current week. The Official Gazette can be browsed by classification or type of patent, for example, utility, design, and plant.

Common Citation Document (CCD):

The Common Citation Document (CCD) application aims to provide single point access to up-to-date citation data relating to the patent applications of the IP5 Offices. It consolidates the prior art cited by all participating offices for the family members of a patent application, thus enabling the search results for the same invention produced by several offices to be visualized on a single page. The creation of the CCD application is part of an ongoing process of technical harmonization at international level aimed at establishing an appropriate infrastructure to facilitate greater integration of the global patent system.

Search International Patent Offices:

To see if your idea has been patented abroad, you'll want to refer to searchable databases made available from other International Intellectual Property offices.

Free online access to patent collections is provided by many countries. Some available databases include:

- European Patent Office (EPO) provides esp@cenet a network of Europe's patent databases- This site also provides access to machine translation of European patents for some languages.
- Japan Patent Office (JPO) - This site also provides access to machine translations of Japanese patents.
- World Intellectual Property Organization (WIPO) provides PATENTSCOPE ® Search Service, which features a full-text search of published international patent

applications and machine translations for some documents as well as a list of international patent databases.

- Korean Intellectual Property Rights Information Service (KIPRIS)
- China National Intellectual Property Administration (CNIPA) - This site also provides access to machine translation of Chinese patents.
- Other International Intellectual Property Offices that provide searchable patent databases
  include: Australia, Canada, Denmark, Finland, France, Germany, Great Britain, India, Israel, Netherlands, Norway, Sweden, Switzerland and Taiwan.

Stopfakes.Gov provides informative Toolkits that give an overview of the Intellectual Property Rights (IPR) environment in various countries around the world.

For additional search resources, contact your local Patent and Trademark Resource Center, visit the USPTO Public Search Facility or the USPTO Main STIC Library. The staff in the Main STIC Library are experts on foreign patents and able to help the public as needed.

Search Published Sequences:

The Publication Site for Issued and Published Sequences (PSIPS) website provides Sequence Listings, tables, and other mega items for granted US patents or published US patent applications.

All sequences (SEQ ID NOs.) and tables for listed patents or publications are available for viewing, without downloading, by accessing the proper document detail page and then submitting a SEQ ID NO or a mega table ID number.

Patent Assignment Search:

Visit the Patent Assignment Search website to search for patent assignments and changes in ownership.

Open Data Portal (ODP):

The Open Data Portal provides public users open-source data, allowing innovators to select and extract data they want through adjustable datasets and Application Programming Interfaces (APIs)

Patent Specification Drafting :

The inclusion of technical information about innovation and the legal boundary of protection makes a patent specification a techno-legal document. Technical and legal jargon are part of the terminology used in patent specifications. An inventor provides the specifics of his invention in a patent specification in return for the government-granted exclusive rights. From a more general standpoint, the government anticipates that a patent specification will reveal the invention specifics so that anyone in the public can create and/or use the invention (after the patent expires), fulfilling the goal of the system.

Although the viewpoint is the foundation of any patent specification, to achieve a high-quality patent, patent applicants, inventors, and patent professionals (henceforth referred to as "patent drafters") must use several additional views when creating a patent specification. In general, the patent drafter must use the

1. Invention perspective. 2. The viewpoint of a third party; and 3. The viewpoint of patentability.

1. Invention perspective: The patent drafter should be sufficiently clear about the invention's nature, its intended use, potential future developments, and other details. The patent drafter should try to broaden the innovation's scope of protection ("X+1" rule, where X is the invention and 1 is the invention's future changes). Assuming that a pen with a cap is the prior art, for instance, the invention might be a "click pen" with a single button that can be used to change the refill's nib from the writing position, where it is outside the pen body, to the closed position, where it is inside the pen body. To create a patent specification, the patent drafter should have the foresight to consider at least a click pen with numerous refills of different colors, a pencil, or a sketch pen using the mechanism.

2. Third Party perspective: A thorough assessment of the possible infringers should be conducted by the patent drafter. A manufacturer, an assembler who puts the manufactured parts together, an end user, or one or more of the company's vendors may find an invention more applicable and useful. To write a patent specification that will unambiguously hold potential infringers accountable for infringement, the patent drafter should take the issue into consideration.

3. Patentability perspective: The patent drafter should always try to broaden the invention's protection, but they should also be careful not to include any unwelcome prior arts that a patent examiner might evaluate during prosecution. The patent drafter should be aware of the previous art that has already been done in the field of the invention in question. They should also stress the invention's uniqueness, utility, and non-obviousness while also droughting the patent specification in a way that sets it apart from the prior art. A patent drafter must use all the previously described viewpoints when writing each portion of a patent specification considering this.

Types of Specifications
1) Provisional specification; and
2) Complete specification.

Provisional Specification
A document that exposes an original concept in a wide, but incomplete, manner is called a provisional specification. When the inventor requires additional time to refine and finalise his invention, the preliminary specification is filed primarily to obtain a "priority date." As a result, the provisional specification rarely provides a clear and comprehensive disclosure of all pertinent information about the invention. It is advised to include as much information about the invention as the inventor or applicant knows at the time of filing in the provisional specification, even though full information is not necessary. This is because the provisional specification will be used later to determine whether the complete specification claims the invention that is included in the provisional specification. Drawings, which relate to the invention, may also be presented with the provisional specification and such illustrations will be deemed as part of the specification.

Complete Specification
A complete specification is a document that, in contrast to a provisional specification, discloses all of the invention's details in a way that is sufficiently clear and comprehensive to allow someone with ordinary competence in the art to practise the invention. Because the full specification must end with a claim or combination of claims, it differs from the provisional specification even further. Understanding that every claim in the entire specification defines an invention is a crucial component of specification draughting. Consequently, a specific priority date is linked to each claim.

Contents of a Specification

It is necessary to prepare a specification and submit it to the Indian Patent Office in Form 2. In contrast to the full specification, a provisional specification will not feature a claim section, as was indicated in the preceding section. The following are the sections.
1) Title.
2) The invention's preamble.
3) Technical domain.
4) Context.
5) Things.
6) A synopsis of the illustrations.
7) A thorough explanation.
8) Statements (for full details); and 9) Synopsis.
Each of the components is briefly covered in the paragraphs that follow, along with the best practices to adhere to when writing those sections.

Title:

The invention's title should appear at the start of the full specification. Certain aspects of the innovation should be fairly captured in the title. The maximum word count should be fifteen (15). Additionally, the title cannot contain the inventor's name, the word "patent," words in foreign languages, the abbreviation "etc," or fancy words. All variations (devices) of the invention should be included in the title. For instance, "A system and a method for ____," "An apparatus and a method for ___," and so forth could be used as titles.

Preamble of the invention

The preamble for a provisional specification should state "The following specification describes the invention". Further, the preamble of a complete specification should state "The following specification principally designates the invention and the manner in which it is to be performed." The preamble along with the title of the invention, name, address and nationality of the applicant(s) should appear in the first page of Form 2.

Technical Field:

The "Technical field" section in the specification will remark as to what field the invention fit in to and particularly states as to the subject matter of the invention. For example, the Technical Field may state "The invention generally narrates to dispensing machines and more chiefly to a machine which distributes coffee".

Background:

The objective of this section is to distinguish the invention at hand from that of what is already being practiced in the industry. The aforementioned objective will be achieved by briefly discussing the teachings of the prior art and drawbacks or disadvantages, if any, of such teachings. This section sets the stage for describing, at a later stage, the invention at hand clearly and in more detail.

For example, if the invention tells to a coffee dispensing machine in which a crusher is comprised, as a novel and inventive concept, to grind the coffee seeds, the disadvantages or drawbacks of existing coffee dispensing machine (assuming that the concept of grinding the coffee seeds in the dispensing machine itself is not contemporary in the existing coffee dispensing machine) may be briefly discussed.

Objects

The objective of this section is to bring about the need of the invention.

This section is aimed at delivery about the objectives, advantages or explanations achieved by employing the invention at hand. It may include statements such as "The prime object of an embodiment of this invention is….; Another object of the embodiment of this invention is……; yet another object of the quintessence if this invention is… and so on.

Brief description of the drawings:
This section will refer to all the figures in "Drawing" part of the description. In this section, a brief argument is presented as to the embodiments portrayed by each of the figures. For example, it may be stated that "Figure 1 is a perspective view of a coffee dispensing engine having a crusher according to an embodiment of the invention; and Figure 2 depicts crusher of figure 1 connected to a collecting chamber and so on.

Detailed description of the invention:
The objective of this section is to deliver sufficient details of the invention. The making and using of the invention and the objectives, advantages or solutions achieved by employing the invention (as discussed in "Objects of the invention "section of the description) should be explained in depth. Further, the details of the invention should be explained with respect to the drawings. The details provided in this section are considered sufficient if a person having ordinary skill in the art is able to practice the invention without undue experimentation. This section may also include examples to facilitate better understanding of the invention. Further, this section should offer or disclose the best method of performing the invention, which is known to the claimant.

Claims:
Claims are the sum and element of the patent specification. The patent moralities are granted to the claimed subject matter. The subject matter which is in the explanation but not claimed will be considered disclaimed and hence is contributed to the public. Each claim is a separate invention and hence all the claims are not held inacceptable for one claim being illegal.

A claim is a verdict and hence should start with a capital letter and end with a full stop. The claims section of the specification should start on a distinct page after the "Detailed description of the invention" section. The prelude to claims section should be, "I claim", "We Claim" or "What is claimed is" and should follow with the claim listings.

Almost always, the first self-determining claim is drafted roughly to cover the important aspects of the invention. Further details of the invention may be covered in dependent claims which will have narrow coverage. Different sets of claims may be conscripted to vary the scope of protection sought.

A claim has to be structured in three parts viz, Introductory phrase, body and a link that joins the introductory phrase and the body.

Claim drafting:
At the heart of a patent application lies its claims. A claim is a signifier of the scope of protection that is sought under the patent. Claims are the first and most important aspect to be examined during prosecution, infringement, and litigation. Every patent application must be accompanied by at least one claim, and usually, an application contains several more.

The language used by patent claims is usually very clear and precise and consists of words that have been interpreted and defined over decades by courts and patent offices. Seemingly innocuous practices such as the use of a synonym, the position of a conjunction, or the choice of a plural, can all be extremely contentious issues in patent infringement suits.

Two-part claims

Patent claim structures are, for the most part, harmonized across patent offices in different countries. However, a few patents office's prefer certain claim formats, one such being the two-part form. Two-part claiming requires that the claim be sectioned into two parts, the parts separated by the transitional phrase "characterized in that", or "characterized by". The general interpretation of such claims is that the section prior to this phrase) describes the state-of-the-art or the prior art, while the post-characterizing portion describes the inventive component of the invention. This note briefly examines two-part claiming practices in different jurisdictions and concludes with best practices for applicants in India.

Europe

The two-part claim is preferred in Europe (EP) as the default format for claims, with Rule 43(1) of the European Patent Convention (EPC) stating that:

"Wherever appropriate, claims shall contain: (a) a declaration indicating the title of the subject-matter of the origination and those technical features which are obligatory for the definition of the claimed subject-matter but which, in combination, form part of the prior art; (b) a characterizing portion, beginning with the expression "characterized in that" or "characterized by" and specifying the procedural features for which, in combination with the features stated under sub-paragraph (a), protection is sought".

The Guidelines for Examination in the European Patent Office ("the Guidelines") explain this requirement further: the pre-characterizing portion must contain a general statement of the subject matter of the invention and 'those technical features which are necessary for the definition of the claimed subject-matter but which, in combination, are part of the prior art". Thus, this pre-characterization portion should claim the state-of-the art, or the non-inventive features of the invention. On the other hand, the post-characterizing section must claim the inventive technical features of the invention which in combination with the non-inventive features describe the scope of the claimed invention.

However, EP does permit fluidity in claim structure. Under the Guidelines, one-part claiming is deemed appropriate wherever strict demarcation into two-parts is likely to cause confusion and ambiguity in the claim. For instance, the Board of Appeals, in T0170/84, concluded that while Rule 29(1) (presently Rule 43(1)) of the EPC) requires that a claim should be formulated in two-part form, when read with Article 84, the two-part form is not appropriate if it would lead to a "complex formulation" of the claim and compromise the clarity of the claim.

United States

The US equivalent of the two-part claim is the "Jepson" claim. Unlike EP, it is not the default format for claims, and is recommended only in special circumstances. This specific claim format describes an improvement over the prior art. 37 C.F.R. 1.75(e) describes such claims thus:

'(Where the nature of the case discloses, as in the case of an improvement, any independent claim should contain in the following order: "(1) A preamble comprising a general description of all the elements or steps of the claimed combination which are conventional or known, (2) A phrase such as "wherein the improvement comprises," and (3) Those elements, steps, and/or relationships which constitute that portion of the claimed blend which the applicant reflects as the new or better portion".

The interpretation of such claims veers on the restrictive side, as the US Manual of Patent Examining Procedure (MPEP) 2129 specifies that: "Conscripting a claim in Jepson format . is taken as an obscure admission that the subject matter of the preamble is the previous artwork of another".

India

In India, two-part claiming is not a prescribed claim format, and in contrast to EP and the US, no specific provisions are described in the Indian Patents Act, 1970 ("the Act"), for such claims. Instead, Section 10(4)(c) of the Act merely requires that:

"Every comprehensive specification shall end with a claim or claims defining the scope of the invention for which protection is claimed".

Section 10(5) adds that, "The claim or claims of a broad specification shall relate to a single invention. Shall be clear and succinct and shall be impartially based on the matter revealed in the specification".

However, two-claim formats are a prevalent practice in India, and some guidance for this can be found in the Manual of Patent Office Practice and Procedure ('the Manual'). Section 05.03.16(n) of the Manual states:

"The invention should be identified very clearly by characterizing the claim with respect to prior art if it is an improvement on a product or a technique that already existed in the prior art. In these situations, the words "characterised by" or "wherein" will be used to divide the two sections of the claim.

The concept of a two-part claim is reiterated in Section 05.03.16(o) of the Manual, which lays down the distinguishing features of the first claim, also known as the "Principal Claim":

"The first claim, sometimes referred to as the "Principal Claim," is always an independent claim... The claim can be accurately described in terms of the "prior art," which includes all the technical aspects that are necessary for the invention or creative idea. The claim should highlight enough information about how the invention works, interacts, or is useful to demonstrate that it accomplishes its goals.

Prosecuting and defending two-part claims in India:

In practice, while there is no specific mandate to draft claims in this format, the Indian Patent Office often requires that claims be amended into the two-part format during the examination of a patent application.

But applicants are generally wary of locking themselves into such claim formats. This is because two-part claims risk a narrow and restrictive interpretation. For instance, in Enercon India Pvt. Ltd. Vs Aloys Wobben [ORA No. 5/2009 dated 18 November 2010; ORA No. 27/2009 dated 2 December 2010, and ORA No. 38/2009 dated 2 December 2010], the Intellectual Property Appellate Board relied on both Article 43(1), EPC and Jepson claims from the US, to conclude that the inventive step lies in post-characterization part of a claim.

In most instances, applicants can successfully argue against the characterization of claims into two-part formats on grounds of lack of clarity, i.e., by arguing that it would result in a confusing claim or that the combination/inter-relationship of the features are such that the inventive step is an outcome of the combination.

Steps for Patent Filing Application in India:

Patent filing application involves a set of processes such as searches, preparing documents, making applications, publishing, examining, and objection response. At each step, originality and the validity of an invention are protected. Filing a patent application in India is a comprehensive process that requires a clear understanding of the legal and procedural requirements. Here's a detailed breakdown of each step:

Step 1: Conduct a Patent Search

Why It's Important: Before filing, conducting a thorough patent search ensures that the invention is novel and does not infringe upon existing patents.

How to do: Search through databases such as Indian Patent Advanced Search System (In PASS) and other international patent databases.

Benefits: Avoids unnecessary rejection due to the existence of prior patents in the same domain.

Step 2: Patent Application Preparation

Provisional Specification: If the invention is still under development, filing a provisional application would help secure an early date for filing.

Timeline: A complete specification must follow within 12 months.

Advantage: Additional time is given to file an improved invention.

Complete Specification: Information about the Invention includes:

> Title and Abstract.
> Previous art or weaknesses in available solutions.
> The Background of the Invention
> Summary of the Invention
> Detailed Description and Claims.
> Drawings, if applicable

Step 3: Lodge the Application

Where to File: Application can be made:

Online: By the website of the Indian Patent Office.

Offline: With the corresponding Patent office located in Delhi, Mumbai, Kolkata and Chennai respectively.

What to Include: All the forms and documents required, which include:

Form 1: Application for grant of patent.

Form 2: Specification-provisional or complete.

Form 3: Statement and undertaking.

Form 5: Declaration of Inventorship.

Power of Attorney if filed through an agent.

Statutory fees.

Step 4: Publication of the Application

When It Occurs: Applications are published in the official patent journal after 18 months from the date of filing.

Early Publication Option: You can apply for early publication by paying extra charges, and the application will get published within a month.

Importance: Publication makes the application public, and any third party can scrutinize it.

Step 5: Application for Examination

How to Apply: File Form 18 for an examination. It must be done within 48 months of the priority date.

Purpose: The application sets in motion the examination process. This is where the Patent Office scrutinizes the application on the aspects of patentability, novelty, and compliance with patent laws.

Step 6: Patent Office Examination

What happens: The Patent Office checks for:

Novelty, inventive step, and industrial applicability.

Legal and technical requirements.

First Examination Report (FER): The examiner raises objections or requires additional information in an FER.

Step 7: Response to Examination Report

Timeline: Overcome FER objections within 12 months.

Amendments: Claims or specifications may be altered, if necessary, to satisfy patentability requirements.

Hearing Opportunity: In case the objections are not overcome, the Controller can provide an opportunity for a hearing to clear up the remaining objections.

Step 8: Pre-Grant Opposition

Who Can Oppose: Any person can oppose the application under Section 25(1) before the patent is granted.

Grounds for Opposition: Novelty, inventive step, or industrial applicability; or non-disclosure of essential information.

Step 9: Grant of Patent

When It Takes Place: After resolving all objections and opposition (if any), the Controller grants the patent under Section 43.

Publication of Grant: Grant published in the official patent journal and public notice of granting such exclusive rights.

Step 10: Post-Grant Opposition

Timeline: Within 12 months from the date of grant. Any person may give notice of opposition. Objective: Permitting the patentees to challenge the patent with regard to validity, novelty or other grounds.

Documents Required for Patent Filing Procedure in India:

The patent application has to be provided with accurate and detailed documents. The required forms, statements, and technical details have to be submitted to conform with Indian patent laws so as to facilitate the processing. The required forms for submission include:

Form 1: Proposal for patent grant

Form 2: Complete or provisional specification

Form 3: Commitment and declaration pertaining to overseas applications.

Form 5: Declaration of Inventorship.

Form 26: Power of attorney (if filed through a patent agent).

Form 18: Request for examination.

Priority Document: If claiming priority from an earlier application.

Abstract: A brief summary of the invention.

Drawings: If applicable, to illustrate the invention.

Advantages of Obtaining a Patent

- A patent provides exclusive rights, and revenue opportunities through licensing, and strengthens the market position of an innovator. It ensures legal protection against unauthorized use.
- Exclusive Rights: The patentee is given exclusive rights to restrain other individuals from using the patented invention without permission.
- Commercialization: Patents may be licensed or sold and provide opportunities for revenue generation.
- Market Position: It enhances market position because it prevents the competitors from exploiting the invention.

Challenges of Patent Filing in India

- The process of patent filing can be difficult, costly, and very time-consuming. This often requires strategic planning to navigate legal and technical requirements.
- Complexity: The process includes complicated legal and technical documentation
- Cost: The filing and keeping of the patents can be very expensive.
- Time-Consuming: The whole process from filing to issuance of a patent can take years.

Reply to Patent Examination Report:

Patent examination is the process by which a patent office assesses a patent application to determine whether it meets the necessary criteria for patentability. The primary goal is to ensure that the invention is new, inventive, and industrially applicable, and that the application complies with all formal requirements.

Key Phases of Patent Examination:
- **Formal Examination:** This initial phase checks whether the application complies with formal requirements, such as proper documentation and payment of fees.
- **Substantive Examination:** This phase involves a detailed review of the invention's novelty, inventive step, and industrial applicability. The examiner reviews prior art to ensure that the invention is not already disclosed or obvious.

Common Reasons for Objections During Patent Examination:
During substantive examination, the patent office may raise several types of objections:
1. **Lack of Novelty** The examiner may object if the invention is not new. This means that the invention has been disclosed in prior art before the filing date. The examiner will compare the invention to existing patents, publications, and other sources.
- **Lack of Inventive Step (Non-Obviousness)** If the invention is deemed obvious to someone skilled in the field based on prior art, the examiner may raise an objection. The invention must involve an inventive step that is not immediately apparent.
- **Insufficient Disclosure** The application must provide a detailed and clear description of the invention. If the examiner finds that the description is inadequate or lacks essential details, they may request additional information or clarification.
- **Claims Deficiencies** Claims define the scope of the patent protection. Objections may arise if the claims are unclear, ambiguous, or do not adequately support the invention as described in the specification.
- **Formal Issues** The examiner may also raise objections related to formal aspects of the application, such as incorrect formatting, missing information, or errors in the drawings.

Crafting a Response to Patent Examination Objections:
Responding to objections effectively is key to advancing the patent application process. Here's how to craft a comprehensive and convincing response:
1. **Understand the Objections** Carefully review the examiner's objections to understand the specific issues raised. This involves analyzing the reasons for the objections and determining the best approach to address them.
- **Gather Supporting Evidence** Collect any additional evidence or documentation needed to support your response. This might include technical data, expert opinions, or revised drawings. Providing clear and relevant evidence strengthens your case.
- **Address Each Objection Individually** Respond to each objection raised by the examiner with a detailed explanation or amendment. Clearly outline how the invention meets the patentability criteria and how the objections have been addressed. Avoid vague or general responses.
- **Revise Claims and Description** If the objections relate to the claims or the detailed description, consider revising them to address the issues raised. This might involve narrowing or amending claims, adding new claims, or clarifying the description.
- **Provide Legal and Technical Arguments** Support your response with well-reasoned legal and technical arguments. Cite relevant legal precedents, prior art, or technical principles to justify why the objections should be overcome.

- **Maintain Professional Tone** Ensure that your response is professional and respectful. Avoid confrontational language or defensive attitudes. A well-crafted, courteous response increases the likelihood of a favorable outcome.
- **Meet Deadlines** Respond within the deadlines set by the patent office. Failure to respond on time may result in the abandonment of the application or further complications.

Example of a Response to Common Objections:

Objection: Lack of Novelty *Examiner's Objection:* "The claimed invention appears to be anticipated by prior art document X."

Response: "We respectfully disagree with the examiner's finding of lack of novelty. Our invention differs significantly from document X in that it includes a novel feature Y, which is not disclosed or suggested in the prior art. We have provided additional evidence (Exhibit A) demonstrating the unique aspects of feature Y, which were not anticipated by document X."

Objection: Lack of Inventive Step *Examiner's Objection:* "The invention appears obvious in light of prior art documents A and B."

Response: "We acknowledge the prior art references but argue that the combination proposed by the examiner does not render our invention obvious. Specifically, the inventive step is demonstrated by feature Z, which provides unexpected benefits and results not suggested by documents A and B. We have provided experimental data (Exhibit B) supporting the technical advantages of feature Z."

Possible Outcomes After Responding to Objections:

After responding to objections, several outcomes are possible:

1. **Application Acceptance** If the examiner is satisfied with the response, they may accept the application, allowing it to proceed to the next stages, such as grant and publication.
- **Further Objections** The examiner may raise additional objections or requests for clarification. In this case, further responses may be required to address the new issues.
- **Application Refusal** If the objections are not adequately addressed, the patent application may be refused. However, there may be opportunities to appeal the decision or amend the application and refile.

Tips for Successful Patent Examination and Objection Reply:

1. **Collaborate with Experts** Work closely with patent attorneys, technical experts, and inventors to ensure a thorough and effective response. Their expertise can help navigate complex issues and strengthen your arguments.
- **Stay Informed** Keep up to date with patent laws, regulations, and practices. Understanding current trends and legal precedents can aid in crafting persuasive responses.
- **Be Proactive** Address potential issues proactively. Conducting a pre-filing patent search and reviewing the application thoroughly can help identify and address potential objections before examination.

Maintenance of Patent:

To maintain a patent and keep it in force, patent owners must pay periodic maintenance fees or renewal fees to the patent office, as per the regulations of the specific jurisdiction where the patent is registered.

Why Maintenance Fees are Necessary?

- **Limited Patent Lifespan:**
  Patents have a limited lifespan, typically 20 years from the filing date for utility patents, and to maintain the exclusive rights granted by the patent, periodic maintenance fees must be paid.
- **Keeping the Patent Active:**
  These fees ensure that the patent remains active and enforceable, preventing it from lapsing before the end of its term.
- **Jurisdictional Differences:**
  The rules and regulations regarding patent maintenance fees can vary significantly from one country to another, so it's crucial to understand the specific requirements of each jurisdiction where a patent is registered.

Types of Maintenance Fees:

- **Annuity Payments:**
These are periodic payments made throughout the life of the patent, often annually, to cover costs associated with maintaining the patent's validity.
- **Renewal Fees:**
These are due when a patent is up for renewal after its initial term has expired.
- **Re-examination Fees:**
These might be required if there is evidence that a previously granted claim should not have been allowed or if new prior art has been discovered that could invalidate existing claims.

Key Considerations:

- **Timely Payment:**
Failure to pay maintenance fees on time can lead to the patent lapsing before the end of its term, leaving the invention open to public use.
- **Grace Periods:**
Some jurisdictions offer grace periods for late payment of maintenance fees, but these periods are often accompanied by surcharges.
- **USPTO (United States Patent and Trademark Office) Requirements:**
In the US, maintenance fees are required for utility patents based on applications filed on or after December 12, 1980, and are due at specific intervals after the patent is granted (3.5, 7.5, and 11.5 years from the date of grant).
- **Indian Patent Office:**
In India, renewal fees are required to be paid in advance for each year (3rd year onwards) to keep the patent in force before the expiration of the succeeding year.

Opposition proceedings to grant of patents:
Patent opposition is a method by which any third party can examine the validity or patentability requirements of both granted and pending innovation. Through the filing of an objection with the Indian Patent Office, the public has the ability to contest both granted and pending patent applications under Indian law. Patent opposition proceedings come in two varieties under

Indian law. Pre-grant and post-grant oppositions are the terms used to describe oppositions filed prior to and following the issuance of a patent, respectively.

In India, the opposition proceedings take place before the Controller General of Patents. The major advantage of opposition proceedings with the Indian patent office is that the whole process is strictly time bound, less costly and quicker than litigation proceedings.

Section 25(1) of the Act deals with Pre-Grant Opposition and Section 25(2) deals with Post Grant opposition.

Pre-Grant Opposition: Section 25(1) of the Patents Act, 1970, states that *where an application for a patent has been published but a patent has not been granted, any person may, in writing, represent by way of opposition to the Controller against the grant of patent* on the following grounds:

a.   wrongfully obtaining the invention.

b.   the claimed invention has been published before the priority date of a claim in any specification filed in India on or after January 01, 1912, or in any other documents in India or elsewhere, subject to the limitations on anticipation under Section 29 Patents Act, 1970.

c.   The invention was previously claimed in India with an earlier priority date, i.e., anticipation by prior date, prior claiming in India.

d.   The invention was already known or in use in India prior to the claim's priority date

e.   Lack of creative step and obviousness.

f.   subject matter that is not patentable.

g.   The invention and the process by which it is to be implemented are not adequately and clearly described in the whole specification.

h.   non-disclosure of information as per requirement by Section 8 or has furnished false information.

i.   where priority of convention application is claimed, the application was not filed within 12 months from the priority date of first application.

j.   nondisclosure or wrong mentioning of the source and geographical origin of the biological material used for the invention.

k.   anticipated by the traditional knowledge in India or elsewhere.

Procedure for Pre Grant-Opposition: Rule 55 of Patents Rule, 2003, lays down the procedure to be followed for pre-grant opposition. *Any person* can file a pre-grant opposition by way of a representation to the Controller against the grant of patent based on any of the grounds mentioned above, wherein:

o   Representation for opposition shall be filed in Form 7(A) may be given at the appropriate office along with a statement and evidence in support of the opposition.

o   The Controller shall forward the notice along with representation to the Applicant. Upon receiving the representation, Applicant, if desires may choose to reply to the representation within three months from the date of notice.

o   Controller may either reject the opposition/ representation or require the amendment of complete specification within one month of receiving the reply from the Applicant.

Post Grant Opposition: Section 25(2) of the Patents Act, 1970 and Rules 55-62 of the Patents Rules, 2003, deal with Post Grant opposition. Post-grant opposition can be filed at the appropriate office by *any interested person*[2] within 12 months from the date of publication of the grant of patent in the Indian Patent Journal.

The grounds for both pre-grant and post-grant oppositions in India are the same. Nevertheless, there are several procedural differences between filing the two types of opposition. In pre-grant opposition, any person may challenge the application for grant of patent, whereas only an interested person can file a post-grant opposition. Notice of opposition is filed in Form 7. Once the notice of post grant opposition is received at the Patent Office:

o   The Controller shall constitute an Opposition Board consisting of three members and nominate one of the members as the Chairman of the Board. An examiner who was involved in the prosecution of the application cannot be a member of the Board.

o   The patentee may reply to the opposition notice within two months of receiving the notice. If the patentee does not reply to the opposition notice, then the Patent is deemed to be revoked.

o   Opponent may also file evidence in reply to the response from the patentee within one month from the date of receipt of reply by the Patentee.

o   The Board conducts an examination of the opposition notice along with replies submitted by the patentee and the opponent.

o   The Board submits a report within three months from the receipt of all the documents and evidence.

A hearing shall be scheduled by the Controller between the patentee and the opponent(s) wherein all the statements and evidence submitted by the concerned parties shall be discussed. Based on the said discussion and recommendation of the opposition Board, the Controller shall decide the outcome of the opposition notice and notify the parties of his decision.

Unlike pre-grant opposition, there is an official fee stipulated for filing a post-grant opposition. However, pre-grant opposition mechanism is faster than post grant opposition. Also, patent opposition in an early stage would only help the patent office to grant quality patents.

Restoration and Lapse of Patents:

To keep patent in force after it has been granted, the renewal fee has to be paid periodically (annually). Failure to pay the renewal fee may lead to lapse of a patent which means that patent ceases to have effect.

Under section <u>60 to 61 of the Indian Patents Act 1970</u>, the lapsed patent can be restored; if it is proved by the patentee that the failure to pay fees was unintentional and pending renewal fees is paid within 18 months from the date on which the patent ceased to have effect. The evidence must support the patentee's claim that the failure to pay fee was unintentional and there has been no undue delay in applying for restoration. The Controller may call for further evidence, which may include letters, deeds etc.

Illustration

The due date for payment of renewal fee is 24th June 2009 and the applicant fails to pay the renewal fee, as a result the patent lapses and ceases to be in force. If the applicant wants to restore the application, he shall make request to restore the application before 24th December 2010 i.e., within 18 months from the date patent ceases to be in force.

After hearing the applicant, if the Controller is *prima facie[1]* satisfied that the failure to pay the renewal fee was unintentional and that there has been no undue delay in the making of the application, he shall publish the application. Any person interested may give notice to the Controller of opposition on the grounds:

1.   That the failure to pay the renewal fee by the applicant was not unintentional; or
2.   That there has been undue delay in the making of the application.

If notice of opposition is given by the opponent to the Controller, the Controller shall notify the applicant, and shall give to him and to the opponent an opportunity to be heard before he decides the case.

If no notice of opposition is given within the period aforesaid or if in the case of opposition, the decision of the Controller is in favor of the applicant, the Controller shall, upon payment of any unpaid renewal fee and such additional fee [as may be prescribed] restore the patent and any patent of addition, which has ceased to have effect on the cesser of that patent.

The Controller may, if he thinks fit as a condition of restoring the patent, require that an entry shall be made in the register of any document or matter which, has to be entered in the register but which has not been so entered.

As, failure to pay renewal fee may lead to lapse of the patent, the time between lapse of patent and date of restoration of patent by the applicant is very crucial and during this time, there is no protection available to the patent in legal sense. During this time, someone may commercialize or use the patented invention assuming that patent has ceased to be in force. In such a case, if anyone has started commercializing the invention and then applicant restores the application and patent comes into force again, situation is extremely sensitive. This situation gives rise to following issues:

- To protect the persons who have begun to use the applicant's invention between the date when the patent ceased to have effect and the date of publication of the application for restoration, every order for restoration should include the provision and the Controller may impose other conditions for protection and compensation of the persons who have begun to use the applicant's invention.

- No suit or other proceeding shall be commenced or prosecuted in respect of an infringement of a patent committed between the date on which the patent ceased to have effect and the date of the publication of the application for restoration of the patent.

WORKING OF PATENTS IN INDIA:

It is a well-established fact that a patent is granted in order to encourage innovation and to ultimately serve the public interest. Most sovereigns accord a patentee exclusive right over an invention subject to certain conditions and limitations. One such condition is: working of the patent locally i.e., commercial exploitation of the invention for which the patent is granted, in the territory for which the patent is granted. The Indian Patent Act, 1970 ("**Act**"), for the purpose of tracking the working of the patent by the Patentees in India, imposes an obligation upon the patentee and patent licensees to disclose information related to the working of their patents in India.

Although this requirement has been part of the Act since in its enactment in 1970, the Indian Patent Office has only recently taken a serious note of the fact that compliance with this provision has been overlooked by a majority of patentees.

In its initiative to collect information on the working of Indian patents, the Patent Office has issued a circular[1] calling upon patentees and licensees to furnish information relating to the working of granted patents before March 31, 2010.

The requirement under the law:

The procedure set out under Section 146(2) of the Act and Rule 131(2) is as follows:

- ➤ Every patentee and every licensee (whether exclusive or otherwise) must furnish a statement describing the extent to which the patented invention has been worked on a commercial scale in India.

> The statement is to be furnished by way of Form 27 to the Patent Office that has granted the patent. Form 27 is to be filed for every patent in respect of every calendar year before March 31st of the succeeding year. No fees are required to be paid along with this Form.

> A separate Form is required to be filed in respect of each patent, even in case of related patents having common patentee.

> The consequences of not filing Form 27 as stated in Section 122(1)(b)[2] of Patents Act is fine which may extend to INR 10,00,000.

> Further, if it is discovered that the information provided in Form 27 is false, the provider of the information is liable to be penalized with imprisonment which may extend to six months, or with fine, or with both under Section 122(2).

> The Controller of Patents under Section 146(1) also has the power to call for information such as periodical statements as to the extent to which the patented invention has been commercially worked in India, as may be specified in the Controller's notice. This notice may be issued at any time during the continuance of the patent. A patentee or a licensee receiving the notice must furnish such information to him within two months from the date of such notice or within such further time as the Controller may allow.

> If the patent has not been worked in India, Form 27 requires disclosure of the reasons for not working of the patent and also steps being taken for working of the invention.

> In case the patent has been worked, then the quantum and value (in Indian Rupees) of the patented product manufactured in India or imported from other countries is to be disclosed.

> The patentee is required to give a declaration as to whether the requirement of the public has been met partly or adequately or to the fullest extent at a reasonable price by the working disclosed in Form 27.

Licensing of patents:

The details of all the licenses and sub-licenses granted during the last calendar year are required to be disclosed in Form 27. If the patent is licensed to a party that does not work the invention disclosed in the patent specification, then the mere act of having granted the license may not be considered as 'working of patent'. However, if the invention is being commercially exploited by the patentee's licensee in the territory of India, the patent is said to be 'worked'.

Registration of the patent license under the provisions of the Act is viewed as a prerequisite by the Patent Offices for filing of Form 27 when the disclosure in the Form relates to working by licensee(s), and it is hence advisable to register the license agreement with the relevant Patent Office before filing Form 27.

Possible consequences of not working a patent in India:

While the consequence of failure to file Form 27 is limited to Section 122(b) discussed above, a patent that has not been worked for 3 years from grant is vulnerable to issuance of a compulsory license.

Any interested party which has been unsuccessful in procuring a voluntary license from the patentee can file an application with the Controller of Patents requesting for a compulsory license after expiry of three years from grant of the patent. Such person needs to establish the occurrence of any of the three conditions in Section 84[3], one of which is 'not worked in the territory of India'. If the Controller is satisfied, he may grant the applicant a non-exclusive compulsory license for the balance term of the patent unless a shorter term is consistent with public interest. The patent can subsequently be revoked after the expiration of two years from the grant of the compulsory license on application by third party or Government if it is established that the compulsorily licensed patent has not satisfied the purpose for which it was granted.

There is no provision for Suo motu revocation by Controller. Neither is 'non-working' a ground for revocation of a patent by a person interested under Section 64 of the Act.

Thus, India does not have any direct provisions to revoke a patent for non-working. It is merely a ground for compulsory licensing under the Act. However, irrespective of whether the patent is worked or not in India, filing of Form 27 is a mandatory annual requirement under the Act, of which every patentee must take note and consider being as important as renewal of a patent itself.

'Compulsory Licenses' Under the Patents Act:

In simple terms, compulsory licenses are authorizations given to a third-party by the Government to make, use or sell a particular product or use a particular process which has been patented, without the need of the permission of the patent owner. The provisions regarding compulsory licenses are given in the Indian Patents Act, 1970 and in the TRIPS (Trade-Related Aspects of Intellectual Property Rights) Agreement at the International level. Although this works against the patent holder, generally compulsory licenses are only considered in certain cases of national emergency, and health crisis. There are certain pre-requisite conditions which need to be fulfilled if the Government wants to grant a compulsory license in favor of someone. Under Indian Patents Act, 1970 the provisions of 'compulsory license' are specifically given under Chapter XVI, and the conditions which need to be fulfilled are given is Sections 84-92 of the said Act.

Section 84 of the Patents Act:

At any time after the expiration of three years from the date of the grant of a patent, any person interested may make an application to the Controller for grant of compulsory license on patent on any of the following grounds, namely:

(a) That the reasonable requirements of the public with respect to the patented invention have not been satisfied, or

(b) that the patented invention is not available to the public at a reasonably affordable price, or

(c) that the patented invention is not worked in the territory of India.

As per Section 84, any person who is interested or already the holder of the license under the Patent can make a request to the Controller for grant of compulsory license on expiry of the three years, when the above conditions are fulfilled.

However compulsory licenses may also be granted, when –

1. Section 92 A- For exports, under exceptional circumstances.
2. Section 92A- In case of national emergency, extreme urgency of public non-commercial use by notification of the Central Government
3. Section 92 A (1) – To a country which has insufficient or no manufacturing power in the pharmaceutical sector to address public health.

India's first case of granting compulsory license:

License was granted by the Patent office in 2012 to an Indian Company called Natco Pharma for the generic production of Bayer Corporation's Nexavar. All the 3 conditions of Sec 84 was fulfilled that the reasonable requirements of the public were not fulfilled, and that it was not available at an affordable price and that the patented invention was not worked around in India. The Government took this decision for the general public benefit. However, it was heavily criticized by the Pharmaceutical Companies as they felt the license should not have been given.

Procedure for processing compulsory licence application:
On filing the application for grant of a compulsory licence along with the relevant facts and evidence, the controller will analyze the *prima facie* case made by the applicant against the patentee. After considering such factors as the nature of the invention, the applicant's ability to work the invention and whether the applicant has made efforts to obtain a licence from the patentee on reasonable terms and, if such efforts have not been successful within a reasonable period (ie, six months from the date of application), the controller will decide whether to grant or reject the compulsory licence.
In case the controller is not satisfied with the applicant's request, a notice will be issued to the applicant regarding rejection of the grant of a compulsory licence. In this scenario, the applicant may request a hearing with the controller, within one month from the date of such notice of rejection. The controller will thereafter decide the fate of the application based on the hearing discussion held with the applicant.

Terms and conditions of a compulsory licence-
- the patentee's investment in the invention.
- the workability of the patentee's invention by the applicant.
- the selling price of the patented articles (at affordable prices); and
- the term of the licence.

The government may, if it is necessary to do so in the public interest, direct the controller at any time to authorise any licensee in respect of a patent to import the patented article or an article or substance made by a patented process from abroad. Such authorization is subject to conditions, including details of royalties and other remuneration, the quantum of import, sale price of the imported article and import period, among other things.

Opposition to the grant of a compulsory licence:
When the controller is satisfied, on consideration of an application under Section 84, that a *prima facie* case has been made out for the making of an order, the applicant will be directed to serve copies of the application to the patentee and any other person appearing from the register (e.g, a licensee mentioned in the register). The application made by the applicant is thereafter published in the *Official Journal*.
The patentee or any other person desiring to oppose the application for the grant of a compulsory licence may, within the prescribed time (two months from the date of publishing the application in the *Official Journal*), file a notice of opposition via Form 14, along with the prescribed fee. The opposition statement should contain statements pertaining to the grounds on which the grant of the compulsory licence is opposed. When such a notice is served, the controller will notify the applicant and give both the applicant and opponent an opportunity to be heard before deciding the case.

Compulsory licence for exporting patented products:
A compulsory licence for exporting goods usually relates to exporting pharmaceutical products, particularly in certain exceptional circumstances. A compulsory licence is available for the manufacture and export of patented pharmaceutical products to any country with insufficient or no manufacturing capacity in the pharmaceutical sector for the concerned product, to address public health problems. Such export is allowed, provided that the compulsory licence has been granted by such country or such country has, by notification or otherwise, allowed the import of the patented pharmaceutical products from India. The pharmaceutical products may be any

patented product or product manufactured through a patented process of the pharmaceutical sector needed to address public health problems and should be inclusive of ingredients necessary for their manufacture and diagnostic kits required for their use. On receiving an application in the prescribed manner, the controller will grant a compulsory licence solely for manufacture and export of the concerned pharmaceutical product to such country under the terms and conditions as may be specified and published.

Termination of compulsory licence:
On an application along with evidence, made by the patentee or any other person deriving title or interest in the patent, the compulsory licence granted under Section 84 may be terminated by the controller when the circumstances considered for grant of the compulsory licence cease to exist. The applicant is thereafter required to serve a copy of the application and evidence to the holder of the compulsory licence and to inform the controller of the date on which the service was made effective.
The holder of the compulsory licence may file his or her objection along with evidence to the application for termination, within one month from the date of the controller's receipt of the application (and evidence). A copy of the objection and evidence is also required to be served to the applicant by the licence holder.
Thereafter, the controller will appoint a hearing for analysing the facts and issuing a verdict. If the controller decides to terminate the compulsory licence, an order setting out terms and conditions (if any) of such termination will be served to both the parties.

1-03: PATENT INFRINGEMENT

INTRODUCTION:
Patent infringement happens when someone manufactures, uses, sells, or imports a patented invention without the patent holder's permission. This permission is usually given through a licensing agreement under which the licensee pays licensing fees to lawfully practice the patented invention. While the Indian Patents Act, of 1970 does not define "patent infringement," it lists the acts that, according to the Act, would constitute infringement such as unauthorized production or commercialization of a patented invention. To use or sell a patented invention without permission of the holder is patent infringement. So, if you patent a new smartphone charger, then no one is able to produce or sell that charger without your permission.

Various Types of Patent Infringement:

The Indian law defines different types of patent infringements:
1. Direct infringement: Making, using, selling, or proposing a patented product or process without the consent of a patent holder is a direct infringement. The direct infringers are restricted from doing these as Section 48 of the Indian Patents Act gives patent holders exclusive rights to prevent these actions.
2. Indirect infringement: This occurs when a person incites or contributes to the infringement of a patent, such as:
3. Contributory Infringement: Supplying components specifically intended for use in an infringing product.
4. Inducing Infringement: Actively persuading another party to infringe on a patent.
5. Literal Infringement: This exists when a product or process matches exactly the patent claims. All the elements must integrate within the accused product to apply literal infringement.
6. Doctrine of Equivalents: A product may infringe even if it does not fall within the patent claims if, in effect, it similarly accomplishes the same purpose to reach the same result. While Indian law has not specifically mentioned a doctrine, courts here have applied its principles to limit liability avoidance in the case of minor alterations.
7. Wilful infringement: In general terms, it is the knowing infringement of a patent. Although Indian law does not mention this particular provision, courts may award higher damages to willfulness in infringement cases.
8. Equivalent infringement: It refers to the use of slightly varied technologies or processes that achieve the patented invention's result, and courts recognize this so that an infringer cannot escape liability by making minor changes.

Laws Related to Patent Infringement in India
Patent infringement in India is treated as a civil offense under Section 48 of the Patents Act, of 1970. This section provides that patent owners generally have the exclusive rights to manufacture, use, sell, or import an invention and can sue for infringement if their rights are violated. International treaties such as TRIPS (trade-related aspects of intellectual property rights) and the Paris Convention, influenced Indian patent law by setting global standards on patent protection

Exceptions to infringement of patents:
Article 30 of TRIPS allows for limited exceptions to the exclusive rights conferred by a patent. The exceptions must not unfairly prejudice the legitimate interests of the patent owner.

Private and Non-commercial Use Exception:
The exclusive rights conferred by a patent do not allow private use or monopoly over commercial activity. If a patentee is neither using nor vending the invention for profit, the Government has the power to grant a license, known as Compulsory License (CL), to a third party to use the patented invention so as to restrict the rights of the patentee for the purpose of preventing the abuse/ misuse of the rights by the property holder and to prevent the negative effect of such action on the public. The concept of CL comes into play when the patented invention is not commercialized in India, or the invention is not available to the public at reasonable prices, or the invention is not manufactured in requisite amount. The provisions of private and non-commercial use exception have been provided under Section 84 (Compulsory licenses), Section 85 (Revocation of patents by the Controller for non-working) and Section 92 (Special provision for compulsory licences on notifications by Central Government) of Patents Act, 1970 (herein after "the Act"). Currently, the provision of CL is seen as the only optimum solution of improving access to costly patented drugs in India while creating an atmosphere that harnesses R&D.

Experimental / Scientific Use Exception:
The experimental use exemption is incorporated under Section 47 of the Act. Under sub section 3 of the said section, the grant of a patent is subject to the condition that any product or process, in respect of which the patent is granted, may be made or used by any person for the purpose merely of experiment or research including the imparting of instructions to pupils.

This is one of the most widely known exceptions to patent rights and it grew up out of the concern that patent rights should not hamper the "bona fide" experiments and scientific processes. This form of experimental use exception permits third parties to carry out experimental or scientific activities relating to the subject matter of the patent without infringing the patent holder's rights.

Regulatory-use/ Prior-use Exemption:
The patent rights, on the one hand, provide economic incentives to innovate, but on the other hand, the exclusive rights they confer result into monopoly and unaffordable pharmaceutical products. Consequently, the Indian Patents (Amendment) Act, 2005 incorporated the regulatory-use or prior-use exemption under section 107A to offer a trade-off between incentives to the innovators, and limited access and costs to consumers.

This exemption is also referred as Bolar Provision and is a statutorily created exemption to patent rights that allows the manufacturers of generic drugs to undertake steps reasonably related to the development and submission of information required for obtaining marketing approval anywhere in the world in respect of a patented product without the consent of the patentee. Some countries permit the generic drug manufacturers to use the technology of a patented drug to generate data and to demonstrate bioequivalence that would assist in the regulatory or marketing approval of the generic product, while the patent is still in force.

This provision allows the generic producers to market and manufacture their goods as soon as the patent term expires. Bolar Provision has been upheld as conforming to the TRIPS agreement and is used in several countries to advance science and technology. However, exemption under Section 107A of the Act does not allow for the use of patented drug to obtain the license to manufacture and distribute the generic drug before the expiry of the term of patent.

Foreign Vessels, Aircraft or Land Vehicles Exception:

As per Article 5 of the Paris Convention, rights conferred by a patent shall not extend to the use of the patented invention on board of vessels when such vessels temporarily or accidentally enter the waters, provided that the invention is used exclusively for the needs of the vessel.

As this exception is not optional for countries party to the Paris Convention, Indian Patents Act, in order to comply, incorporated the said exception under Section 49. According to the said section, the patent rights are not infringed when the patented invention is used exclusively for the needs of foreign vessels, aircraft, or land vehicles and other accessories thereof, when such foreign vessels, aircraft, or land vehicles temporarily or accidentally comes into India.

The term "Temporarily" not only includes the accidental and unintentional entry but also the intentional and regular going into a port, provided that the vessels, aircraft, or land vehicles does not remain permanently in the territorial waters or the territory of the country. This exception is beneficial in facilitating uninterrupted international travel and reducing tensions between countries over the treatment of vessels flying their flag.

Exhaustion of Patent Rights:

The *Doctrine of Exhaustion or First Sale Doctrine* refers to the exhaustion of the exclusive rights of the patent holder once the patented invention is sold without any restriction. As per this Doctrine, the first unrestricted sale of a patented item exhausts the patentee's further control over that particular item.

The rationale behind the patent holder *exhausting* their rights once they have sold the patented product is that, by first sale of the patent invention the Patent holder has already used the exclusive rights to prevent others from making, using, selling, offering for sale in the territory of patent grant or importing an invention into the territory of patent grant and therefore has already reaped the benefits conferred by a patent.

Defenses available in Infringement:

The common defenses to patent infringement include:

> **Non-infringement**: Your product or process is not the same as the one protected by the patent in question.

> **Invalidity**: The patent in question is invalid as obvious or anticipated by prior art. Every patent is assumed to be valid based on the USPTO examination before it is awarded. Therefore, to invalidate a patent as obvious or anticipated requires convincing and clear evidence that prior art already exists.

> **Inequitable conduct**: A defense of inequitable conduct asserts:
> The patent owner misled the examiner on purpose.
> The patent owner withheld information they knew was important.
> The patent is not valid, and no infringement can be had.
> Honesty rules of some kind were broken.

> **First Sale Doctrine**: You are reselling an item legally sold to you. This defense is available because patent rights exhaust on a specific item once that item is sold.

> **Repair Doctrine**: You are repairing a device by replacing components that are not patented. This defense does not permit you to completely rebuild an invention.

> **Patent misuse**: The following examples are considered misuse of a patent:
> Using it to violate antitrust.
> Using it to crush competition.
> Using it to engage in business practices that are unethical, such as price fixing.

> **Licensing**: The patent holder granted permission or rights to use the patent to you and you have used the invention in compliance with said rights or permission.

> **Patent Exhaustion**: The accused's supplier upstream has legally purchased the patented invention from either the patent holder or a licensee of the same. Current

laws forbid a patent holder from attempting to collect payment from multiple levels of a supply chain for a single patented invention.

> **Estoppel**: There are two forms of estoppel:
File Wrapper Estoppel: If the inventor disclaimed rights or admitted to any limitations of rights in their patent application, those disclaimed rights cannot be used as part of a patent infringement case.
Equitable Estoppel: The patent holder led you to believe that there would be no enforcement of the patent. This can occur either from promises or failure to enforce. It means that the accused counted on that belief or assurances in continuing their business practices.

> **Experimental use**: You can use a patent invention if it is related to the development of information. You can also use it if it is related to the submission of the same under Federal laws regulating the use, sale, and manufacture of drugs.

Penalties to offences to patent infringement:

Patent infringement, the unauthorized use of a patented invention, can lead to civil penalties like monetary damages, injunctions to stop infringement, and potentially, costs and attorney's fees for the patent holder. Here's a more detailed breakdown of the penalties for patent infringement:

Civil Penalties:

- **Monetary Damages:**
  - **Actual Damages:** The patent holder can recover the actual financial losses suffered due to the infringement, including lost profits.
  - **Reasonable Royalty:** If the patent holder can prove a reasonable royalty rate, the infringer may be required to pay that amount for the unauthorized use of the patent.
  - **Enhanced Damages (Treble Damages):** In cases of willful or egregious infringement, the court may award up to three times the actual damages as a deterrent.
- **Injunctions:**
  - **Temporary Injunctions:** The court can issue a temporary injunction to prevent the infringer from continuing their infringing activities while the case is pending.
  - **Permanent Injunctions:** If the infringer is found liable, a permanent injunction can be issued to permanently stop the infringing activity.
- **Costs and Attorney's Fees:**
  The losing party may be ordered to pay the costs of the lawsuit, including court fees and attorney's fees, especially if the infringement was willful or egregious.
- **Destruction of Infringing Goods:**
  The court may order the destruction of infringing goods or materials.

Criminal Penalties (Limited):

- While patent infringement is primarily a civil matter, there are some specific offenses under the Indian Patents Act, 1970 that can lead to criminal penalties.
- **Examples of Criminal Offenses:**

- o **Contravention of Secrecy Provisions:** Failing to comply with secrecy orders related to certain inventions can lead to imprisonment for up to two years, fine, or both.
- o **Falsification of Entries in Register:** Falsifying entries in the patent register can lead to imprisonment for up to two years, fine, or both.
- o **Unauthorized Claim of Patent Rights:** Falsely claiming patent rights can lead to a fine of up to one lakh rupees.
- o **Providing False Information:** Furnishing false information or statements can lead to imprisonment for up to six months, fine, or both.
- o **Practicing as a Patent Agent Without Registration:** Practicing as a patent agent without proper registration can lead to a fine of one lakh rupees for the first offense and five lakh rupees for subsequent offenses.
- o **Falsely Representing that an article is Patented:** Falsely representing that an article sold is patented can lead to a fine of up to one lakh rupees.
- o **Failure to Submit a Statement of Working of a Patent:** Refusal or failure to submit a statement of the working of a patent can lead to a fine of up to ten lakh rupees.
- o **Submitting False Information in Statement of Working of a Patent:** Submitting false information in the statement of working of a patent can lead to imprisonment up to six months, or fine, or both.

Legal Remedies for Patent Infringement:
In case of infringement of patents, there are several legal remedies available to a patent holder. These remedies may vary with the jurisdiction, but they generally fall into the following categories:

1. Injunctive Relief:
Injunctive relief is one of the main remedial measures regarding patent infringement. It usually involves an order that a court issues to prevent an infringer from continuing in any infringed activity. It is granted in cases where there is a large possibility that the patent holder will prevail at trial and if the patent holder suffers irreparable harm. There are two forms of injunctions:
Pre-Trial Injunction: A court order restraining further infringement until the case is tried.
Permanent Injunction: A court order permanently prohibiting the infringer from continuing in the infringing activity after the court has found infringement.

2. Monetary Damages:
Compensation by monetary damages is given to the patent holders. Monetary damages include:
Actual Damages: The losses in actual money that the patent holder incurred due to the infringement.
Statutory Damages: These are awarded at the discretion of the law.
Enhanced Damages: it's their enhanced value, which happens if willful infringement is established, multiplied according to how the court sees fit, usually threefold of actual damages.

3. Royalty Payments:
In some jurisdictions, the infringer may be ordered to pay the patent owner a royalty to use the patented invention. This amount can be agreed upon between the parties or established by the court.

4. Costs of Litigation:

The winning party in a patent infringement case may be awarded costs of litigation, which can include attorney's fees, in some jurisdictions. This occurs most often when the infringement is egregious.

5. Confiscation of Infringing Products:
In some cases, a patent holder may seek the seizure of infringing goods, especially in cases where the goods are being sold or imported illegally.

6. Criminal Sanctions:
In some jurisdictions, patent infringement can result in criminal penalties, including fines or imprisonment, especially in cases of willful infringement or counterfeiting.

1-04: LANDMARK CASES

SECTION 3(d) OF THE PATENTS ACT, 1970

Section 3 of the Act stipulates, "What are not inventions" as per the Act. The main aim of the amendments of the Patents (Amendment) Act of 2005 is to prohibit ever-greening of drug patents and bring within the ambit of patentability, the patents on variants of those chemical compounds that show significant enhancement in therapeutic efficacy.

Section 3(d) of the Act recites as follows:

"The mere discovery of a new form of a known substance which does not result in the enhancement of the known efficacy of that substance or the mere discovery of any new property or new use for a known substance or of the mere use of a known process, machine or apparatus unless such known process results in a new product or employs at least one new reactant.

Explanation - For the purposes of this clause, salts, esters, ethers, polymorphs, metabolites, pure form, particle size, isomers, mixtures of isomers, complexes, combinations and other derivatives of known substance shall be considered to be the same substance, unless they differ significantly in properties with regard to efficacy".

Thus, Section 3(d) of the Act stipulates that in an invention claiming an already known substance, having established medicinal activity, such substance shall be deemed to be treated as a same substance, and thus, shall fall foul of patentability, <u>unless the invention is able to demonstrate significantly improved therapeutic efficacy with respect to that known compound.</u>

Often misunderstood, Section 3(d) of the Act, does not in fact act as an impediment in the patentability of pharmaceutical inventions. The Supreme Court of India in a landmark judgement[1] in 2013, has emphasized on the positive construction of Section 3(d) in the patentability of pharmaceuticals as a second tier of qualifying standards for pharmaceutical products in order to leave the door open for true and genuine inventions, but at the same time, to check any attempt at repetitive patenting or extension of the patent term on spurious grounds.

The provision of Section 3(d) of the Act is adjudicated meticulously and with utmost care by the IPO. To enable Applicants to substantiate the therapeutic efficacy of their invention, in various matters, Controllers have permitted the Applicants to produce additional data and experimental results during the proceedings, even in cases where said data and results were not directly referenced in the specification of the application.

GLEEVEC CASE:

<u>Introduction</u>
- This case is the landmark case of Section 3(d) of the Patent Act, 1970.
- This case deals with the patent that can be granted to the product if it shows **novelty and non-obviousness** of the invention.

<u>Facts</u>
- A big pharmaceutical company called Novartis AG (Appellant) wanted to get a patent registered for a cancer drug named **'Glivec'** or **'Gleevec'** which they created using a specific form of a substance called "Imatinib mesylate".

- The Assistant Controller determined that the appellant's claimed invention had been pre-emptively disclosed in a prior publication of a similar product named Zimmermann patent.
- At first, the request of the appellant was denied under a law called **Section 5 of the Patents Act, 1970** which said, "Inventions were only methods or processes of manufacture patentable".
- Later, when the law changed in 2005, the appellant tried again, but the Madras Patent office and the Intellectual Property Appellate Board rejected it.
- They said Glivec did not show better effectiveness than an earlier drug called 'Zimmermann' from the US.
- Because of this, it did not meet the requirements for a new invention under Section 3(d) of the Patent Act, 1970.
- Hence, the company appealed to the Supreme Court of India.

Issues Involved

- Whether the invention "Beta crystalline form of imatinib mesylate" claimed by Novartis is more efficacious than the substance that it was derived from i.e. "Imatinib mesylate"?
- What is the test of efficacy in the context of Section 3(d) of the Patent Act, 1970?

Observation

- The Court said the product is not a new substance, just a **different version** of an existing substance.
- To get a patent, it must meet the rules in **Section 3(d) of the Patent Act, 1970** which says the new version must improve its "known efficacy."
    - They explained "efficacy" as meaning **therapeutic effectiveness.**
- So, in this case, the company should have proven that the new version works better for treating diseases than the old one. The term "efficacy" is crucial here.
- The SC said Section 3(d) aims to stop "evergreening," where companies try to extend their patent by making small changes.
- If a new invention does not pass the Section 3(d) test, it cannot get a patent. They also clarified that this case does not mean Section 3(d) blocks all small improvements.

Conclusion

- The Court finally held that beta crystalline form of Imatinib Mesylate is not a new form of known substance and **dismissed the appeal** by Novartis AG.

SECTION 84 CASES

- Section 84 of IPC deals with the **act of a person of unsound mind** whereas the same provision has been covered under **Section 22 of the Bhartiya Nyaya Sanhita, 2023 (BNS).**
- It states that nothing is an offence which is done by a person who, at the time of doing it, by **reason of unsoundness of mind, is incapable of knowing the nature** of the act, or that he is doing what is either wrong or contrary to law.
- Section 84 IPC is **one of the general defenses** available under the IPC and provides for the defense of insanity.
- The foundation for the law of insanity was laid down by the House of Lords in 1843, in what is popularly **known as the M'Naghten case.**
- The word **'insanity' is not used** in Section 84 of IPC.

- It uses the expression 'unsoundness of mind', which is **not defined in the Code.** However, the courts in India have treated the expression '**unsoundness of mind' as equivalent to 'insanity'.**
- This section is **legal insanity and not medical insanity.** The crucial point of time for deciding the legal insanity is the material time when the offence took place.
- In order to seek protection under Section 84 of IPC, it is necessary for an accused to prove that he, because of unsoundness of mind, was **incapable of knowing the nature of the act or that the act was contrary to law.**
- The crucial point of time of such incapability due to unsoundness of mind is the **time when he committed the offence.**
- His insanity prior to or subsequent to the commission of the offence is **not in itself adequate to absolve him** from the criminal liability.

Case Law:

- In **Rattan Lal v. State of M.P(2002), Supreme Court** held that the crucial point of time at which the unsound mind should be established is the time when the **crime is actually committed** and whether the accused was in such a state of mind as to be entitled to benefit from Section 84 of IPC can **only be determined from the circumstances that preceded, attended and followed the crime.**

Essentials of section 84 of IPC:

  o   The act needs to be finished through a person of unsound thoughts.
  o   Such person needs to be impotent of judging and knowing:
  o   The actual nature of the act finished through him, or
  o   The act devoted through him is inconsistent with the regulation of the land, or the act finished through him become wrong.
  o   The impotency accordingly caused to the individual need to be because of the one-of-a-kind purpose of unsoundness of Mind.
  o   The impotency stated above in Paras2 should exist on the time of doing the act constituting an offence.
  o   In order to efficaciously plead the defense of 'unsoundness of thoughts', the necessities are required to be proved earlier than the courtroom docket of regulation past an inexpensive doubt.

NEXAVER CASE :

Introduction:

The case of Bayer Corporation Vs. Union of India and Others involved the Indian Intellectual Property Appellate Board (IPAB) upholding the decision to grant India's first compulsory license for the cancer drug Sorafenib (Nexavar). The IPAB found that Bayer had not met the reasonable requirements of the public, as the drug was neither accessible nor affordable. The ruling emphasized that the patentee must make the benefits of patented inventions available at reasonable prices, balancing public health interests with patent rights. Following the IPAB's decision, the Bombay High Court confirmed the findings, and the Supreme Court of India dismissed Bayer's appeal, reinforcing the importance of compulsory licensing in ensuring public access to essential medicines.

FACTS:

Bayer Corporation patented Sorafenib, a drug used for treating liver and kidney cancer, in India. The drug was marketed under the brand name Nexavar, priced at approximately 280,438 INR per month. In contrast, the Indian generic manufacturer CIPLA offered a generic version, Soranib, for about 27,960 INR. Amid ongoing legal disputes with CIPLA, Natco Pharma sought a compulsory license to produce Sorafenib, arguing that Bayer's pricing and availability did not meet public needs. The Controller of Patents granted the license, stating Bayer failed to satisfy the requirements of the Indian Patent Act. Bayer appealed this decision, leading to the IPAB's ruling that upheld the compulsory license, allowing Natco to produce the drug at a lower cost while increasing Bayer's royalty from 6% to 7% of profits.

LEGAL ISSUES:

> Whether Bayer adequately met the reasonable requirements of the public for the patented drug Sorafenib.
> Whether the pricing of Nexavar was considered affordable for the average patient in India.
> Whether Bayer was actively working the patent in India as required by the Patents Act.
> Whether the Controller of Patents followed proper procedures in granting the compulsory license to Natco Pharma.
> Whether the grounds for granting a compulsory license were satisfied based on the evidence provided.
> Whether the decision to grant a compulsory license would set a precedent affecting future patent rights and public health considerations.

CONTENTIONS OF BAYER CORPORATION:

Bayer Corporation contended that it had fulfilled its obligations under the Patents Act by making the patented drug Nexavar available in India, albeit at a high price. Bayer argued that the pricing reflected the research and development costs associated with bringing the drug to market. The company claimed that the presence of CIPLA in the market, selling a generic version, indicated that the reasonable requirements of the public were being met. Bayer also asserted that Natco Pharma's request for a compulsory license was not valid, as it had not properly sought a voluntary license before applying for the compulsory one, which is a prerequisite under Section 84 of the Patents Act. Furthermore, Bayer maintained that it had not failed to share technical knowledge with potential licensees, as it was not obligated to do so without a formal licensing agreement in place.

CONTENTIONS OF NATCO PHARMA:

Natco Pharma contended that Bayer had not satisfied the reasonable requirements of the public regarding the availability and affordability of Nexavar. Natco highlighted that Bayer's pricing made the drug inaccessible to many patients who needed it for cancer treatment. The company argued that the high cost of Nexavar was a significant barrier to access, and thus, a compulsory license was necessary to allow Natco to produce a more affordable generic version. Natco also claimed that Bayer had not adequately worked the patent in India, as evidenced by the limited availability of the drug. Additionally, Natco maintained that it had made a good faith effort to negotiate a voluntary license with Bayer, which was rejected, thereby justifying its application for a compulsory license under the provisions of the Patents Act.

JUDGMENT:

The Intellectual Property Appellate Board (IPAB) delivered its judgment on March 4, 2013, upholding the Controller of Patents' decision to grant India's first compulsory license for the drug Sorafenib, marketed by Bayer as Nexavar. The IPAB affirmed that Bayer had not adequately met the reasonable requirements of the public, nor had it made the drug available at an affordable price. The Board emphasized that the patentee has an obligation to ensure that the patented invention is worked in India and made accessible to the public.

The IPAB clarified that the term "patented invention" under Section 84 of the Patents Act refers to inventions that must be made available to the public, satisfy public needs, and be worked within the territory of India. It noted that Bayer's high pricing and limited availability of Nexavar did not fulfill these criteria.

While the IPAB acknowledged Bayer's rights as a patentee, it stressed that the public interest must take precedence, particularly in matters of health. Consequently, the IPAB allowed Bayer's appeal to the extent that the royalty rate for the compulsory license was increased from 6% to 7% of the profits made by Natco Pharma. The judgment underscored the balance between patent rights and public health, setting a significant precedent for future cases involving compulsory licensing in India.

AFTERMATH:

The aftermath of the Bayer v. Natco Pharma case had significant implications for the landscape of patent law and public health in India. Following the IPAB's decision to grant the compulsory license for Sorafenib, several key developments occurred:

Confirmation by Higher Courts: On July 15, 2014, the Bombay High Court upheld the findings of the IPAB, reinforcing the legitimacy of the compulsory license granted to Natco Pharma. Bayer's subsequent special leave petition to the Supreme Court of India was dismissed, further solidifying the precedent set by the IPAB's ruling.

Impact on Compulsory Licensing: The case marked a turning point in the application of compulsory licensing in India. It demonstrated that the Indian legal framework could be utilized to prioritize public health over patent rights, encouraging other generic manufacturers to explore similar avenues for obtaining compulsory licenses for essential medicines.

Subsequent Applications: Following the landmark ruling, there were several applications for compulsory licenses filed by other companies. However, despite the precedent established by the Bayer case, the Controller of Patents rejected a subsequent application by BDR Pharma for a compulsory license on Dasatinib, citing a lack of a prima facie case and failure to seek a voluntary license first. This indicated that while the Bayer case opened doors for compulsory licensing, each application would still be scrutinized on its individual merits.

Public Health Advocacy: The case galvanized public health advocates and organizations, highlighting the need for affordable access to medicines in India and other developing countries. It underscored the importance of balancing intellectual property rights with the urgent health needs of populations, particularly in the context of life-threatening diseases like cancer.

Global Implications: The ruling attracted international attention and sparked discussions about the role of patent law in public health. It served as a reference point for other countries grappling with similar issues of access to medicines and the enforcement of patent rights, influencing global conversations about the TRIPS Agreement and its implications for public health.

Ongoing Challenges: Despite the positive outcomes of the Bayer case, challenges remain in the realm of compulsory licensing. The reluctance of some companies to grant voluntary licenses and the complexities involved in navigating the patent system continue to pose barriers to access for essential medicines.

ANALYSIS:

The Bayer v. Natco Pharma case represents a landmark decision in the realm of patent law and public health in India. The IPAB's ruling underscores the critical balance between the rights of patent holders and the need for public access to essential medicines. By granting a compulsory license for Sorafenib, the IPAB recognized the pressing need for affordable cancer treatment in a country where many patients cannot afford high-priced medications.

The decision also highlights the importance of the obligations imposed on patentees under the Indian Patent Act. The IPAB's interpretation of Section 84 emphasizes that patent holders must actively work their patents and ensure that their inventions are accessible and affordable to the public. This ruling sets a precedent that could influence future cases, encouraging more generic manufacturers to seek compulsory licenses when they believe that public health needs are not being met.

Furthermore, the case illustrates the complexities involved in the intersection of intellectual property rights and public health. The IPAB's decision reflects a growing recognition of the need for flexibility in patent law to address public health crises, particularly in developing countries where access to life-saving medications is often limited by high costs.

CONCLUSION:

In conclusion, the Bayer v. Natco Pharma case is a pivotal moment in the evolution of patent law in India, particularly concerning compulsory licensing. The IPAB's ruling affirms the principle that patents should serve the public interest, especially in the healthcare sector. By allowing Natco Pharma to produce a generic version of Sorafenib, the IPAB not only facilitated greater access to essential cancer treatment but also reinforced the notion that patent rights must be balanced with the needs of society.

1. Neem Patent Case

Neem extracts can be used against hundreds of pests and fungal diseases that attack food crops;t he oil extracted from its seeds can be used to cure cold and flu; and mixed in soap, it providesr elief from malaria, skin diseases and even meningitis.

In 1994, European Patent Office (EPO) granted a patent to the US Corporation WR Grace Company and US Department of Agriculture for a method for controlling fungi on plants by the aid of hydrophobic extracted Neem oil.

In 1995, a group of international non-govenrmental organizations (NGOs) and representatives of Indian farmers filed legal opposition against the patent. They submitted evidence that the fungicidal effect of extracts of Neem seeds had been known and used for centuries in Indian agriculture to protect crops, and therefore was a prior art un-patentable.

US Claimed:
- ➤ That product i.e. a particular medicine is an example of American Discovery.
- ➤ It satisfies the requirement of United States Code (USC) section 101 102 103.
- ➤ i.e. it is novel, of industrial usefulness and is non obvious.
- ➤ That what they are doing will help the Indian economy.

India Claimed:
- ➤ Neem's pesticidal properties have been known in India for years. The communities in India had already discovered storage stable mixtures of pesticides therefore Grace's patent is obvious.
- ➤ They are actually stealing the indigenous practices, knowledge of Indian peopleand c ausing harm to farmer's right to do business.

Held :
In 1999, the EPO determined that according to the evidence all features of the present claim were disclosed to the public prior to the patent application and the patent was not

considered to involve an inventive step. The patent granted on Neem was revoked by the EPO in May 2000.

2. Turmeric (Haldi) Patent Case:
The rhizomes of turmeric are used as a spice for flavoring Indian cooking. It also has properties that make it an effective in regional cooking as well as having a central place in Ayurvedic and Chinese medicine to treat various ailments. Its use within the medicinal field has been found to help against among other things inflammations, digestive disorders, liver diseases and cancer.

Fact of the Case and India's Challenge:
In 1995, two Indians at the University of Mississippi Medical Centre (Suman K. Das and HariHar P. Cohly) were granted a US Patent on use of turmeric on wound healing by administeri ngturmeric to a patient afflicted with a wound.

The Council of Scientific and Industrial Research (CSIR) of India challenged the patent in 1996.CSIR claimed that the patent lacked novelty as the use of Turmeric as a method for healing wounds was age old in India and therefore a part of the prior art. CSIR presented 32 references, some of them over a hundred years old, to support that the claims of the patent wer ewell known and part of the prior art. The process was non-novel and had in fact been traditionally practiced in India for thousands of years, as was eventually proven by ancient Sanskrit writings that documented turmeric's extensive and varied use throughout India's history.

Held:
In April 1998, the USPTO upheld the objections raised by CSIR, which were based on the argument—supported by decades-old documentary evidence—that turmeric had been used by Indian people since ancient times, and consequently cancelled the patent.

3. CASE STUDY: The San people and the Hoodia Plant

The forebears of the San people settled in the southern African region some 150,000 years ago. The San currently number about 100,000 and live in the Kalahari region of South Africa, Botswana and Namibia. The San have used the hoodia plant as an appetite suppressant for many centuries, especially during hunting expeditions where little food was available for many days. In 1963, CSIR became aware of the plant's traditional uses, from a 1937 paper by a Dutch ethnobiologist, and from San trackers who had worked for the South African military. In the 1980s, the CSIR revived its interest in the plant and isolated its active ingredient, a compound called P57, which it then patented in 1995. In 1997 the CSIR licensed P57 to a small British biotech company, Phyto pharm, which conducted double blind clinical trials of the chemical, confirming its appetite suppressing qualities. In a phase I trial, obese people were given P57 or placebo, and the group receiving the active compound spontaneously reduced their daily food intake by 1000 calories.4 Phytopharm then sub-licensed the product to Pfizer for $21 million.
A lawyer representing the San people in the contemporaneous land negotiations with the South African government found out about the license to Phytopharm of the CSIR P57 patents. The lawyer also became aware that the head of Phytopharm believed that the Khomani San had disappeared.

When the Phytopharm CEO was informed of his error, he expressed concern about proper compensation for the San community, "I honestly believed that these bushmen had died out and am sorry to hear they feel hard done by. I am delighted that they are still around and have a recognizable community. The ownership of medicinal plants is extremely complex, but I have always believed that this type of knowledge is the most valuable asset of indigenous tribes. Instead of weaving baskets and taking tourists around, royalty payments from medicines could transform their prospects."5 At CSIR, the head of the P57 project said that he had intended to tell the San about the drug development once a successful product had emerged, so as not to raise false hopes.

The attorney representing the San in the land claims communicated the news of the patents to the newly established San political organization, which decided to challenge the lack of compensation for their traditional knowledge. An urgent meeting was called between the Working Group of Indigenous Minorities in Southern Africa (WIMSA), representing San people in several countries in the region, and representatives of CSIR in June 2001. The attorney described the timing of the patent issue as opportune, since the San had recently organized politically to address the land claims and other heritage problems, and so were in a good position to enter negotiations. Under the auspices of WIMSA, a South African San Council was formed in November 2001, which represented the claims regarding traditional knowledge and benefit sharing in negotiations with CSIR. The San did not challenge the patent itself (which could have resulted in loss of profitability as the commercial knowledge then became public) but rather demanded some form of benefit from the commercial development process. In response the CSIR immediately acknowledged that some form of compensation was appropriate and began negotiations with the indigenous people's representatives. As a result, the San Council and the CSIR entered into a memorandum of understanding in February 2002 recognizing the San contribution in the form of traditional knowledge. WIMSA reports that benefits will be shared not only with the South African San but also with San peoples in other countries in the region: Namibia, Botswana, Angola, Zambia and Zimbabwe. Reaching an agreement took three years of "tough negotiations," to quote the San Council chair. Under the terms of the agreement reached between CSIR and the San, announced in March 2003, CSIR will pay 6% of all milestone payments (estimated to be $0.9 to $1.4 million) it receives from Phytopharm, and 8% of all royalties from products developed from P57. Milestone payments are paid upon completion of agreed technical performance targets over a three-to-four-year period. Royalties would be based on sales, which were not anticipated before 2008. Payments are to be made to a trust fund established for the San, the San Hoodia Benefit-Sharing Trust. The Trust includes representatives of CSIR, the regional San Councils, WIMSA, and an observer from the South African Department of Science and Technology. The trust fund can then be used for local development projects in the community. The San plan to use the money for education, jobs, and preservation of their language. As described in a press release, the trust is set up "to use income received from the CSIR for general upliftment, development and training of the San Community as approved by the Board of Trustees." The agreement has been hailed as a landmark in more equitable sharing of benefits from traditional knowledge. At a ceremony celebrating the agreement a San participant, said "I am happy that others can benefit from our plants." But a San community development facilitator replied: "But it would be wrong if fat white people overseas get slim thanks to us while our children go hungry and uneducated." However, as of August 1, 2003, Pfizer discontinued its development program for P57 and returned the sublicense rights to Phytopharm. The Phytopharm Chief Executive commented that considerable clinical and preclinical data have been obtained and that his company is now seeking other partners for commercial development. The drug has been through phase IIa trials and is reported to have clinical promise in the growing market for anti-obesity compounds. The hoodia plant has already made it to the "gray" market of internet sales of natural products, although the quality of these unrefined and untested supplements is unknown.

02-05: TRADEMARKS & INDUSTRIAL DESIGN

Introduction:
In this competitive business environment, protecting a business' specific identities has become the need of the hour. Such specific identities include business name, logo, any other specific design, mark or word of identification that gives it distinctive identity from its other competitors. Any symbol, word, design or logo can be protected through trademark registration. If a business has multiple trademarks representing it, a different application needs to be filed separately for each of them. For example, say a business wants to get its brand name and logo both protected under trademark, it will then have to file separate applications for trademark registration of its brand name and logo.

What is a Trademark?
The Indian Trademark Act, 1999 under Section 2 (zb) defines a trademark as a vital Intellectual Property that marks and distinguishes products/services from others using a recognizable symbol, design, or expression. Any legal entity i.e., individual, or business, can own a trademark.

Anyone who wants to use a brand name for business purposes must file for a trademark registration for the same and get it done properly. This registration legally binds others for not using the same name for their brand, or products/services. Trademark registration of your brand name, logo, or any special identity marks it as your intellectual property that can't be utilized by others.

A trademark is used to denote the origin of a business's brand. There are different types of Trademarks in India that help in detecting the quality and origin of a product, or service, thereby preventing confusion among customers for recognizing a brand. It is used to create an identity for the business that makes it stand out differently from its competitors and helps increase consumer loyalty.

Types of Trademarks in India:
The purpose of different types of trademark registration is to assure distinction of a business, product/service and make its source, owner, or producer recognizable. When it comes to the types of trademarks in India, an individual or entity has a large variety to choose from including name, logo, shape, design, tagline, etc. However, using an existing mark is prohibited. Soft drink firms, for example, are not permitted to use Coca-Cola-like logos or names for their products.

Types of Trademarks in India

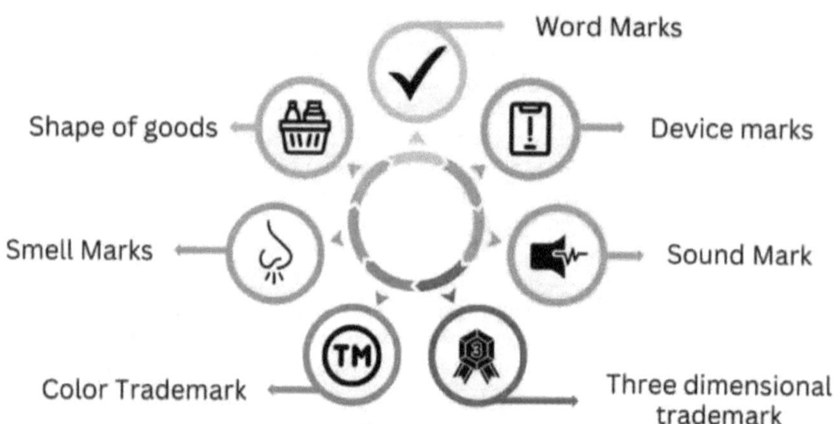

<u>Different types of trademarks in India</u>

1. Word Marks:

This type of trademark includes one or more words, letters, numerals or anything written in standard character like brand name , slogan , tagline. In simple words where one wants to register only the letters, words or combination of words or numerals without any artistic and pictorial representation can register the trade under word mark category. Flexibility is the biggest benefit that the word mark provides as after the registration of the mark; it can be used in any design, style and font. Some good examples of this type of trademarks are Microsoft, Tata, KFC, IBM.

2. Device marks:

It is one of its own types of trademarks that includes any label, sticker, monogram, logo or any geometrical figure with or without word element in it. Device marks may also include colors but if the registration is made along with colors, then the same combination of colors have to be used to claim trademark protection.

Device marks are eye-catching and attractive which makes it easy for the public to remember. When unique devices are used it helps in recognition of the business because people may not remember the name, but they can easily remember the logo. The Apple logo is a good example of device mark.

3. Sound Mark:

Sound marks are features acquired by hearing and characterized by their unique sound. It is a type of trademark where sound is used to perform the trademark function of uniquely distinguishing the commercial source of products or goods and services.

According to the new provision the sound submitted should be in MP3 format and it should not exceed 30 seconds of length and visual representation of the sound notations.YAHOO was the first company to register a sound trademark across the globe.In India ICICI bank was the first to register sound as a trademark.Some of the registered sound marks in India are:

1. Yahoo – (Human voice yodelling Yahoo)
2. National Stock Exchange – (Theme song)
3. ICICI Bank – (Corporate jingle – Dhin Chik Dhin Chik)
4. Britannia Industries (Four note bell sound)
5. Cisco – (Tune heard on logging in to the conferencing service Web Ex)
6. Edgar Rice Burroughs – (Tarzan Yell by its toy action figure)
7. Nokia – (Guitar notes on switching on the device)

4.Three-dimensional trademark:

It includes both shapes of goods or packaging.It is a non-conventional trademark and to get its registered the shape of goods or its packaging must be distinctively different from the competitors in the market and is enough for the public to recognise the origin of the goods , without the aid of other word marks on it.In simple words it must be able to perform the function of the trademark.

5.Color Trademark:

Trademark act permits registration of combination of colors to represent the goods and services.When the distinctiveness is claimed in the combination of colors with or without device it is called color mark.In trademark law the color could be considered to acquire distinctiveness when the purchasing public recognises the product or brand by particular combination of color only.In this case the brand is the color.

According to section 10 of the Trademark Act,1999, Colour trademark can be of a single color or combination of colors, but Section 2(1)(m) of the Trademarks Act, 1999 requires a mark to be a 'combination of colors' shows the intention of the legislature to not allow single-color trademarks.Thus it is suggestible to file for a combination of colors as a trademark but where a trade mark is registered without limitation of color, it shall be deemed to be registered for all colors.

6.Smell Marks

When the smell is distinctive and cannot be mistaken for another product, a smell mark can be recognized. Consider perfumes.

7.Shape of goods

Trademarks can be registered in shape or goods if they have a distinctive shape. But it cannot be registered if the -Shape of goods which results from the nature of goods themselves; Shape of goods which is necessary to obtain a technical result; Shape of goods, which gives substantial value to the goods.

Shape of goods are also non-conventional types of trademarks. In a nutshell, Consumer recognition and acquired distinctiveness becomes an important factor in granting a non-conventional trademark like Shape of goods, 3-dimensional trademark, sound mark, smell mark. In granting registration of the non-conventional trademark, the Registry needs to evaluate the balance of convenience of the Applicant of the mark with the other traders who may be using elements of such trademarks in good faith.

Selection of Brands and its overview:

Not all brands are alike. Some brand names have greater impact than others. Your brand's place on the so-called 'spectrum of distinctiveness' defines this. Trademarks ranging from generic and descriptive to suggestive, arbitrary, and fanciful. Let's understand better the notions of uniqueness so that any individual or a business entity can select a strong brand for their future goods and services or determine whether the present brand is inherently strong.

1. **Generic Mark:** The Generic mark, is considered as the brand's weakest form as it refers to the class of product or services. A brand becomes generic once it enjoys immense popularity and widespread recognition and the consuming public starts recognising the class of product and services with the brand itself and it loses its connection with the company that first or originally created it.

   In most cases, it is just a generic phrase that everyone uses to refer to a certain product or service that you offer. Some brands start as ordinary brands and then become generic as they are utilized as band aid.

2. **Descriptive Mark:** The trademark in this category no longer refers to goods and services by the common word but they refer to characteristics of a product or its quality.

   You may seek the registration in descriptive marks by illustrating that your brand has earned distinctiveness, that is, you can show that when people hear or see your brand, they think of your products or services, not just any product or service with particular features.

   Brands with descriptive types of trademarks have a significant market reach, allowing them to become acceptable trademarks for their owners. Some examples of such type of trademark include KFC, American Airlines, Whirlpool, Louis Vuitton, and Pepsi.

3. **Suggestive Mark:** They outperform generic and descriptive marks together. This type of mark provides suggestions to the consumer to connect with products or services. They make considerably more precise references to the traits and characteristics of the goods and services. Good example of this type of trademark is the telephone logo of Whatsapp LLC.

4. **Arbitrary Mark:** Arbitrary marks are dictionary phrases used to categorize goods and services that have nothing to do with the words themselves. The most well-known examples are 'Apple' and 'Adobe.' In layman's language, arbitrary markings are seen as essentially effective marks because they have nothing to do with the goods or services they are meant to represent.

5. **Fanciful Mark:** Finally, these marks are defined coin words or coined terms that have no meaning other than to indicate certain items or services and has never been used for product or services KODAK, for example, denotes nothing more than a photography brand; similarly, Twitter denotes nothing more than the name of a social media platform. More examples are available to help you understand. Walmart, Pepsi, Marlboro, Audi, and Ola, uber are all excellent examples of fanciful marks.

Companies and Trademark experts should use aforementioned types of trademarks depending on their business nature as well as requirement. If you want to create a new brand, your brand objective should reflect from your products or services.

Distinctiveness vs Descriptiveness of Trademarks

A successful trademark is a valuable asset that can boost the reputation of a brand and affect the preferences of its consumers. We opt for trademarks when we form a new, distinct meaning to the current word. Besides, we can also use it when we coin a new term to prevent customer confusion on the market and also to distinguish the origin of the products and services. Now, let us look into the difference between the distinctiveness and descriptiveness of the trademark.

Distinctiveness:
The Trade and Merchandise Marks Act 1958 states that a trademark that is not a distinctive mark is not registrable in Part A of the register. Distinctiveness means we should be able to differentiate a product from other products in the market. Furthermore, it should also ensure no such mark exists during the registration process. However, we can also register a mark in Part B, even if it was not "distinctive" but "capable of distinguishing" between its owner's and others' goods.

In ***The Imperial Tobacco Co. of India Ltd. v. The Registrar of Trademarks [AIR 1977 Cal. 413],*** the Calcutta High Court stated that distinctiveness means *'some quality in the trademark which earmarks the goods so marked as distinct from those of other producers of such goods.'* Distinctiveness is the inherent capacity to differentiate between your products and services from those which provide the same goods and services. Hence, we cannot register the signs that identify the product or services to be distinguished.

For example, let us consider the mark 'diet ice cream.' The business offers products such as ice cream, cold drinks, shakes, etc. First, in this mark, the word 'ice cream' means the product itself, and 'diet' means it contains fewer calories. So, we cannot register it under the trademark act.

The 1999 Act incorporates Part A and Part B of the 1958 Act. We can register a trademark under the 1999 Act if its existence is distinctive, meaning it should be capable of distinguishing between the goods or services of one person and that of another.

Trademark distinctiveness is an essential concept of the law applicable to trademarks and service marks. Therefore, we can consider a mark "distinctive" because of its ability to "identify and differentiate" goods or services.

The spectrum of distinctiveness:
Registering trademarks without distinctive characters are complex, and the United States' protection depends upon this spectrum.

1. *Generic Marks*: We use the term generic marks to designate a class or category of product or service. In *M/s. Three-N-Products Pvt. Ltd. v. M/s Kairali Exports and Anr.*, Delhi Court ruled that *"a generic mark requires a greater degree of proof and burden of proof on one who claims the distinctiveness is much higher."*

2. *Descriptive Marks*: These trademarks only describe the goods or services we use.

3. *Suggestive Marks*: Suggestive mark enables the consumer to exercise his imagination or perception about the goods, *T.V Venogopal Vs. ushodaya Enterprises Ltd. &Anr 2011*

4. *Arbitrary Marks*: These marks have a specific meaning, but they have no connection to the goods or services of the business.

5. *Fanciful Marks*: Businesses often come up with fanciful trademarks to represent their products or services, and these marks have no other significance.

Descriptiveness:

Most trademark controversies are on whether the trademark is specifically descriptive of products or services. Furthermore, we usually do not register descriptive words as trademarks; a trademark is descriptive if it transmits information directly.

In ***Consim Info Pvt. Ltd. v. Google India Pvt. Ltd. [2013 (54) PTC 578 (Mad) (D.B.) p. 606]***, the court stated that a *"descriptive mark was a word, picture, or another symbol that directly describes something about the goods or services in connection with which it was used as a mark. Such a term may be descriptive of the desirable characteristics of the goods"*. In short, descriptiveness in a mark directly describes the product or services to which we apply the mark.

To register a descriptive trademark, the owner must also persuade the Examiner that the applied trademark has gained secondary meaning and is subject to protection under Section 32 of the Act.

We are often left with the question of how to prove that any mark has gained distinctiveness or secondary significance. Hence, to justify the use of the mark, the proprietor of the mark must submit invoices, advertisements, and other related promotions.

There are three types of evidence that we can use to show secondary meaning:
– claims of ownership of similar trademarks with similar goods or services that were registered already,
– Five years of continuous use and actual evidence.

Determining mark descriptiveness:

One should consider the following factors while determining the descriptiveness of a mark:
- ➤ **Dictionary meaning** is one of the considerations when deciding if a trademark is descriptive. Nevertheless, the lack of definition is impossible if it is proved that the word has an understood and accepted meaning.
- ➤ **The first user of the mark** – If the applicant is the sole user of any trademark, it does not justify the trademark registration if he uses it descriptively.
- ➤ **Intended user** – We can consider a trademark descriptive if it describes the category of people who use the products or services.

    Thus, when deciding to use a mark for specific goods or services, we should see that it has acquired a distinctive character even though the mark looks merely descriptive. Clearly, to avail protection for a trademark, it should be distinct and have a secondary meaning. We can calculate the degree of distinctiveness or descriptiveness based on particular products or services, and you can always get in touch with experts to register your mark.

Similarities in Trademarks:

Deceptive similarity under trademark law refers to a scenario where one trademark is so similar to another that it is likely to mislead or confuse the public. This term indicates that even though two marks may not be identical, their resemblance in appearance, sound or meaning could cause consumers to mistakenly associate the marks with each other.

This potential for confusion suggests that the later mark might be capitalizing on the goodwill and reputation established by the original mark holder. The legal framework, such as Section

2(1)(h) of the Trademark Act, assesses whether marks are "deceptively similar" by evaluating their phonetic, visual and conceptual likeness.

To assess whether two trademarks are deceptively similar, several key factors should be considered:

- **Nature and Purpose of Goods:** Evaluate the similarity in the nature and purpose of goods offered under the rival trademarks.
- **Characteristics of the Marks:** Examine the nature of each mark, which could include words, created words, descriptive or non-descriptive names or geographical names.
- **Usage of the Marks:** Consider the types of goods that are currently associated with the trademarks or likely to be associated in the future.
- **Similarity in Mark Features:** Assess the degree of phonetic, visual and conceptual similarity between the marks, focusing on their essential features.
- **Consumer Profile:** Analyse the demographic and psychographic characteristics of potential buyers, including their level of education, intellect and the degree of attention likely to be exercised during their purchasing decision.
- **Purchasing Methods:** Reflect on the means by which the goods are purchased, or orders are placed, as this can influence the perception of the marks.

Nature of Deception in Trademarks:

Deception of trademarks can manifest in various ways, impacting consumer decisions. Firstly, deception concerning the goods occurs when a mark similar to a registered trademark is used on different goods, leading consumers to mistakenly believe they are buying a product from a brand they trust. Secondly, deception about the trade origin involves consumers recognising a mark and wrongly assuming that the goods come from a familiar source.

Lastly, deception concerning the trade connection happens when non-identical goods share similar marks, causing consumers to erroneously think there is an association or connection between the different brands. These deceptive practices can mislead consumers about the nature, source or affiliation of products, influencing their purchasing choices.

Different Types of Similarity Found in the Marks:

When assessing trademark similarities, it's important to consider different types:

- **Visual Similarity:** This involves comparing visual elements of the marks, including any common syllables, suffixes, prefixes, shapes and overall length. This type of similarity focuses on how the trademarks appear visually to the consumer.
- **Phonetic Similarity:** This type of similarity evaluates how trademarks sound when spoken. Marks that sound alike, such as 'Zegna' and 'Zenya' or 'Fevikwik' and 'Kwikheal', can confuse consumers, especially in oral communication or advertising.
- **Conceptual Similarity:** This similarity assesses the ideas or concepts conveyed by the trademarks. Marks that suggest similar ideas or themes can lead to consumer confusion even if they are visually or phonetically distinct. Examples include 'Gluvita' and 'Glucovita' or 'Lakme' and 'Likeme', which might evoke related images or concepts in the minds of consumers.

INDUSTRIAL DESIGN:

There are many factors of the article or product that helps to attract the consumer hence affecting the sales of that particular article or product. Consumers often get influenced by the appearance of the article. The appearance or design of the product plays a very vital role in the sale of the product. Many times, it has been seen that people get attracted by a design that has artistic merit. The designs of some articles or products are so much attractive that it attracts the public and within a short period of time, the whole stock may be sold in the market. Hence, the design of the goods helps in increasing profits by attracting customers. Some intellectuals work very hard by putting a lot of time and money to find out an attractive design for an article that would help to increase sales.

Industrial Design (ID) is the professional practice of designing products, devices, objects, and services used by millions of people around the world every day. Industrial designers typically focus on the physical **appearance, functionality, and manufacturability** of a product, though they are often involved in far more during a development cycle. All of this ultimately extends to the overall lasting **value and experience a product or service provides for end-users.**

In India, Intellectual property laws cover the rights related to trademarks, copyrights, patents, designs, and geographical indications of goods. Under Intellectual Property, Industrial design protects the physical appearance of an article. E.g., The Piaggio 'Vespa' Scooter, The Coca-Cola 'Contour' Bottle, The Volkswagen 'Beetle', The Apple iMac

Historical perspective of design law in India:
The industrial revolution in Europe, lead to the legal protection for textile designs in the U.K. The first enactment for the protection of designs was made in the U.K in the year 1787. In 1839 and 1842 more new acts were enacted for the protection of designs in the U.K. After that in 1883, the Patents, Designs, and Trademarks Act,1883 was made in the U.K. and after 1905, the separate Trademarks Act of 1905 was enacted due to which Patents and Designs law remained together.

In British India, the first legislation that governs a design was made as to the Patents and Designs Act, 1872. To give protection to inventions and designs the Inventions and Designs Act, 1888 was made. The Indian Patents and Designs Act 1911 was enacted on the basis of the British Patents and Designs Act, 1907. The enactment of the new Patent Act, 1970 repealed the provisions of the patents from the Patents and Designs Act, 1911. Thereafter the designs in India are dealt with by the Designs Act, 1911 and Designs Rules, 1933. The Designs Act, 2000 which has come into force from 11.05.2001 has been enacted by repealing the Designs Act, 1911. The new Act contains most of the provisions as were contained in the Designs Act, 1911, except some minor changes and contained some provisions that are based on the TRIPS Agreement and other International Conventions. Designs Rules, 2001 have been made as per the provisions of the Designs Act,2000.

Meaning of design under design act, 2000:
A Design is defined under section 2(d) of the Design Act, 2000. Design means only the features of shape, pattern, configuration, an ornament which is applied to any article in three forms namely two dimensional, three dimensional or both with the help of any industrial process, whether mechanical, manual, chemical, separate, or combined further resulting in the finished article and is judged solely by the eyes but it does not include any mode of construction or anything which is in substance a mere mechanical device and any trademark or property mark or any artistic work.

Essential requirement for the registration of design:

There are some prior requirements which are needed to be fulfilled in order to get the registration of the design. They are as follows-

1. It should be novel and original:
The design in order to be registered must be both novel and original which means it should be produced for the first time. It can be considered for the registration only if that particular design is unique. A combination of two or more previously published designs can be registered only if the combination produces new visuals or designs.

2. It should not be published previously:
The design which is intended for registration should not be published previously. If a copy of the publication is already available in the public library that may be sufficient to constitute publication. So, in order to get the registration, the design should not be publicly accessible.
In Kemp and Company and others v. Prima Plastics Ltd. 2000 PTC 96 Bom1
In this case it was held that if the proprietor of a design discloses it to any other person in good faith, it is not deemed to be a publication Subsequently, if the registration is obtained of the said design, the earlier disclosure would not invalidate the copyright thereof.

3. Design should not be contrary to order and morality:
The design must not be contrary to morality and order or prohibited by the Government of India or any authorized institution. The design which can cause disturbance or breach of public order and peace cannot be considered for registration.

Trademark Classes in India: A trademark class refers to the classes in which various products and services are divided under the NICE classification. There are 45 trademark classes. Each class consists of goods and services of a particular nature.

Sr. No.	Trademark Class	Description
1	Trademark Class 1	Chemical used in industry, science, photography, agriculture, horticulture and forestry, unprocessed plastics, chemical substances for preserving foodstuffs
2	Trademark Class 2	Paints, varnishes, preservatives against rust and against deterioration of wood, colorants, metals in foil and powder form for painters, decorators, printers and artists
3	Trademark Class 3	Bleaching preparations and substances for laundry use, cleaning, polishing, abrasive preparations, soaps, perfumery, essential oils, cosmetics, hair lotions
4	Trademark Class 4	Industrial oils and greases, lubricants, dust absorbing, wetting and binding compositions, fuels (including motor spirit) and illuminants, candles, wicks
5	Trademark Class 5	Pharmaceutical, veterinary and sanitary preparations, dietetic substances adapted for medical use, food for babies, disinfectants, fungicides, herbicides

6	Trademark Class 6	Common metals and their alloys, metal building materials, small items of metal hardware, pipes and tubes of metal, goods of metal not included in other classes
7	Trademark Class 7	Machines and machine tools, machine coupling and transmission components, agricultural implements other than hand-operated, incubators for eggs
8	Trademark Class 8	Hand tools and implements (hand-operated), cutlery, side arms, razors
9	Trademark Class 9	Scientific, electric, photographicl, measuring, apparatus for recording, transmission or reproduction of sound or images, data processing equipment and computers
10	Trademark Class 10	Surgical, medical, dental and veterinary apparatus and instruments, artificial limbs, eyes and teeth, orthopaedic articles, suture materials
11	Trademark Class 11	Apparatus for lighting, heating, steam generating, cooking, refrigerating, drying ventilating, water supply and sanitary purposes
12	Trademark Class 12	Vehicles, apparatus for locomotion by land, air or water
13	Trademark Class 13	Firearms, ammunition and projectiles, explosives, fire works
14	Trademark Class 14	Precious metals and their alloys and goods in precious metals, jewellery, precious stones, horological and other chronometric instruments
15	Trademark Class 15	Musical instruments
16	Trademark Class 16	Paper, cardboard and goods made from these materials, printed matter, stationery, brushes, typewriters and office requisites, plastic materials for packaging
17	Trademark Class 17	Rubber, asbestos, mica and goods made from these materials, plastics in extruded form for use in manufacture, packing, stopping and insulating materials, flexible pipes
18	Trademark Class 18	Leather and imitations of leather, animal skins, hides, trunks and travelling bags, umbrellas, parasols and walking sticks, whips, harness and saddlery
19	Trademark Class 19	Building materials, (non-metallic), non-metallic rigid pipes for building, asphalt, pitch and bitumen, non-metallic transportable buildings, monuments, not of metal.

20	Trademark Class 20	Furniture, mirrors, picture frames, goods of wood, cork, reed, cane, wicker, horn, bone, ivory, whalebone, shell, amber, mother- of-pearl, meerschaum or of plastics
21	Trademark Class 21	Household or kitchen utensils and containers, combs and sponges, articles for cleaning purposes, unworked or semi-worked glass, glassware and earthenware
22	Trademark Class 22	Ropes, string, nets, tents, awnings, tarpaulins, sails, sacks and bags, padding and stuffing materials(except of rubber or plastics), raw fibrous textile materials
23	Trademark Class 23	Yarns and threads, for textile use
24	Trademark Class 24	Textiles and textile goods, not included in other classes, bed and table covers.
25	Trademark Class 25	Clothing, footwear, headgear
26	Trademark Class 26	Lace and embroidery, ribbons and braid, buttons, hooks and eyes, pins and needles, artificial flowers
27	Trademark Class 27	Carpets, rugs, mats and matting, linoleum and other materials for covering existing floors, wall hangings(non-textile)
28	Trademark Class 28	Games and playthings, gymnastic and sporting articles not included in other classes, decorations for Christmas trees
29	Trademark Class 29	Meat, fish, poultry and game, meat extracts, preserved, dried and cooked fruits and vegetables, jams, fruit sauces, eggs, milk and milk products, edible oils and fats
30	Trademark Class 30	Coffee, tea, cocoa, sugar, rice, tapioca, sago, bread, pastry and confectionery, ices, honey, treacle, yeast, baking powder, salt, mustard, vinegar, spices, ice
31	Trademark Class 31	Agricultural, horticultural and forestry products and grains, live animals, fresh fruits and vegetables, seeds, natural plants and flowers, foodstuffs for animals, malt
32	Trademark Class 32	Beers, mineral and aerated waters, and other non-alcoholic drinks, fruit drinks and fruit juices, syrups and other preparations for making beverages
33	Trademark Class 33	Alcoholic beverages(except beers)

34	Trademark Class 34	Tobacco, smokers' articles, matches
35	Trademark Class 35	Advertising, business management, business administration, office functions.
36	Trademark Class 36	Insurance, financial affairs, monetary affairs, real estate affairs.
37	Trademark Class 37	Building construction, repair, installation services.
38	Trademark Class 28	Telecommunications.
39	Trademark Class 39	Transport, packaging and storage of goods, travel arrangement.
40	Trademark Class 40	Treatment of materials.
41	Trademark Class 41	Education, providing of training, entertainment, sporting and cultural activities.
42	Trademark Class 42	Scientific, design and technological services, industrial analysis and research services, design and development of computer hardware and software.
43	Trademark Class 43	Services for providing food and drink, temporary accommodation.
44	Trademark Class 44	Medical services, veterinary services, hygienic and beauty care for human beings or animals, agriculture, horticulture and forestry services.
45	Trademark Class 45	Legal services, security services for the protection of property and individuals, personal and social services rendered by others to meet the needs of individuals.

Classes of Industrial Design :Locarno Classification:

The International Classification for Industrial Designs ("the Locarno Classification") published by the WIPO is the system adopted for classifying design articles. The class and sub-class of the registered design records show the classification of the articles at the time of registration of the designs. They will not be re-classified in accordance with the latest edition of the Locarno Classification published by WIPO. The Locarno Classification is "solely of an administrative character"; it facilitates design searches and obviates substantial reclassification work when documents are exchanged at the international level.

According to the Locarno Classification, Class 32 sub-class 01 is the class to which the items "graphic symbols and logos, surface patterns, ornamentation" belong. Under section 2 of the Registered Designs Ordinance (Cap. 522), "design" is defined as "features of shape, configuration, pattern or ornament applied to an article by any industrial process ..." and "article" means "any article of manufacture and includes any part of an article if that part is made and sold separately".

Accordingly, if you wish to apply for registration of a design in respect of "graphic symbols and logos, surface patterns, ornamentation" (or any of the above items), you need to specify the article(s) to which the relevant Class 32 sub-class 01 items are to be applied and state the class and sub-class of the article(s) in accordance with the Locarno Classification. For example, if you wish to seek registration of a design in respect of an "ornamentation" and the ornamentation is to be applied to handbags, the article and the classification may be stated as "ornamentation for handbags" and "3-01" respectively in Application Form D1 instead of "ornamentation" and "32-01" respectively.

If you file an application for registration of design and wish to claim priority in your application based on a previous application for registration of the same design filed in a Paris Convention country or a World Trade Organization member, you are required to specify the article and the class in your application form as mentioned in the preceding paragraph even if such previous application is classified in Class 32.

Class 1 FOODSTUFFS
Class 2 ARTICLES OF CLOTHING AND HABERDASHERY
Class 3 TRAVEL GOODS, CASES, PARASOLS AND PERSONAL BELONGINGS, NOT ELSEWHERE SPECIFIED
Class 4 BRUSHWARE
Class 5 TEXTILE PIECE GOODS, ARTIFICIAL AND NATURAL SHEET MATERIAL
Class 6 FURNISHING
Class 7 HOUSEHOLD GOODS, NOT ELSEWHERE SPECIFIED
Class 8 TOOLS AND HARDWARE
Class 9 PACKAGING AND CONTAINERS FOR THE TRANSPORT OR HANDLING OF GOODS
Class 10 CLOCKS AND WATCHES AND OTHER MEASURING INSTRUMENTS, CHECKING AND SIGNALLING INSTRUMENTS
Class 11 ARTICLES OF ADORNMENT
Class 12 MEANS OF TRANSPORT OR HOISTING
Class 13 EQUIPMENT FOR PRODUCTION, DISTRIBUTION OR TRANSFORMATION OF ELECTRICITY
Class 14 RECORDING, TELECOMMUNICATION OR DATA PROCESSING EQUIPMENT
Class 15 MACHINES, NOT ELSEWHERE SPECIFIED
Class 16 PHOTOGRAPHIC, CINEMATOGRAPHIC AND OPTICAL APPARATUS
Class 17 MUSICAL INSTRUMENTS
Class 18 PRINTING AND OFFICE MACHINERY
Class 19 STATIONERY AND OFFICE EQUIPMENT, ARTISTS' AND TEACHING MATERIALS
Class 20 SALES AND ADVERTISING EQUIPMENT, SIGNS
Class 21 GAMES, TOYS, TENTS AND SPORTS GOODS
Class 22 ARMS, PYROTECHNIC ARTICLES, ARTICLES FOR HUNTING, FISHING AND PEST KILLING

Class 23 FLUID DISTRIBUTION EQUIPMENT, SANITARY, HEATING, VENTILATION AND AIR-CONDITIONING EQUIPMENT, SOLID FUEL
Class 24 MEDICAL AND LABORATORY EQUIPMENT
Class 25 BUILDING UNITS AND CONSTRUCTION ELEMENTS
Class 26 LIGHTING APPARATUS
Class 27 TOBACCO AND SMOKERS' SUPPLIES
Class 28 PHARMACEUTICAL AND COSMETIC PRODUCTS, TOILET ARTICLES AND APPARATUS
Class 29 DEVICES AND EQUIPMENT AGAINST FIRE HAZARDS, FOR ACCIDENT PREVENTION AND FOR LIFE SAVING
Class 30 ARTICLES FOR THE CARE AND HANDLING OF ANIMALS
Class 31 MACHINES AND APPLIANCES FOR PREPARING FOOD OR DRINK, NOT ELSEWHERE SPECIFIED
Class 32 GRAPHIC SYMBOLS AND LOGOS, SURFACE PATTERNS, ORNAMENTATION, ARRANGEMENT OF INTERIORS AND EXTERIORS

Legal Requirement of Designs:
The Purpose of obtaining the design registration under the Designs Act is to safeguard a novel or innovative design to be applied to a specific article under the manufacturing process through an Industrial Process or mode. At times, we see that customers' buying behaviour towards some articles for consumption is inclined not only by their actual product quality but also by the design of their appearance, e.g., a mobile phone or goggles.
The main objective of obtaining a design Registration is to make sure that the particular artisan, creator, craftsman, engineer or the designer of that design having a unique appearance is not deprived and deceived of his bonafide reward by some copycats, who might tend to use his design to their goods.

IMPORTANCE OF DESIGN REGISTRATION:
Designs play a significant role in attracting attention to products and articles. Unique and appealing designs make them easily recognizable and enhance their commercial value. Registering a design provides various benefits and protection to designers.
Enhancing Commercial Value:
Industrial design adds style, appeal, and attractiveness to a product or article, making it stand out. Registering a design increases its commercial value as it becomes exclusive to the owner. This exclusivity helps consumers identify the product with a particular brand. Registered designs can be sold or used as assets for business purposes, such as paying liabilities.
Protection and Legal Rights:
Registering a design gives the owner legal rights and protection against unauthorized copying or imitation by others. In case of infringement, the owner can file a lawsuit to recover losses and protect their market position and reputation. Additionally, owners can license or sell their registered designs to generate income or expand their production capacity.
DESIGN REGISTRATION PROCESS:
To register a design, an application must be submitted to the Office of the Controller General of Patents, Designs, and Trademarks located in Kolkata, under the Department of Industrial Policy and Promotion in the Ministry of Commerce and Industry. The office investigates and grants registration if the application meets all the necessary formal and substantive requirements outlined in the Designs Act.

Basic Requirements for Design Registration in India:
To register and protect a design under the Design Act of 2000, the following essential elements must be fulfilled:

> **Novelty Aspect:**
> The design must possess a novelty aspect, meaning it should be new and not previously registered. A combination of registered designs can be considered if it produces a new visual appearance.

> **No Prior Publication:**
> The design should not have been disclosed or published to the public anywhere in India or internationally through prior use or any other means.

> **Application of Design to an Article:**
> The design should be applied to the article itself. Registration cannot be granted without an actual article.

> **Compliance with Public Order, Morality, and Security:**
> The design should not go against public order, morality, or the security of India. Designs that the government or any authorised institution prohibits, or those contradicting public sentiment, may not be eligible for registration.

DOCUMENTS REQUIRED FOR DESIGN REGISTRATION:
The following documents are necessary to register a design in India:

> **Applicant's Name and Address:**
> The applicant's name and detailed address must be provided.

> **Nature/Legal Status of the Applicant:**
> The applicant should specify their legal status, such as being a natural person or a company. Start-ups need to provide a certificate of registration.

> **Description of the Article:**
> A description of the article and its identification as per the classification system should be included in the application.

> **Images/Drawings of the Article:**
> At least four images or drawings of the article from different angles need to be submitted along with the application.
> Steps Involved in Design Registration under the Design Act, 2000

> **Prior Art Search:**
> The applicant conducts a search to determine if any similar design has been previously registered. Online databases like IP India's public design search platform and WIPO's Global design database can assist in this search. If no similar design is found, Form no – 7 is filed along with a fee of Rs. 1000.

> **Representation and Classification of Designs:**
> The applicant identifies the appropriate class of design based on the function of the article using the Locarno classification. A representation or diagram of the design is prepared on white A4 size paper, clearly indicating the design details and applicant's information. It is important to adhere to the A4 size requirement to avoid delays. Applicant details include name, address, and the article on which the design is applied. Foreign applicants must provide an address for services in India.

> **Statement of Novelty:**
> The statement of novelty is a crucial part of the application and is placed below the representation sheet. It expedites the examination and registration process. An example statement could be: "The novelty of the 'XYZ design' resides in its unique shape and configuration as illustrated."

> **Disclaimer:**
> To distinguish the design from a trademark, a disclaimer is necessary. It clarifies that the registration does not claim any exclusive rights to words, letters, or trademarks depicted in the representation. If there are any powers of attorney, they should also be specified. A sample disclaimer draft could be:
> "This registration does not claim any right to the exclusive use of the words, letters, or trademarks appearing in the representation."

> **Claiming a Priority Date:**
> The applicant can claim a priority date in India if the application is filed in a conventional country or a member country of intergovernmental organizations. This date will be the application's filing date in any such country, provided that the application is made within 6 months in India.

> **Payment of Fees:**
> Fees can be paid by cheque, draft payable at the Kolkata head office, or in cash. The application fee for registration is Rs. 1000, and for renewal, it is Rs. 2000.

> **Initial Processing of Application:**
> The applicant is allocated a registration number upon filing the application with all the required documents and fees. The application can be filed at the Design Office in Kolkata or its branches in Delhi, Mumbai, or Chennai. The examination officer conducts a substantive examination, and a report is issued within 2 months.

> **Objection Stage:**
> If the applicant receives any formal objections, they have the opportunity to respond by filing a written reply addressing those objections. A hearing may be scheduled if the examination officer is not satisfied with the written reply. If the applicant fails to overcome the objections, the design may be declared as non-registrable. This stage should be completed within 6 months from the filing date.

> **Final Stage of Registration and Publication:**
> The application will be registered and published in the patent office if the applicant clears all stages. A certificate of registration will be issued. The registered design is valid for 10 years and can be renewed for an additional 5 years. The entire process, from filing to registration, typically takes 8 to 12 months.

TRADEMARK CASES IN INDIA:

A trademark is a unique identifier legally protecting a business's name, logo, or slogan. It signifies the origin and quality of goods and services, gaining consumer trust and brand recognition. However, deceptively similar marks can infringe upon this valuable asset, leading to confusion and potential harm. Such infringement dilutes brand identity, misleads consumers, and ultimately affects business reputation and revenue.

7 Trademark Cases on Similarity of Goods and Services in India:

Below, you'll find real-time trademark cases illustrating how the Indian judiciary interprets and approaches the concept of deceptively similar trademarks.

1. Parle Products Pvt. Ltd. v JP & Co

Parle, a biscuit maker, had a trademark for their "Parle's Glucose Biscuits" wrapper. When they noticed a similar wrapper used by JP & Co in 1961, they took legal action. The Supreme Court decided that despite minor differences, the resemblance was enough to cause confusion, highlighting the importance of avoiding confusion in trademark infringement cases.

2. Proctor and Gamble v Joy Creators

This case is centered on Proctor and Gamble's "OLAY TOTAL EFFECT" anti-ageing cream and Joy Creators' "JOY ULTRA LOOKS TOTAL EFFECTS" advertised in 2008. Despite Joy Creators using the label since 2001, the Delhi High Court sided with Proctor and Gamble, emphasizing the substantial resemblance due to extensive use of key features and the likelihood of consumer confusion.

3. Sony Corporation vs. K. Selvamurthy

Sony Corporation filed a trademark infringement suit against a tour and travel business named Sony Tours and Travels. The court ruled in favor of the defendant, stating that the businesses were distinctly different, and consumers weren't likely to be confused. Moreover, the plaintiff's delay in taking legal action was noted, resulting in costs awarded to the defendant.

4. Starbucks Corporation v. Sardarbuksh Coffee & Co

This case involves Starbucks objecting to Sardarbuksh Coffee & Co's logo and name. Despite receiving a cease-and-desist letter, Sardarbuksh continued operations, leading to a trademark infringement lawsuit.

5. Mondelez India Foods Private Limited (formerly Cadbury India Ltd.) V. Neeraj Food products

Cadbury India Limited sued over a deceptively similar mark, 'JAMES BOND,' used for chocolates. The Delhi High Court ruled in favor of Cadbury, granting an injunction and damages due to the likelihood of consumer confusion.

6. Vishnudas Trading v. Vazir Sultan Tobacco Co. Ltd.

It involves the use of the 'CHARMINAR' trademark for different products. Despite both products being tobacco-related, the court ruled that they were distinct enough to warrant separate trademark registrations.

7. Himalaya Drug Company vs S.B.L Limited

Himalaya Drug Company sued over the use of 'LIV-T,' claiming it resembled their 'LIV-52' trademark for liver tonics. However, the court ruled that generic terms like 'LIV' couldn't be exclusively claimed as trademarks, especially in the pharmaceutical industry.

How to Avoid the Trademark Cases in India?

Use the following procedure to classify your trademark to prevent legal consequences and penalties.

1. Conduct a Thorough Trademark Search: Before adopting a new trademark, conduct a comprehensive trademark search through the Indian Trademark Registry and other online databases to identify any existing marks with potential similarity. Consider both phonetic and visual similarities and the meaning and target audience.

2. Choose a Distinctive Mark: Select a unique and creative mark that differentiates your brand from competitors. Avoid using generic terms, descriptive elements, or elements already associated with other brands.

3. Understand Trademark Classification: Classify your goods and services accurately under the relevant Trademark Classes. This helps ensure you're not infringing on existing marks in similar categories.

4. Consult a Trademark Attorney: Seeking professional guidance from a qualified trademark attorney is crucial. They can advise on the legal risks associated with your chosen mark, assess its registration, and guide you through the registration process.

5. Register Your Trademark: Registering your trademark with the Indian Trademark Registry helps you get exclusive legal rights and strengthens your brand protection. It also simplifies legal action against infringers.

6. Monitor Trademark Use: Regularly monitor the marketplace and online platforms for potential infringements. Use the online trademark monitoring tools and stay updated on changes in the trademark landscape.

7. Enforce Your Trademark Rights: Take prompt action against any suspected infringement. This might involve sending cease-and-desist letters, filing opposition proceedings with the Trademark Registry, or initiating legal action.

Trademark Cases in India - Consequences & Penalties

Having a deceptively similar trademark in India can lead to several negative consequences and penalties, both civil and criminal. Here's a breakdown:

Civil Consequences:
- **Injunction:** The aggrieved party may seek a court order to restrain the infringer from using the deceptive mark, effectively stopping them from doing business under it.
- **Damages:** The court can order the infringer to compensate the trademark owner for the financial losses incurred due to the infringement. This can include lost profits, damage to brand reputation, and legal expenses.
- **Accounts of Profits**: The court may order the infringer to surrender all profits earned through the use of the infringing mark.

Criminal Consequences:
- **Imprisonment:** The Indian Trademarks Act of 1999 prescribes imprisonment of up to 3 years for intentionally using a deceptively similar trademark. In case of subsequent offenses, the imprisonment term can be extended to 5 years.
- **Fine:** The infringer may be liable to pay a fine of up to Rs. 2 lakhs, which can be extended to Rs. 3 lakhs for subsequent offences.

LANDMARK CASES OF DESIGN INFRINGEMENT IN INDIA:

Landmark design infringement cases combine creativity, intellectual property, and legal restrictions. These instances feature disagreements over the unauthorized duplication or usage of classic architectural designs, calling into question the basic nature of intellectual property rights in the area of built environments. The legal landscape around design infringement has been a focal topic for both legal practitioners and creative professionals as society increasingly appreciates the importance of distinctive architectural icons.

Section 11 in The Designs Act, 2000

11. Copyright on registration.—

(1)When a design is registered, the registered proprietor of the design shall, subject to the provisions of this Act, have copyright in the design during ten years from the date of registration.(2)If, before the expiration of the said ten years, application for the extension of the period of copyright is made to the Controller in the prescribed manner, the Controller shall, on payment of the prescribed fee, extend the period of copyright for a second period of five years from the expiration of the original period of ten years.

1.Carlsberg Breweries A/S vs Som Distilleries and Breweries:
Carlsberg Breweries A/S, the owner of the well-known trademark "TUBORG" for beer, launched a major legal struggle against Som Distilleries and Breweries Ltd. Carlsberg claimed that Som Distilleries' beer bottle, advertised as "Tuborg Strong Beer," not only infringed on its registered design for the TUBORG beer bottle but also constituted an act of passing off.
In an extraordinary ruling, the Delhi High Court gave Carlsberg the ability to pursue a composite suit against Som Distilleries for both violation of the registered design and passing off. The reasoning behind this decision was that both causes of action originated from the same selling transaction executed by Som Distilleries, and they had common legal and factual issues. When it came to the specifics, the Court found clearly in favor of Carlsberg. It ruled that Som Distilleries had definitely breached Carlsberg's copyrighted design for the TUBORG beer bottle. The Court thoroughly studied the general look of Som Distilleries' beer bottle and decided that it bore a misleading resemblance to Carlsberg's iconic bottle. This research substantiated Carlsberg's infringement allegation, showing the potential customer misunderstanding caused by the two drinks' close visual similarities.
The Court also examined the issue of passing off in relation to Som Distilleries' use of the word "Tuborg" on their beer bottle. The court highlighted that such use amounted to passing off because it was likely to deceive customers into thinking there was a connection between Som Distilleries' product and Carlsberg. The Court emphasized the risk of customer confusion, stating that Som Distilleries' use of the moniker "Tuborg" could lead customers to mistakenly associate the brand with the well-known Carlsberg.
The Delhi High Court's historic ruling not only recognized Carlsberg's claims of infringement and passing off, but also established a critical precedent by enabling the prosecution of a composite claim in circumstances where both causes of action originate from a single transaction and share common characteristics. This decision is a significant milestone in intellectual property law, emphasizing the significance of protecting registered designs and trademarks against unlawful use and potential consumer confusion.

2.Reckitt Benckiser (India) v Wyeth Ltd:
Reckitt Benckiser (India) Ltd. v. Wyeth Ltd. in the Delhi High Court addressed a critical issue of design infringement and the influence of prior publication in foreign countries on the validity of a registered design in India.
The controversy included Reckitt Benckiser's registered design for an S-shaped spatula used in the administration of hair removal cream. The company alleged that a competitor, Wyeth, had infringed on their design by creating and marketing a similar spatula.
Reckitt Benckiser's design, Wyeth maintained, was not unique or creative because it had already been published in nations such as the United States and the United Kingdom. According to Wyeth, Reckitt Benckiser's Indian design registration was declared invalid due to earlier publication in foreign countries.
The Delhi High Court took a strong opinion on this issue in a landmark verdict. The court ruled that prior publication of a design in a foreign country did not automatically render a registered design in India invalid. The court stressed that the Designs Act of 2000 was intended to safeguard distinctive and original designs, regardless of whether they had previously been disclosed in other countries.
This decision emphasizes the notion that the Designs Act's protection is intended to protect original and distinctive designs within India's jurisdiction. The mere publication of a design in other countries does not constitute grounds for rejecting a registered design in India. The court's

ruling reaffirms the premise that each country's intellectual property laws operate independently, with protection provided based on the merits of the design within that country's specific legal framework.

The decision has major consequences for Indian intellectual property law, creating a precedent that the novelty and originality of a design within Indian jurisdiction are paramount, regardless of the invention's prior disclosure in foreign jurisdictions. This case clarifies the protection granted to designs in India and helps to a greater understanding of the interaction between international intellectual property rights and state legal systems.

3.Sree Vishnu Bottles v State of Tamil Nadu:

In Sree Vishnu Bottles v. The State of Tamil Nadu, a disagreement arose between two organizations engaged in the business of purchasing empty beer and paper bottles from small merchants in Tamil Nadu and transporting them to Karnataka and Madhya Pradesh for recycling. The petitioners stated that they have been conducting their company legally for more than 30 years. They claimed, however, that certain government officials, especially the Regional Transport Officer and the local Inspector of Police, were blocking their activities without legal justification.

The petitioners asked the Madras High Court for a writ of mandamus ordering the defendants to stop interfering with their right to transport empty beer and brandy bottles from Tamil Nadu to other states.

After hearing both sides' arguments, the High Court dismissed the petitioners' writ petitions. The petitioners had failed to support their assertions of arbitrary interference by the respondents, according to the court. The petitioners had not presented any concrete examples or proof to back up their claims.

The court also highlighted that the petitioners had not exhausted all alternative remedies before turning to the High Court. They could have filed an appeal or sought recourse from the competent authorities in accordance with the applicable legislation.

The court explained that to demonstrate prior publication, the design must have been published in a tangible form, such as a real thing or a book, and must have been accessible to the public in India. The mere presence of a design in the records of a convention country's registrar of designs would not constitute previous publication.

4.Whirlpool of India Ltd vs Videocon Industries Ltd:

Whirlpool of India Ltd. v. Videocon Industries Ltd. was a watershed moment in Indian design law, addressing the issues of design infringement and passing off. The dispute revolved around the "Pebble," a semi-automatic washing machine introduced by Videocon Industries Ltd. that showed a remarkable resemblance to Whirlpool's registered design for its "Ace" washing machine.

Whirlpool sued Videocon, stating that the Pebble's design was a forgery of its Ace washing machine, infringing on its registered designs and confusing customers. Videocon denied the charges, claiming that its design was distinct from Whirlpool's and that there was no risk of consumer confusion.

After reviewing the evidence, the Bombay High Court found that Videocon's Pebble washing machine did indeed infringe on Whirlpool's registered designs. The court found that the two washing machines had a strikingly similar general look, particularly in terms of the design and structure of the wash and spin areas.

The court also determined that Videocon's objective was to capitalize on Whirlpool's goodwill and reputation by mimicking the design of its popular washing machine. Videocon's acts were considered to be passing off since consumers were likely to be deceived into thinking the Pebble washing machine was a Whirlpool product.

The Bombay High Court issued a permanent injunction prohibiting Videocon from manufacturing, selling, or offering for sale the Pebble washing machine in its decision. Whirlpool was also granted damages for infringement of its copyrighted designs and passing off.

The Whirlpool vs. Videocon decision established a precedent in Indian design law, highlighting the necessity of preserving original designs and avoiding unfair competition through design imitation. It also emphasized the importance of corporations exercising due diligence while designing products in order to avoid future infringement lawsuits.

5.Havells India Limited vs Panasonic Life Solutions India:
The case of Havells India Limited vs. Panasonic Life Solutions India Pvt. Ltd. & Anr. (CS(COMM) 261/2022) concerned a design infringement and passing off dispute between two major electrical goods manufacturers. The lawsuit focused on Havells' Enticer series of ceiling fans, which were noted for their distinctive design, which included creative patterns on the trims.

Panasonic's Venice Prime line of ceiling fans, according to Havells, were deceptively similar to its Enticer series, infringing on its copyrighted designs and confusing consumers. Panasonic denied the charges, claiming that its design was distinct from Havells' and that there was no risk of consumer confusion.

After reviewing the evidence, the Delhi High Court determined that Panasonic's Venice Prime series did not infringe on Havells' registered designs. While there were significant similarities between the two designs, the overall appearance was not substantially similar, according to the court.

However, the court determined that Panasonic's use of Havells' Enticer series' color scheme and trade dress constituted passing off. The court stated that Panasonic's adoption of these elements was likely to lead customers to believe that the Venice Prime series was manufactured by Havells.

The Delhi High Court ordered an injunction prohibiting Panasonic from using the color scheme and trade dress of Havells' Enticer series in connection with its Venice Prime series in its verdict. Havells was also given monetary damages for passing off.

The case of Havells v. Panasonic emphasizes the necessity of safeguarding original designs and preventing unfair competition through design imitation. It also stresses the importance of businesses carefully considering the possibility of passing off when utilizing similar color schemes and trade attire.

Introduction:
Copyright is a legal right granted to creators, giving them exclusive control over the use and distribution of their original works of authorship, such as books, music, and software, for a limited time. Copyright is a form of intellectual property law that protects original works of authorship, including literary, dramatic, musical, and artistic work.

What it protects?
Copyright protects the expression of an idea, not the idea itself. This means you can't copyright a fact or an idea, but you can copyright the way you express that fact or idea (e.g., the words you use, the images you create).

Types of Work under the Copyright section:
Section 13 of Chapter III within the Copyright Act, 1957 outlines the various types of works eligible for copyright protection in India. Below, you can find a brief overview of each work with copyright status. It helps you to know which category your work falls under,

1. Literary Works:
Copyright protects original written creations in form and expression, not just ideas or facts. This covers novels, poems, scripts, articles, essays, blog posts, website content, and even reference works like dictionaries. However, titles, short phrases, and factual information aren't protected. The essential factor is originality in the arrangement, selection, or wording of your writing. Protection lasts for the author's life plus 60 years in India, allowing you to control reproduction, distribution, derivative works, and public display of your creation. Remember, copyright doesn't prevent others from writing about similar topics but gives you exclusive rights over your unique expression.

2. Artistic Works:
Copyright for artistic works safeguards the original expression captured in a tangible form, not the underlying concept. Whether it's a painting, sculpture, photograph, drawing, graphic design, or diagram, originality in its visual creation is important. The copyright protects your specific artistic choices, not the object itself. You can't copyright a common object like a chair, but a unique sculpture representing that chair could be protected. Remember, ideas and titles are not protected but unique expressions made by your creativity and labour.

3. Musical Works:
Musical works include compositions of melodies, harmonies, and rhythms, whether vocal or instrumental. Under copyright, musical works are protected from unauthorized reproduction, distribution, performance, and adaptation. This includes both the musical notation and any recorded performances. Copyright ensures that composers, songwriters, and music publishers have control over the use of their creations, allowing them to earn royalties for their work and maintain artistic integrity.

4. Cinematographic Works:
Cinematographic works involve the creation of audiovisual content, including films, videos, and documentaries. Copyright protection extends to audiovisual presentation, including the screenplay, visuals, sounds, and performances. This grants filmmakers, producers, and distributors exclusive rights to control their films' reproduction, distribution, public performance, and adaptation. Copyright ensures creators can profit from their creations and maintain creative control over their works.

5. Architectural Works:

Architectural works encompass the design and construction of buildings, structures, and architectural plans. Your architectural drawings, plans, and models, as well as the built structures can be protected. This protection allows architects and designers to control their designs' reproduction, distribution, and adaptation, preventing unauthorized copying or replication. It helps the architects receive recognition for their creative contributions and can benefit financially from their designs.

6. Software's:

Software refers to computer programs and applications, including source and object codes. The protection extends to the underlying code and the software's user interface and functionality. This protection allows software developers and companies to control their programs' reproduction, distribution, and modification. With this protection, developers can monetize their software through licensing agreements and protect against unauthorized copying or distribution.

7. Databases:

Databases consist of organized collections of data or information, such as directories, catalogues, or compilations. Copyright protection extends to data selection, arrangement, and presentation within a database. This protection prevents unauthorized copying or extraction of substantial parts of the database, ensuring that creators or database owners can control access to and use of their valuable collections of information.

8. Choreographical works:

Choreographical works involve the composition and arrangement of dance movements and routines. It includes the sequence of movements, formations, and patterns. This protection allows choreographers and dance companies to control the performance, reproduction, and adaptation of their choreographic works.

9. Performing Arts:

Performing arts encompass live performances of music, dance, theatre, and other forms of entertainment. The original scripts, music scores, or choreography also come under protection. Performers, playwrights, composers, and choreographers have control over the use and distribution of their performances, ensuring they receive recognition and compensation for their artistic contributions.

How to Copyright the Works in India?

The following is the standard procedure to copyright your works in India,

Steps 1 - Eligibility: Ensure your work is original and falls under a protected category like literary works, music, software, or artistic creations. Ideas, facts, and common expressions are not protected.

Step 2 - Choose Your Form: Different forms exist for different work types. Visit the Copyright Office website to select the right one based on your creation.

Step 3 - Application Details: Carefully complete the form with accurate information, including title, author/creator name, creation date, and a brief description. Attach copies of your work (e.g., manuscript pages, music score, artwork images) or a description if copying is difficult.

Step 4 - Fee Payment: Fees vary depending on the work type and other factors. Check the website for current details and pay online or through offline methods.

Step 5 - Submit your application: Submit online through the e-filing portal or by mail to the Copyright Office in Delhi.

Step 6 - Processing and Wait: The office will process your application and may request additional information. Processing time typically takes 2-3 months.

Step 7 - Receive Your Certificate: Upon successful registration, you'll receive a copyright registration certificate – proof of ownership.

Benefits of Copyright Registration:
If you produce an original work, it will be protected automatically. But, having copyright registration provides you with the following benefits,

- ➢ **Presumption of Ownership:** A registered copyright acts as prima facie evidence of ownership in court, making it easier to prove your rights and seek legal action in case of infringement.
- ➢ **Stronger Legal Position:** In infringement cases, registration shifts the burden of proof to the infringer, strengthening your legal position and potentially reducing legal costs.
- ➢ **Access to Statutory Remedies:** Registration allows you to claim enhanced statutory remedies like injunctions, damages, and criminal prosecution against infringers.
- ➢ **Licensing:** A registered copyright allows you to license your work to others for commercial gain, generating income through royalties or fees.
- ➢ Fundraising and Investment: Registration enhances the value of your work, making it easier to attract investors or secure funding for creative projects.
- ➢ **Customs Protection:** You can record your registered copyright with Indian Customs to prevent the import of infringing copies.

Copyrights of Software's:
In today's digital age, computer software plays a vital role in almost every aspect of our lives. Whether it's the operating system on our personal computers or the apps on our smartphones, software is the driving force behind modern technology. As software becomes increasingly valuable, protecting intellectual property through computer software copyright has become essential. In this blog, we will explore the concept of computer software copyright, its importance, and the legal framework surrounding it.

Computer Software Copyright:
Computer software copyright refers to the legal protection granted to creators of computer programs or software. It is a form of intellectual property law that grants exclusive rights to the original creators or owners of software, preventing others from copying, distributing, or modifying their work without permission.
Copyright protection extends to both the source code (the human-readable instructions that make up the software) and the object code (the machine-readable version of the software). It covers various types of software, including applications, operating systems, databases, video games, and more.

Importance of Computer Software Copyright:
1. **Incentivizing Innovation:** Software copyright provides creators with the motivation and economic incentive to invest time, effort, and resources in developing new and innovative software. Copyright protection allows them to enjoy the benefits of their work by ensuring that others cannot simply copy and profit from their creations.
2. **Encouraging Competition:** While copyright protection grants exclusive rights, it also encourages competition by preventing unauthorized copying or distribution. Competitors are required to develop their own original software or

obtain proper licenses, leading to a more competitive and innovative software market.

3. **Promoting Economic Growth:** The software industry is a significant contributor to the global economy. By protecting software through copyright, governments promote economic growth by attracting investment, fostering job creation, and facilitating technological advancements.

Legal Framework for Computer Software Copyright

Copyright protection for computer software is primarily governed by national laws, but there are international agreements that establish minimum standards of protection. One such agreement is the Agreement on Trade-Related Aspects of Intellectual Property Rights (TRIPS), administered by the World Trade Organization (WTO). TRIPS sets out standards for copyright protection, including software copyright, among its member countries.

In many jurisdictions, software is automatically protected by copyright as soon as it is created in a fixed form. However, registering software with the relevant copyright office provides additional benefits, such as the ability to seek statutory damages and establish a public record of ownership.

It's worth noting that copyright does not protect ideas or functionality but rather the specific expression of those ideas in software. Therefore, while someone can create similar software with different code, they cannot directly copy the original code without permission.

Authorship & Ownership of Copyrights:

Authorship under Indian Copyright Law:

The Indian copyright law distinguishes between authorship and ownership of copyright in India. An author is someone who actually writes, composes or creates the work utilizing his or her creativity, imagination and intellectual abilities. The author of a particular copyrighted work can also be owner of the work if such work is not created under the employment or direction from some other person.

The ownership of a copyrighted work can vary depending on the conditions surrounding its creation, but an author will always remain the creator of the work because the authorship has been rewarded in order to appreciate the efforts that an author put into the creation of the work. The copyright Act, 1957 establishes a general rule that the author is the first owner of a copyright and the exceptions to this rule has been laid down under section 17 of the act, which also explains the difference between the authorship and the ownership of a copyright.

The rights of a copyright owner in India are wide, including the right to reproduce the work, the right to convey the work to the public, the right to adapt, translate, and many more. Whereas the author of the work does not have such a broad range of rights, the author's rights are limited to the right of receiving remuneration for the work created and the moral rights of being known as the creator of the work (right to paternity) and protecting the work from exploitation (right to integrity).The creator of a literary or dramatic work is referred to as the author in general, but under the copyright act, any individual who causes a work to be done is the author of that particular work. Section 2(d) of the Copyright Act of 1957 establishes a list of authors for various types of work protected by copyright. The section reads as follows:

- The author of a literary or dramatic work shall be the author.

- In musical works, the composer is the author.

- In artistic works, the artist is the author.

- The author of a photograph is the person who takes the photograph.

- The producer of a cinematographic film is the author.
- The author of a sound recording shall be the producer of such sound recording.

Ownership under Indian Copyright Law:

As previously stated, the author of the work may also be the owner of the work; but, if the work is created in exchange for any consideration or in the course of employment, the person under whose direction the work is created becomes the owner of the work.

For instance, if a person X hires another person Y, who is an application developer, to develop an application for his business under a service agreement, then X will be the owner of such an application and Y, who developed the application under X's employment in exchange for monetary compensation, will have authorship of the application. On the contrary, if Y had created the application for himself or his business, he would have been both the author and the owner of the application.

Exceptions to the General Rule – 'Author is the first Owner'

The exceptions to the general rule that the author is the first owner of copyright is laid forth in Section 17 of the Indian Copyright Act, 1957, which states that a person who pays or provides resources for a work to be created is the first owner of such work. Let us take a closer look at these exceptions.

Section 17	Subject matter
Clause (a)	Literary, dramatic & artistic work
Clause (b)	Photograph, painting, engraving, cinematographic film
Clause (c)	Work made under course of employment
Clause (cc)	Lectures delivered in public in behalf of another
Clause (d)	Work assigned by government
Clause (dd)	Work made on behalf of a public undertaking
Clause (dd)	Work of certain international organization

• Section 17(a) – Literary, Dramatic & Artistic Work

This clause states that if an author creates a literary, dramatic, or artistic work while working for the owner of a newspaper, magazine, book, or other publication under a contract for publishing such work, the owner of such newspaper or magazine becomes the first owner of the copyrighted work, unless an agreement to the contrary is in place.

Illustration – A journalist or writer working in a newspaper house is never the owner of the work he produces; only authorship is his.

- **Section 17(b) – Photograph, painting, engraving, cinematographic film**

This paragraph states that anytime a photographer is paid to take photographs, a painter is hired to paint, and a cinematographer is hired to shoot a film, the person who hired or caused such work to be done becomes the first owner of the copyright.

Illustration – A painter hired by a school to paint the school's boundary walls with storytelling paintings presenting social and moral values will not be the first owner of the paintings he made, but the school that hired the painter will be.

- **Section 17(c) – Work made under course of employment**

This section states that if a work is made during the course of employment or a service contract, the employer becomes the first owner of such copyrighted work.

In the well-known case of V.T. Thomas and Others vs Malayala Manorama Co. Ltd, the employee, an artist, created a cartoon character prior to his employment with the publishing house Manorama and continued to use it after his job terminated. The publishing house claimed that they were the first owners of the copyright because the cartoon was utilized while the artist was working for them. Although the cartoon was utilized by Manorama, it was not created by the artist during his employment with them; hence he was the sole owner of the artwork.

In another case of Neetu Singh vs Rajiv Saumitra, the court agreed that the defendant had served as a director of a company for two years, but the plaintiffs were unable to prove that the literary work authored by the defendant was part of his employment obligations.

- **Section 17(cc) – Lectures delivered in public on behalf of another**

This clause states that if a person provides a speech in public on behalf of another person, the person on whose behalf the speech was delivered is the original copyright owner, not the person giving the speech.

- **Section 17(d) – Work assigned by government**

If a copyrightable work is created as a result of a government tender, the government will be the first owner of the copyright deriving from and accruing to such works.

For example, the Indian government owns the copyright on the "statue of unity," not the engineers or architects who designed or built it.

- **Section 17 (dd) – Work made on behalf of a public undertaking**

In the absence of an agreement to the contrary, if a work is created or first published by or under the control or direction of a public undertaking, that public undertaking will be the original owner of Copyright.

- **Section 17(dd) – Work of certain international organization**

If an international organization commissions someone to create a copyrightable work on its behalf, that organization will be the original owner of the work.

OWNERSHIP & TERMS OF COPYRIGHTS:

The duration of protection for copyright works varies according to the type of work and the date of creation of the work. It is divided as follows:

Literary, dramatic, musical or artistic works:

The Copyright expires after 60 years from the end of the calendar year in which the author dies. Where a work has a joint author/co-author, it expires 60 years from the end of the calendar year in which the co-author dies. Where the author's identity is unknown, copyright expires 60 years from the end of the calendar year in which the work was first published. In a case where there are joint authors/co-authors, and the identity of one author is known and the identity of the other is unknown, the copyright expires 60 years from the end of the calendar year in which the known author dies.

Cinematograph films:
The Copyright shall subsist until 60 years from the beginning of the calendar year following the year in which the film is made available to the public.

Sound Recording:
The Copyright shall subsist until 60 years from the beginning of the calendar year following the year in which the sound recording is made available to the public. Further, the author's moral right, which is a right against distortion, is available even after the expiry of the term of copyright.

The ownership of copyright is dependent on various factors. The concept of "first owner" is quite important and may be determined as follows:

In the case of a literary, dramatic or artistic work (which includes a photograph, painting or a portrait) created during the course of employment or under a contract of service or apprenticeship, for the purpose of publication in a newspaper, magazine or similar periodical, the author of such a publication shall, in the absence of a contract to the contrary, be the first owner of copyright.

However, such ownership shall vest with the proprietor of the publication only for the limited purpose of publishing the work or a reproduction of the work in a publication and, for all other purposes, the copyright shall vest with the author of the work.

If a photograph, painting or portrait has not been made for the purposes of publication in a periodical but has been made for any other purpose, then in the absence of a contract to the contrary, the copyright in such work shall vest with the person at whose instance the work was created.

In the case of a cinematograph film, in the absence of a contract to the contrary, the copyright in the cinematograph film shall vest with the producer of the film (i.e. the person at whose instance the film was made for a valuable consideration).

In the case of a work made during the course of employment or under a contract of service or apprenticeship, the employer shall, in the absence of a contract to the contrary, be the first owner of copyright. In the case of a government work, the copyright in the work shall vest with the Government.

The copyright can be jointly owned as well. As per the Act, work of joint authorship means a work produced by the collaboration of two or more authors in which the contribution of one author is not distinct from the contribution of the other author or authors. Joint authors fully enjoy all of the rights granted by the Act, as mentioned previously. The term of copyright of a work of joint authorship is calculated with respect to the author that dies last.

RIGHTS OF THE COPYRIGHT OWNER

The copyright protection is provided by the Copyright Act,1957 in India. These protections are enjoyed by the copyright owner in two following ways:

1. Economic right of the author, and
2. The moral right of the author

Moreover, the Rights of the copyright owner are classified in detail hereunder:

1. Right to Assignment:

The copyright owner of existing work or the prospective owner of the copyright in a future work have the right to assign copyright to anyone either wholly or partially and generally subject to limitation and either for the whole term of the copyright or any part of the term.

However, in case of future assignment of copyright will take effect only when the work comes into existence. Thus, Copyrights in future work cannot be assigned effectively, unless it comes into existence.

In the Judgment of *Srimagal & co. Vs. Books (India) Pvt. Ltd.,* the court held that "no particular form of assignment of under Section 19 is required it will suffice if the assignment can be culled out in writing from some documents.

2. Right to the author to relinquish copyright:

By giving notice to the registrar of copyrights the author has the right to relinquish all or any of the rights of the work. The effect of such notice is that from the date of the notice, all his rights cease to exist for that work. However, the copyright owner can only relinquish those rights which he can, on his own, without affecting the rights of other persons like assignees.

3. Right to reproduce work:

It is a general rule given in the Copyright Act,1957 that the only author of the work has the right to reproduce his work or authorize others to reproduce his work. No one other than the author can reproduce his work without his prior permission.

In the case of, *Star India (P) Ltd. v. Leo Burnett India (P) Ltd.,* the court briefly discussed where can the works of writing be copied in cinematography. Tide came out with the logo 'Kyon Ki Bahu Bhi Kabhi Saas Banegi' which broke out a controversy because it is as same as the title of a show 'Kyon Ki Saas Bhi Kabhi Bahu Thi'. The court held that it was against the law.

4. Right to broadcast work:

The term 'broadcast' is communication to the public by any means of wireless diffusion, whether in any one or more of the forms of signs, sounds, or visual images; or by wire and includes a re-broadcast.

The author has additional rights to preserve and protect his moral rights. The author can protect his intellectual property under copyright law.

5. Right to grant Licenses:

The Owner of the copyright of any existing work may grant or allow his interest in the right by license in writing duly signed by him. Even the owner of any future copyrighted work can also allow or grant the license in respect of such work, provided that the license will take effect only after the accomplishment of that future work.

6. Other Rights:

Apart from the above, the copyright Act,1957 also provides some other kinds of rights to the author of the work like performer's right, right to sue for infringement of copyright, right to resale original copies, right to distribute copies of work or commercial rental, right of public performance and *Sui Generis Rights,* etc.

RECENT DEVELOPMENT IN COPYRIGHT LAW:

Globally, Piracy of work is one of the major problems that have been seen in recent days after the boom in internet usage, there are numerous items on the internet that have a varying degree of copyright protection such as photos, graphics, e-books, videos, news, articles, games, etc. The decentralization of the internet is one of the major reasons to make it possible for the users to disseminate a work endlessly from cyberspace through endless numbers of ways, which results in difficult to understand whether the work is a duplicate or copy of a protected work, which gave rise to global piracy.

Assignment of Copyrights in India:

Section 18 of the Copyright Act discusses "assignment of copyright." The owner of the copyright in an existing work or the prospective owner of future work has the right to assign to any person the copyright of that work. Since copyright per se is a bundle of rights, assignment of copyright could be:

1. Whole or partial,
2. Subject to certain conditions/limitations,
3. For the whole term of the copyright or any part thereof.

If the work is not yet in existence at the time of assignment (future work), the assignment shall take effect only when the work comes into existence.

Essentials of a Copyright Assignment agreement in India:

An assignment agreement shall have the following essentials:

1. It shall be made in writing and identify the work assigned.
2. It shall specify the scope of rights assigned and consideration.
3. It shall mention the duration and territorial extent of such assignment.

It is sufficient if the assignment is made in writing bearing the signature of the author or their authorized agent. Furthermore, in case where the duration of the assignment is not mentioned, as per law, it is deemed to be five years from the date of the assignment and in the case where the territorial extent of such assignment is not mentioned, as per law, it is presumed to extend within India. The assignment shall be exercised within one year from the date of assignment failing which the rights so assigned shall be deemed to have lapsed.

Recordal of Assignment of Copyrights in India with Registrar of Copyrights:

An assignment can be carried out prior to filing the copyright application or even registered copyright can be assigned. This is to be done only if the author/creator of the work is not filing the application and it is being done by a third-party who is now the owner of the work. The formalities in the event of the former have already been dealt with under "Application for Registration of Copyright."In case of the latter where the assignment is subsequent to registration, a request under Form XV (registration of changes in particulars of copyright) has to be filed with the following documents as attachments:

1. Notarized copy of the Assignment Deed.
2. An affidavit to the effect, attesting that there is no case pending in any court of law relating to the Assignment.
3. A Power of Attorney (POA), in original, if the application is filed through an authorized agent.
4. Attested Copy of the Death Certificate if the original copyright holder is deceased.

LEGAL FRAMEWORK FOR ASSIGNMENT OF COPYRIGHT

SECTION 18: ASSIGNMENT OF COPYRIGHT

Section 181 provides for the assignment of copyright. Section 18(1) allows for the owner of the copyright in an existing work or the prospective owner of the copyright in a future work to assign to any person the copyright in the work. Such assignment can be either wholly or partially and either generally or subject to limitations. Further the assignment can be either for the whole term of the copyright or any part thereof. The agreement must specify the rights being transferred, the duration of the transfer, and the territorial extent.

SECTION 19: MODE OF ASSIGNMENT

Section 192 outlines the legal requirements for a valid copyright assignment, which are:

In writing: Section 19(1) lays down that for an assignment of the copyright in any work to be valid it must be in writing and signed by the assignor or by his duly authorized agent. It emphasizes the need for a written document that clearly outlines the terms of the assignment, including the work and rights assigned, and details the duration, territorial extent, and consideration payable.

Specify the work and terms: Section 19(2) mandates that the assignment of copyright in any work shall identify such work and shall specify the rights assigned and the duration and territorial extent of such assignment.

Royalty: Section 19(3) the assignment of copyright shall specify the details of royalty or consideration mutually agreed upon by the parties.

Lapse automatically: Section 19(4) states that the assignment will lapse if the assignee fails to exercise the rights assigned to him within one year from the date of assignment unless the assignment specifically states otherwise.

Term: Section 19(5) – If the period of assignment is not specified, the assignment is deemed to be for a period of five years from the date of assignment.

Territorial Extent- Section 19(6) if the territorial extent of assignment of the rights is not specified, it shall be presumed to extend within India.

In addition to the above, Section 19(8) states that in cases where the author of the work is a member of copyright society, the assignment of copyright in any work contrary to the rights already assigned to such society shall be void.

A copyright transfer agreement should mainly include the following:

- Identify the work/subject of the copyright.
- The rights being transferred.
- The duration and geographical extent of the transfer.
- Any payment or royalties' conditions.
- Obligations of both parties.
- A dispute resolution mechanism.

Rights of Broadcasting of Copyrights:

The emergence of technology has revolutionized the world of broadcasting, presenting a multitude of opportunities and challenges for both content creators and distributors alike. In India, broadcasting organizations are protected by copyright law, which provides a comprehensive framework that aims to strike a balance between the interests of creators and broadcasters. This article delves into the rights that are granted to broadcasting organizations in India, as well as the legal landscape that governs them, offering an in-depth analysis of the subject matter.

Legal Framework

In India, the Copyright Act of 1957 is the main legal framework that provides for the safeguarding of intellectual property rights. This includes the protection of broadcasting organizations' rights. Section 37 of the Act is a provision that deals with the specific rights of broadcasting organizations in this regard.

Rights of Broadcasting Organizations

1. **Rebroadcasting Right:** To safeguard their creative output and maintain control over the dissemination of their content, broadcasting organizations are granted the exclusive right to permit or prohibit the rebroadcasting of their broadcasts. This ensures that the original broadcaster has full authority over their content and prevents any unauthorized rebroadcasts from taking place.
2. **Communication to the Public:** Organizations that produce and distribute media content are vested with exclusive rights to transmit their content to the public. This includes not only the initial broadcast, but also any subsequent communication of the

content to the public through various mediums such as cable, satellite, or online platforms. These organizations have the power to authorize or prohibit the use of their content by other parties and can take legal action against those who infringe upon their rights. The exclusive rights granted to media organizations are aimed at safeguarding their creative works and ensuring they have control over the distribution and use of their content.

3. **Fixation and Reproduction:** Broadcasting organizations are granted certain rights that allow them to create sound or visual recordings of their broadcasts. These recordings can be reproduced and stored, which enables broadcasters to preserve and archive their content for future use. In other words, this right provides broadcasters with the ability to retain a permanent record of their broadcasts, which can be accessed and used later. This is particularly important for historical purposes, as well as for maintaining a comprehensive record of significant events and developments. Overall, this right is crucial for ensuring that broadcasting organizations can maintain the integrity of their content and preserve it for future generations.

4. **Distribution Right:** The distribution right is a legal concept that provides broadcasting organizations with the sole authority to control the distribution of copies of their broadcasts. This exclusive right guarantees that the original broadcaster retains the power to determine how and where their content is disseminated, preventing others from reproducing or distributing their content without permission. The distribution right is essential for broadcasters to maintain control over their intellectual property and to monetize their content effectively. This right applies to various forms of broadcasting, including radio, television, and streaming services, and has become increasingly important in the digital age, where content piracy and unauthorized distribution are prevalent.

5. **Commercial Rental Right:** Broadcasting organizations play a crucial role in producing and distributing content to a wide audience. They invest significant resources and creative efforts in developing high-quality programming that entertains, informs, and educates viewers. To protect their investment and preserve the value of their content, broadcasting organizations hold a unique and exclusive right to determine whether the commercial rental of copies of their broadcasts should be allowed or prohibited.

   This right gives broadcasting organizations greater control over the commercial exploitation of their content, enabling them to exercise greater autonomy and ensure fair compensation for their creative efforts and investments. By prohibiting unauthorized rental and distribution of their broadcasts, broadcasting organizations can prevent competitors from profiting off their content without permission and protect their economic interests.

   In practical terms, this right allows broadcasting organizations to license their content to third-party distributors, such as cable and satellite companies, streaming services, and other media outlets. By negotiating licensing agreements, broadcasting organizations can ensure that they receive fair compensation for the use of their content and retain control over its distribution and commercial exploitation.

   Overall, the exclusive right of broadcasting organizations to determine the rental and distribution of their content serves as an essential tool for preserving the economic value of broadcast content while providing broadcasters with the necessary control over its commercial exploitation. It ensures that broadcasting organizations can continue to invest in high-quality programming and remain competitive in a rapidly evolving media landscape.

6. **Moral Rights:** Broadcasting organizations are granted not only economic rights but also moral rights to safeguard the quality and credibility of their broadcasts. These moral rights serve as a crucial mechanism to ensure proper attribution and protect against any derogatory treatment or misuse of the broadcast that may harm the reputation of the broadcaster. The purpose of granting moral rights is to protect the interests of broadcast organizations and maintain the integrity of their content by preventing any unauthorized or unethical use of their broadcasts. Thus, these rights serve as a vital tool in promoting fairness, accuracy, and accountability in the broadcasting industry.

Enforcement and Remedies:

When broadcasting organizations face infringement issues, they have legal options available to protect their rights. These options may include seeking injunctions from the court to prevent further infringement, which is a legal order that prohibits the infringing party from continuing the infringing activity. Additionally, they may also seek damages or an account of profits to compensate for the losses incurred due to the infringement. Damages refer to the monetary compensation that the infringing party is required to pay to the broadcasting organization, while an account of profits refers to the monetary value of the profits that the infringing party has earned using the unlawfully copied material. Finally, the broadcasting organization may also request the delivery-up or destruction of infringing copies to prevent any further dissemination of the infringing material.

Copyrights Registration Process:

While the copyright registration for your work under copyright law isn't obligatory, it's highly recommended for several compelling reasons. Copyright registration provides the creator with a specific set of fundamental rights over their work and assures that their creative efforts cannot be replicated for a designated period. This sense of security and legal protection fosters motivation and encourages creators to continue their artistic endeavors and produce more content.

Benefits of Copyright Registration:

Copyright registration offers several advantages to creators and intellectual property owners, including the following:

- ➤ **Safeguarding the Owner:** Copyright registration provides copyright owners exclusive rights over their work, encompassing reproduction, distribution, adaptation, dissemination, and translation.
- ➤ **Legal Protection:** Creators benefit from legal protection with copyright registration, ensuring their work cannot be reproduced without proper authorization.
- ➤ **Enhancing Brand Value:** A registered copyright serves as proof of ownership, allowing creators to use it for marketing purposes and contributing to goodwill creation.
- ➤ **Global Reach:** Copyright protection extends internationally. If a work is copyrighted in one country, it enjoys similar privileges in other countries, including India.
- ➤ **Copyright as an Asset:** Copyright is considered an intellectual property asset, making it an intangible resource that can be sold or licensed, adding economic value.
- ➤ **Owner Visibility:** Copyright registration raises the work profile, making it accessible worldwide and searchable in copyright registries. It also prevents unauthorized use of the work once registered.

➢ **Economic Stability:** Copyright registration promotes economic stability, enabling creators to reproduce and monetize their art in various forms, contributing to their financial well-being.

Copyright Symbol:

Once you've obtained copyright registration, you can use the copyright symbol (©) to indicate that your work is protected by copyright. This symbol serves as a clear notice to others that the work is under copyright protection and can help deter unauthorized use or reproduction of your creative work.

Legal Rights of a Copyright Owner:

As a copyright owner, you are entitled to a range of legal rights with the copyright registration for your work, which include:

➢ **Claiming Authorship:** You can claim authorship of your published work, asserting your paternity over the creation.

➢ **Reproduction and Storage:** Copyright registration gives exclusive privilege to the owner to reproduce the work in any tangible form and store it in any medium through electronic means.

➢ **Control Over Publication:** You can decide where and where not to publish your work, exercising the publication right.

➢ **Public Performance and Communication:** The owner may publicly perform or communicate the work to the public through copyright registration. You also have the authority to create translations or adaptations of the original work.

➢ **Protecting Reputation:** In case of any potential harm to your image or reputation, you have the right to take necessary preventive actions.

➢ **Selling or Transferring**: The owner can sell or transfer the copyright, granting others the rights to use, reproduce, or adapt the work as specified in the transfer agreement. These copyright registration and legal rights empower copyright owners to manage and protect their creative works while allowing them to control their intellectual property.

Step-by-Step Copyright Registration Process:

Securing copyright registration involves a systematic process that includes the following key steps:

Step 1: Access the official website.

Visit the Official website of the Copyright Office. Log in with your valid User ID and Password. If you still need to register, click on "New User Registration. Make sure to note down your User ID and Password for future reference.

Step 2: Submission of Application

An application containing all the necessary particulars and a statement of the particulars must be prepared in the prescribed format (FORM XIV).

After logging in, click the "Click for Online Copyright Registration" link. The online "Copyright Registration Form" requires completion in four steps:

Fill out Form XIV, then click "SAVE" to save your entered details, and proceed to Step 2

Prepare a scanned copy of your signature for uploading.

Complete the "Statement of Particulars" and click "SAVE" to save your entered details.

Fill out the "Statement of Further Particulars. This form applies to "LITERARY/DRAMATIC, MUSICAL, ARTISTIC, AND SOFTWARE" works. Click "SAVE" to store your entered details and proceed.

Make Payment: This application and the requisite fees outlined in Schedule 2 of the Copyright Act are then forwarded to the copyright registrar. Use the Internet Payment Gateway to make the required payment.

It's important to note that a separate application is necessary for each distinct work. Additionally, the applicant and an Advocate holding a Vakalatnama, or a Power of Attorney (POA) must sign every application.

Step 3: Dairy Number Issuance:

Upon receiving the application, the registrar will issue a Dairy Number, marking the initiation of the copyright registration process. Subsequently, there is a mandatory 30-day waiting period for any potential objections to be submitted. Finally, print one hard copy of each of the "Acknowledgement Slip" and the "Copyright Registration Form" and send them by post to the following address:

Copyright Division
Department For Promotion of Industry and Internal Trade
Ministry of Commerce and Industry
Boudhik Sampada Bhawan,
Plot No. 32, Sector 14, Dwarka, New Delhi-110078
Email Address: copyright[at]nic[dot]in
Telephone No.: 011-28032496

Step 4: Copy Right Objection Handling:

If no objections are raised within 30 days, a scrutinizer will assess the application for any discrepancies. If no differences are found, the registration will proceed, and an extract will be provided to the registrar for entry into the Register of Copyright.

Step 5: Objection Resolution

If objections are received, both parties will receive a notification from the examiner outlining the objections. A hearing will be arranged to address these objections.

Step 6: Application Scrutiny

Following the hearing and the resolution of objections, the scrutinizer will meticulously review the application if applicable. Subsequently, they will either approve or reject the application, depending on the specific circumstances.

Step 7: Get a Copyright Registration Certificate

Once the application is approved, the relevant authority will issue the copyright registration certificate. In the usual course of events, the entire process typically takes approximately 2 to 3 months to complete.

Checking the Status of Copyright Registration Application:

To verify the status of your Copyright registration application, follow these simple steps:
Visit the website of the Copyright registrar and locate the "Status of Application" section.
Provide the diary number you received upon submission, which is also referred to as the acknowledgment number. Submit this information, and you will receive the current status of your application.

ECONOMIC & MORAL RIGHTS OF COPYRIGHTS:

To understand how copyright works it is important to understand the rights that make up copyright protection, and how they vary depending on the type of material. There are three types of rights in copyright:

1. **Economic rights**
2. **Moral rights**
3. **Performer's rights**

Economic rights:

The main group of rights granted by the *Copyright Act* allows the copyright owner to restrict the reuse of their material by other people without their consent. These rights are often referred to as 'economic rights.

The copyright owner has the right to prevent uses that would infringe copyright in their material. They also have the right to authorise others to use the work by granting a licence or to transfer or assign their rights to another party. And in some cases, copyright owners also have the right to be paid for the use of the work, such as through royalties from statutory licenses.

Economic rights vary depending on whether the material is a work or other subject matter.

Economic rights in works

The same rights apply to literary, dramatic and musical works whereas artistic rights have fewer rights. The economic rights in other subject-matter are similar to the economic rights in Works but they aren't exactly the same.

Economic rights for literary, dramatic and musical works

The copyright owner of a literary, dramatic and musical work has the exclusive right to:

- **Reproduce the work** in a material form.
- **Publish the work.**
- **Perform the work in public.**
- **Communicate the work to the public**, such as by making it available online or electronically transmitting the work to the public, including by broadcasting it.
- **Make an adaptation** of the work.

With respect of any adaptation of a copyright owner's literary, dramatic or musical work, they also enjoy the exclusive right to reproduce the adaptation in a material form, publish the adaptation, perform the adaptation in public and communicate the adaptation to the public.

Any literary work (other than a computer program), musical work or dramatic work that is reproduced in a sound recording also attract the right to commercially rent the sound recording. Computer programs attract the right to commercially rent the computer program.

Economic rights for artistic works

Artistic works do not attract the public performance or adaptation rights that literary, dramatic and musical works enjoy. Owners of artistic works have the exclusive right to:

- **reproduce the work** in a material form.
- **publish the work.**
- **Communicate the work to the public**, such as by making it available online.

Economic rights in other subject matter
The economic rights in other subject matter depend on whether the material is a sound recording, film, broadcast or a published edition of one or more works.
Economic rights in sound recordings and films
The copyright owners of sound recordings and films have the exclusive right to:

- **make a copy** of the sound recording or film.
- cause the sound recording to be **heard in public** or cause the visual images of the film to be **seen in public** and/or the sounds of the film to be heard in public.
- **Communicate the sound recording or film to the public**, such as by broadcasting it or making it available online.

Copyright owners of sound recordings also have the right to enter into a commercial rental arrangement in respect of the recording.

Economic rights in broadcasts:
The rights enjoyed by a copyright owner of a broadcast depend on the type of broadcast. Copyrights owners of both television broadcasts and sound broadcasts (i.e. radio broadcasts) have the exclusive right to:

- **re-broadcast** the broadcast
- **Communicate the broadcast to the public** by some other means other than broadcasting it, such as by make it available online.

Copyright owners of sound broadcasts (i.e., radio broadcasts) also have the exclusive right to:

- **make a sound recording** of the sound broadcast.
- **copy that recording** of the sound broadcast.

Copyright owners of television broadcasts also have the exclusive right to:

- **make a film** of the visual images of the television broadcast.
- **copy that film** of the visual images of the television broadcast.
- **make a sound recording** of the sounds of the television broadcast.
- **Copy that sound recording** of the sounds of the television broadcast.

Economic rights in published editions of works:
Owners of published editions of one or more literary work have the right to **make a facsimile copy** (i.e., an exact copy) of the edition.
Duration of economic rights
The economic rights copyright owners get under copyright law continue for the full duration of copyright in the material. More information about how long copyright lasts is available in 'Duration of copyright'.
Infringement of economic rights
As a general rule, an infringement of economic rights happens when someone else uses copyright-protected material in a way that is within the scope of the copyright owner's exclusive rights. More details on infringement of copyright (economic rights) is available in 'Infringement of copyright'.
Moral rights of authors of works and films.
Most copyright-protected works and films also attract moral rights. They relate to a creator's personal connection to their creations, ensuring they are identified as the creator and that their material is not used in a way that is contrary to their wishes. These rights allow the author of literary works, dramatic works, musical works and artistic works or the director, producer or

screenwriter of films (collectively called filmmakers) to take certain actions to preserve and protect their connection with their work.

In Australia, there are three moral rights. They are:

- **the right of attribution** of authorship
- **the right not to have authorship falsely attributed**
- **The right of integrity** of authorship of a work.

In Australia moral rights occur automatically when a literary, dramatic, musical or artistic work or a film is created. They apply in addition to any other rights and in relation to use of the whole work or a substantial part of it.

Only individuals have moral rights. Where two or more people are joint authors of a literary, dramatic, musical or artistic work or two or more people were the principal directors, producers or screenwriters of a film each has moral rights individually.

Authors and filmmakers cannot assign, transfer or sell their moral rights. But they can give consent for their work to be used in specific ways. While moral rights are not transmissible by assignment, will or devolution by operation of law, all moral rights of authorship except the right of integrity of authorship in respect of a film can be exercised and enforced by the author's or filmmaker's legal personal representative.

The right of attribution of authorship

An author of a literary, dramatic, musical or artistic work and a filmmaker of a film has a right of attribution of authorship which gives them the right to be identified as the creator of the material. Generally, the right comes into play any time an attributable act occurs in relation to the work or film.

It is an attributable act when a literary, dramatic and musical works is:

- **reproduced** in a material form.
- **published**
- **performed in public.**
- **communicated to the public**, such as by making it available online.
- **Adapted.**

For artistic works, attributable acts occur when the works is:

- **reproduced** in a material form.
- **published**
- **exhibited to the public.**
- **Communicated to the public**, such as by making it available online.

Attributable acts in relation to films occur when the film is:

- **copied** in a material form.
- **exhibited in public.**
- **Communicated to the public**, such as by making it available online.

The author or filmmaker may be identified by any reasonable form of identification. However, if a creator has made known a particular way they wish to be identified, and the identification of them in that way is reasonable in the circumstances, the attributing party must comply. Making a preferred way of being identified can be made generally or specifically to a person who is required to identify the author or filmmaker.

An identification of the author or filmmaker must be clear and reasonably prominent. When a work is reproduced, an adaptation is made of a literary, dramatic or musical work, or a copy of a film is made, occurs when the identification of the author or filmmaker is included on each reproduction of the work or of the adaptation or on each copy of the film, in such a way that a person acquiring the reproduction or copy will have notice of the author's identity.

The right not to have authorship falsely attributed:
The right of attribution is about being acknowledged as the creator, whereas the right against false attribution allows the author or filmmaker to prevent someone else falsely claiming or implying they are the author of a work or maker of a film. The right comes into play any time an act of false attribution occurs in relation to the work or film.

In relation to a literary, dramatic and musical works, it is an act of false attribution when:

- a person's name is inserted or affixed in or on the work or a reproduction of it in such a way as to falsely imply that the person is the author or an author of the work or the work is an adaptation of a work of the person, including authorizing someone else to do so.

- dealing with the work or a reproduction of the work with a person's name inserted or affixed where the person required to attribute knows that the person whose name is inserted or affixed is not an author of the work or that the work is not an adaptation of a work of the person.

- performing the work or communicating it to the public as a work of which a person is the author or as being an adaptation of a work of a person where the person required to attribute knows that the person whose name is inserted or affixed is not an author of the work or that the work is not an adaptation of the work of the person.

An act in relation to an artistic work works is an act of false attribution when:

- a person's name is inserted or affixed in or on the work or a reproduction of it or a person's name is used in connection with the work or a reproduction of it, in such a way as to falsely imply that the person is the author or an author of the work or the work is an adaptation of a work of the person, including authorizing someone else to do so.

- dealing with the work or a reproduction of the work with a person's name inserted or affixed where the person required to attribute knows that the person whose name is inserted or affixed is not an author of the work or that the work is not an adaptation of a work of the person.

- Communicating the work to the public as a work of which a person is the author where the person required attributing knows that the person is not an author of the work.

Acts of false attribution in relation to films occur when:

- a person's name is inserted or affixed in or on to insert or affix on the film or on a copy of the film in such a way as to imply falsely that the person is the director, producer or screenwriter of the film, including authorizing someone else to do so.

- dealing with the film or a copy of the film if a person's name has been inserted or affixed where the person required to attribute with the work knows that the person whose name has been inserted or affixed is not the director, producer or screenwriter of the film.

- Communicating the film to the public as being a film of which a person is the director, producer or screenwriter where the person required to attribute knows that the person whose name has been inserted or affixed is not the director, producer or screenwriter of the film.

If the work, reproduction of a work or film in question has been altered by a person other than the author of the work or the filmmakers, then it is an act of false attribution to deal with the altered work, reproduction or copy of the film as if it is the unaltered work, reproduction of the work or the unaltered film if the person dealing with the work, reproduction of film knew it was an altered version.

The right of integrity of authorship:
Authors of literary, dramatic, musical and artistic works and filmmakers also get a right of integrity of authorship in respect of the work which allows them to stop the work or film from being subjected to derogatory treatment. For all works and films that is doing anything that results in a material distortion of, mutilation of, or a material alteration to the work or film that is prejudicial to the author's or filmmaker's honour or reputation or doing of anything else in relation to the work or film that is prejudicial to the author's or filmmaker's honour or reputation. For artistic works two additional acts may also be a derogatory treatment:

- doing anything that results in the destruction of the artwork that is prejudicial to the author's honour or reputation.
- Exhibiting the artwork in public where the exhibition is prejudicial to the author's honour or reputation because of the manner or place in which the exhibition occurs.

Moral rights of performers (Performers' rights)
Performers in a live performance or recorded performance also attract moral rights with respect to their performances. This includes performances of:

- **dramatic works** (including improvisations), such as theatre, puppetry, dance, circus acts and an expression of folklore.
- **musical works** (including improvisations)
- a **reading, recitation or delivery of a literary work,** or part of a literary work, and the recitation or delivery of an improvised literary work.

For musical works that were conducted by a conductor, the conductor is also a performer of the work.

The right of attribution of performership
Performers have a right of attribution of performership which gives them the right to be identified as a performer in the performance. Generally, the right comes into play any time an attributable act occurs in relation to the performance.
It is an attributable act when a live performance is:

- **communicated to the public,** such as by making it available online.
- **Staged (put on) in public.**

For recorded performance, attributable acts occur when the performance is:

- **copied**
- **Communicated to the public,** such as by making it available online.

The performer may be identified by any reasonable form of identification. However, if a performer has made known a particular way they wish to be identified, and the identification of them in that way is reasonable in the circumstances, the attributing party must comply. Making a preferred way of being identified can be made generally or specifically to a person who is required to identify the performer. Where a performance is presented by performers who use a group name, then identification by using the group name is sufficient identification of the performers in the group.

An identification of a performer must be clear and reasonably prominent or reasonably audible. When a copy of a recorded performance is made, reasonably prominent identification of the a performer or group of performers occurs when the identification of the performer or group of performers is included on each copy of the recorded performance, in such a way that a person acquiring the copy will have notice of the author's identity.

The right not to have performership falsely attributed.
Like authors of works and makers of films, performers have a right against false attribution to stop someone else falsely claiming they are a performer of a work. The right comes into play when an act of false attribution occurs in relation to the work.

Acts of false attribution in relation to live performances occur when, immediately before, during or immediately after the performance is put on (staged), a person putting on (staging) the performance (i.e. the person that makes the arrangements necessary for the performance to take place) states or implies falsely to the audience or intended audience that a person is, was or will be a performer in the performance or that a group of performers is, was or will be presenting the performance, including authorizing someone else to do so.

For recorded performances, an act is an act of false attribution when:

- A person's name or a group name is inserted or affixed in or on a record embodying the performance in such a way as to falsely imply that the person is a performer in the performance, including authorizing someone else to do so.

- dealing with a record embodying the performance with a person's name or a group name is inserted or affixed where the person required to attribute knows that the person whose name is inserted or affixed is not a performer in the performance or the group whose name is inserted or affixed are not performers in the performance.

- Communicating the performance to the public as a performance in which a person is a performer or a group are performers where the person required to attribute knows that the person is not a performer in the performance, or the group are not performers in the performance.

If a recorded performance has been altered by a person other than a performer in the performance, then it is an act of false attribution to dealing with the altered copy of the recorded performance as if it were not an altered copy if the person dealing with the copy knew it was an altered copy.

The right of integrity of performership:
Each performer in live or recorded performances have a right of integrity of performership in respect of the performance, meaning they have the right not to have the performance subjected to derogatory treatment. For both live and recorded performances a derogatory treatment is the doing of anything that results in a material distortion of, mutilation of, or a material alteration to, the performance that is prejudicial to the performer's reputation.

Duration of moral rights:
The duration of moral rights depends on the right in question and whether the person involved is an author of a work, a maker of a film or a performer in a performance. Generally, moral rights in a work, film or performance continue for the duration of copyright in the material, however more details on the duration of moral rights is available in 'Duration of copyright'.

Infringement of moral rights:
As a general rule, an infringement of moral rights happens when:

- An attributable act occurs in relation to a work, film or performance and the author, filmmaker or performer was not identified and it was not reasonable in the circumstances not to do so.
- an act of false attribution occurs in respect of a work, film or performance.
- a work, film or performance is subjected to derogatory treatment, and it was not reasonable in the circumstances to do so.

Exclusion & Fair Use of Copyright:
Much has been written about the fair use exception to copyright. It is simply not possible to discuss it in great detail here. What we provide is an overview of the fair use exception to provide the reader with enough information to get a high-level understanding of what the fair use exception is and how it applies.

What Is Fair Use?
Fair use is an affirmative defense to an action for copyright infringement. It is potentially available with respect to all manners of unauthorized use of all types of copyrighted works in all media. The fair use exception permits a party to use a work without the copyright owner's permission and without compensating the copyright owner for such use in certain circumstances. The copyright law identifies certain types of uses, including criticism, comment, news reporting, teaching, scholarship, and research as examples of activities that may qualify as a fair use.

There is no bright line test for determining when a particular use constitutes a fair use under the law. Whether a particular use constitutes a fair use is determined on a case-by-case basis. In each case a court, in determining whether a particular use made of a work is considered to be a fair use, will look at:

(1) The purpose and character of the use, including whether such use is of a commercial nature or is for nonprofit educational purposes.

(2) The nature of the copyrighted work.

(3) The amount and substantiality of the portion used in relation to the copyrighted work as a whole; and

(4) The effect of the use upon the potential market for or value of the copyrighted work. Each of these factors is briefly discussed below.

Factor 1: The Purpose and Character of the Use
Historically the first factor has played a significant role in fair use determinations. In more recent cases that role seems to have dramatically increased to the point where it may be the predominant reason for a finding of fair use. The first factor considers whether use is for commercial purposes or nonprofit educational purposes. On its face, this analysis does not seem too complex. However, over the years a relatively new consideration called "transformative use" has been incorporated into the first factor. Transformative uses are those that add something new, with a further purpose or different character, and do not substitute for the original use of the work. If the use is found to be a transformative use, it is almost always found to be a fair use. In recent years, the dividing line between the type of transformations of a work that fall within the derivative use right and the types that are considered to be a transformative use has grown unclear. Safe to say, this is an evolving area of the law that has made the already murky doctrine of fair use even murkier.

Factor 2: The Nature of the Copyrighted Work
Of the four fair use factors, this factor is the least complex and thus also the easiest to evaluate. The more creative a copyrighted work, the less likely there will be a finding of fair use. Thus, when the copyright work being used is a work of fiction this factor favors the copyright owner,

but when the work is a factual work it favors a fair use finding. The publication status of the work also plays a role with this factor. When the copyrighted work is unpublished the use is less likely to be a fair use.

Factor 3: The Amount Used

This factor considers the amount of the copyrighted work that was used in relation to the copyrighted work as a whole. Where the amount used is very small in relation to the copyrighted work, this factor will favor a finding of fair use. On the other hand, where the amount used is not insignificant in relation to the copyrighted work, this factor will favor the copyright owner. There are several important factors to consider here:

- This factor not only considers how much quantitatively was used but also what qualitatively was used. So, for example, if the portion used was the "heart" of the work, this factor will likely weigh against a finding of fair use even if that portion was otherwise a very small amount.
- Historically, using an entire work was generally not a fair use. However, there have been some recent cases that have called this tenet into question.
- This amount used is considered in relation to the copyrighted work, not in relation to the alleged infringing work. As a result, whether the amount used constitutes a small or large percentage of the alleged infringing work is irrelevant to this factor.

Factor 4: The Effect of the Use on the Market

Historically this has been the most significant of the four fair use factors. However, this may no longer be the case as many recent court decisions have been focused more on whether the use is considered to be "transformative" under the first fair use factor. This factor not only considers whether the defendant's activities may harm the current market, but also considers whether the use may cause any harms to potential markets that could be exploited by the copyright owner if the use were to become widespread.

INFRINGEMENT AND LANDMARK CASES OF COPYRIGHTS

Copyright infringement occurs in various instances when someone uses, reproduces, or distributes copyrighted material without the permission of the copyright owner. Here are shared instances:

- **Unauthorized Copying:** Reproducing, photocopying, or duplicating copyrighted content without permission.
- **Piracy:** Illegally distributing or selling copyrighted material, such as movies, music, or software.
- **Plagiarism:** Presenting someone else's work as one's own, without proper attribution or permission.
- **Online Sharing:** Sharing copyrighted material on online platforms without authorization, including social media, websites, or file-sharing networks.
- **Adaptation or Derivative Works:** Creating adaptations, remixes, or derivative works without permission from the original copyright owner.
- **Performing Rights Violation:** Performing copyrighted works publicly without obtaining the necessary licenses or permissions.
- **Commercial Use without Permission:** Using copyrighted material for commercial purposes without obtaining proper licensing or permission.
- **Digital Reproduction:** Unauthorized reproduction or distribution of digital content, including e-books, software, or digital artwork.

- **Unauthorized Translation:** Translating copyrighted works without the copyright owner's permission.
- **Rebroadcasting:** Broadcasting or streaming copyrighted content without proper authorization.
- **Artwork Reproduction:** Reproducing visual art, photographs, or illustrations without the artist's permission.
- **Educational Use without Fair Use:** Using copyrighted material in educational settings without qualifying for fair use or obtaining the necessary licenses.
- **Failure to Attribute:** Not providing proper attribution or credit to the original creator when using their copyrighted work.
- **Using Copyrighted Software Illegally:** Using software without adhering to licensing agreements, such as using unauthorized copies or distributing software without permission.
- **Public Display:** Displaying copyrighted material in public without proper authorization.
- **Architectural Works:** Copying or reproducing architectural designs without permission.
- **Fashion Design Infringement:** Copying or replicating unique and original fashion designs without permission.

Famous Copyright Cases in India:

1. YRF vs Sri Sai Ganesh Productions

YRF initiated a copyright infringement lawsuit against Sri Sai Ganesh Productions, alleging that their movie 'Jabardasht' copied essential elements from YRF's 'Band Baaja Baaraat.' The court applied a test of originality, focusing on foundational aspects, substance, and kernel to determine if an average viewer would perceive one work as a copy of the other. The court found that Sri Sai Ganesh Productions had blatantly replicated YRF's film, leading to a verdict of copyright infringement.

2. Hawkins Cooker Ltd. vs Magi cook Appliances

Hawkins Cooker Ltd. filed a lawsuit against Magicook Appliances for unlawfully utilizing their copyrighted label on the popular pressure cooker line. The court prohibited Magicook Appliances from using Hawkins Cooker Ltd's cookbooks and mandated compensation for damages related to the alleged unauthorized use of books, products, and articles in the production of the infringing goods.

3. Super Cassettes Industries Limited vs YouTube and Google

Super Cassettes Industries Limited (SCIL) asserted that YouTube's business model profits significantly from the unauthorized use of copyrighted works without approval or royalty payment. The court directed YouTube and Google to cease the distribution, reproduction, display, or transmission of any audio-visual works exclusively owned by SCIL on their platform.

4. Ratna Sagar (P) Ltd. V. Trisea Publications & Ors., 1996 Ptc (16) 597

In the legal matter of Ratna Sagar (P) Ltd. versus Trisea Publications & Ors. (1996 Ptc (16) 597), the examination centered on the safeguards for copyright protection as per Order 39, Rules 1 and 2 of the Civil Procedure Code, 1908. It emphasized the necessity of safeguarding the prior publication of the work. The court deemed the party's right to the work, based on the author's assignment, irrelevant at this point. Consequently, the court issued an injunction to prevent copyright infringement under Sections 14 and 19 of the Act.

5. Star India (P) Ltd. V. Piyush Agarwal & Ors, C.S. (O.S.) No. 2722/2012, Del Hc

Star India Pvt. Ltd. (STAR) initiated legal actions against Piyush Agarwal (Cricbuzz), Idea Cellular (IDEA), and On Mobile Global Ltd. (ONMOBILE). Despite the Board of Cricket Control in India (BCCI) being named as a common defendant, it is supporting STAR, asserting primary rights over all information from cricket events due to its role in organizing and promoting cricket in India. STAR and BCCI argue that, through an agreement on 10.08.2012, BCCI exclusively assigned a set of rights, including s Mobile Rights and s Mobile Activation Rights, to STAR. STAR alleges a violation of these rights by the defendants and seeks an interim injunction.

6. Najma Heptulla V. Orient Longman Ltd., Air 1989 Del 63

This case pertains to obtaining a temporary injunction under Order 39 for the publication of books. The plaintiff asserts her status as the legal heir of Maulana Azad, the book's author, and has initiated legal action seeking an account rendition and injunction. The primary relief is sought against Orient Longman Limited, a publishing company, and Professor Humayun Kabir, a close associate of Maulana Azad.

7. Eastern Book Company & Others V. D.B. Modak & Another, Air 2008 Sc 809

Eastern Book Company, a partnership, and EBC Publishing Private Limited were involved in publishing legal books, including 'Supreme Court Cases' (SCC) since 1969. This compilation comprised non-reportable, reportable, and short judgments of the Supreme Court, enriched with user-friendly elements like formatting, numbering, cross-references, and additional contributions. It featured headnotes, footnotes, and long notes. In 2004, Spectrum Business Support Limited (Respondent-1) and Regent Datatech Private Limited (Respondent-2) released 'Grand Jurix' and 'The Laws' software, respectively, allegedly copying the entire SCC module onto CD-ROMs, leading to accusations of IP rights infringement by the appellants.

8. The Chancellor, Master, and Scholars of the University Of Oxford & Ors. V. Rameshwari Photocopying Services and Anr., Cs (Os) 2439/2012

In 2012, Oxford University Press, Cambridge University Press (UK), and Taylor & Francis Group (UK), along with Cambridge University Press India Pvt. Ltd. and Taylor & Francis Books India Pvt. Ltd., initiated a legal action for copyright infringement against Rameshwari Photocopy Service and the University of Delhi in the Delhi High Court. The lawsuit gained significant backing from students, professors, and activists who rallied in support of Rameshwari Services.

Several petitions were submitted to join the defense, with entities like the Association of Students for Equitable Access to Knowledge (ASEAK) and the Society for Promoting Educational Access and Knowledge (SPEAK) seeking inclusion as defendants. Consequently, they were formally included as defendants' number three and four in the case.

9. Sajeev Pillai v. Venu Kunnapalli & Anr

In this case, Sajeev Pillai, a film director and scriptwriter, researched the historical festival 'Mamankam' and wrote a script for a film. He signed an MoU with Kavya Film Company to produce the film. However, after two shooting schedules, he was replaced as the director. Pillai alleged that the script was altered, leading him to file a civil suit seeking various reliefs. He also filed an interim injunction application to prevent the film's release without proper authorship credits. The District Judge denied the injunction, prompting Pillai to appeal to the Kerala High Court, which issued its order a day before the scheduled movie release.

10. UTV Software Communication Ltd., v.1337X.TO and Ors

In a unilateral decision, the Delhi High Court issued a groundbreaking dynamic injunction in India, allowing the injunction holder to utilize a single court order to block websites hosting infringing content, eliminating the need for separate suits for each instance of infringement. This ruling emerged from a case seeking an injunction against 'rogue websites' disseminating pirated versions of cinematograph films.

The court found these websites culpable of hosting copyright-infringing material, denying them exemptions under the Indian Copyright Act, 1957, and the safe harbor principle for intermediaries under the Information Technology Act, 2000. Additionally, the court directed the Ministry of Electronics and Information Technology (MeITY) and the Department of Telecommunications (DoT) to consider formulating a technically feasible policy to issue warnings to viewers engaging in content infringement. Section 79 of the Information Technology Act, 2000 addresses intermediary liability and provides safe harbor exemptions.

11. Sarla A. Saraogi & Ors Vs. Krishna Kishore Singh

The New Delhi High Court declined to impose an interlocutory order against the distribution and broadcast of **cinematograph films copyright** supposedly relating to SSR (Sushant Singh Rajput) because SSR's parents failed to establish prima facie evidence, and the ratio of advantage was in favor of the respondents. 'NYAY the Law,' 'Suicide or Death,' and 'Roughly in the Middle,' according to the plaintiffs in the lawsuit, must be inducted and prohibited from being disclosed, printed, and conveyed to the world. The Complainant claimed violations of publicity and security rights and the right to due process, slander, and infringement of the Indian Constitution's Article 21.The Complainant struggled to create a legitimate argument for copyright infringement of SSR's famous person or licensing because the Claimant was unaware of the subject matter of the movies, the plaintiffs were not taking SSR's appearance, similarities, or title, and the movies had suitable provisos, the Court concluded after evaluating the facts and findings further showed. It further stated that famous rights may cease to exist after the demise of the star and those plaintiffs may use information from the official information without responsibility. Finally, the Court concluded that a libel claim is hypothetical with no access to the offensive content.

The Court further stated that no breach of the legal right to a fair trial might be considered a result of news or film coverage. It continued to say that when it comes to material that is part of the public domain, freedom of speech and expression takes precedence over Article 21. While rejecting the order, the Court requested the plaintiffs provide accounts to reimburse any losses.

Geographical Indications (GIs) are one of the most important types of intellectual property (IP) that connect products to certain regions. These products have qualities or characteristics determined by their origin from a particular region. GIs protect the reputation of regional products, preserve traditional knowledge, and offer economic benefits to local communities. Only those products that genuinely originate from a particular region are allowed to use its name.

What Are Geographical Indications?
A Geographical Indication in IPR is a sign that identifies a product as originating in a particular geographical region. The qualities, like taste, texture, and aroma, of such a product are closely linked to its place of production. These include geographical and natural factors, as well as human ones, like know-how and tradition, of the region concerned.
For instance:
Darjeeling Tea has a specific taste that characterizes the region in India due to its particular climate and soil.
Champagne is only produced in France and is a sparkling wine.
GIs distinguish these products and assure consumers of quality and originality in the market.

IMPORTANCE OF GEOGRAPHICAL INDICATIONS IN IPR:
GIs help protect regional products, thereby fostering local economies. Here are some of the main reasons why GIs become important:
1. Protection of Regional Identity
GIs preserve the cultural and historic significance of products connected with a particular region. Thus, they ensure only those who follow the age-old methods can produce and market such a product, keeping it distinct.
2. Economic Benefits to Local Producers
By providing legal protection, GIs prevent unauthorized producers from using the names of famous regional products. This gives local producers a market advantage because they will receive fair compensation for their efforts and investments. Higher demand for authentic GI products often leads to higher prices, which is beneficial to the local economy.
3. Consumer Confidence
GIs assure consumers about the quality and authenticity of the products they purchase. The GI in the IPR label assures consumers. It guarantees the product is authentic and meets quality standards. So, they can make informed decisions.
4. Rural Development
Many GI products have their origins in rural areas. Registering a GI brings the product to national and international markets. It creates jobs, builds infrastructure, and improves living standards in rural areas.

REQUIREMENT FOR FILING OF GI APPLICATION
1. **Name of GI :** To file logo of along with GI for better identification and Protection of GI Rights.

2. **Details of applicant:** Name and Address of the Applicant , Documentary evidence relating to legal status of an Association of Producers to be provided such as Memorandum and Articles of Association, Bye-laws, Registration certificates etc.,

3. **Name of the goods and class:** As per Section (2) (1) (f) of G.I. Act 1999. ,Agricultural, Natural, Handicrafts, Industry, Manufactured goods & Food Stuffs , Classification of Goods as per Schedule 4 mentioned in GI Act, 1999.

4. **GI AREA:** certified copy of area map : The GI area may be indicated by giving details of the longitude and latitude of the production area. The provided certified map (three copies) issued from a competent statutory authority giving details of the longitude and latitude of the production area.

5. **An affidavit to represent the producers :**The Applicant to file a notarized affidavit in original stating how the applicant claims to represent and safeguard/protect the interest of producers of proposed GI; Approximate Annual Turnover. The date, month & year of execution of the affidavit should be mentioned.

6. **Proof of origin:** Brief description about the origin and the evolution of the GI. Documentary evidence (such as gazetteers, published books & records) relating to proof of origin (historical proof) of product along with usage of Name of GI.

7. **Method of production:** The general good practices of Production adopted by the producers in the GI Area to be provided. The specific standards of Quality and process of sequence of production along with the characteristics which make the product Unique to be provided.

8. **Specification & description :**Specification of GI product to be to be provided with detailed and clear characteristic and technical specification.

9. **Uniqueness:** Peculiar features that makes the GI different from other similar goods. The human skill of producer in making of this unique product to be provided.

10. **Particulars of inspection body :** The inspection structure should be strengthened with an independent Neutral agency to maintain the quality and regulating the use of Geographical Indications.

STEPS FOR GI REGISTRATION:

STEP 1 : Filing of application.

Please check whether the indication comes within the ambit of the definition of a Gl under section 2(1)(e).

The association of persons or producers or any organization or authority should represent the interest of producers of the concerned goods and should file an affidavit how the applicant claims to represent their interest.

- Application must be made in triplicate.
- The application shall be signed by the applicant or his agent and must be accompanied by a statement of case.
- Details of the special characteristics and how those standards are maintained.
- Three certified copies of the map of the region to which the GI relates.
- Details of the inspection structure if any to regulate the use of the GI in the territory to which it relates.
- Give details of all the applicant together with address. If there is a large number of producers a collective reference to all the producers of the goods may be made in the application and the G.I., If registered will be indicated accordingly in the register.

Please sent your application to the following address in India.

Geographical Indications Registry

Intellectual Property Office Building

Industrial Estate, G.S.T Road
Guindy, Chennai – 600 032
Phone: 044 – 22502091-93 & 98
Fax: 044 – 22502090
E-mail: gir-ipo[at]nic[dot]in
Website: ipindia.gov.in
The applicant must have an address for service in India. Generally, application can be filed by
(1) a legal practitioner (2) a registered agent.

STEP 2 and 3: Preliminary scrutiny and examination
- The Examiner will scrutinize the application for any deficiencies.
- The applicant should within one month of the communication in this regard, remedy the same.
- The content of statement of case is assessed by a consultative group of experts will be versed on the subject.
- They will ascertain the correctness of particulars furnished.
- Thereafter an Examination Report would be issued.

STEP 4: Show cause notice
- If the Registrar has any objection to the application, he will communicate such objection.
- The applicant must respond within two months or apply for a hearing.
- The decision will be duly communicated. If the applicant wishes to appeal, he may within one month make a request.
- The Registrar is also empowered to withdraw an application, if it is accepted in error, after giving on opportunity of being heard.

STEP 5: Publication in the geographical indications Journal
Every application, within three months of acceptance shall be published in the Geographical Indications Journal.

STEP 6: Opposition to Registration
- Any person can file a notice of opposition within three months (extendable by another month on request which has to be filed before three months) opposing the GI application published in the Journal.
- The registrar shall serve a copy of the notice on the applicant.
- Within two months the applicant shall sent a copy of the counter statement.
- If he does not do this shall be deemed to have abandoned his application. Where the counterstatement has been filed, the registrar shall serve a copy on the person giving the notice of opposition.
- Thereafter, both sides will lead their respective evidence by way of affidavit and supporting documents.
- A date for hearing of the case will be fixed thereafter.

STEP 7: Registration
- Where an application for a GI has been accepted, the registrar shall register the geographical indication. If registered the date of filing of the application shall be deemed to be the date of registration.
- The registrar shall issue to the applicant a certificate with the seal of the Geographical indication's registry.

STEP 8: Renewal
A registered GI shall be valid for 10 years and can be renewed on payment of renewal fee.

STEP 9: Additional protection to notified goods.
Additional protection for notified goods is provided in the Act.

The Registration Process - FLOW CHART
- In December 1999, Parliament passed the Geographical Indications of Goods (Registration and Protection) Act 1999. This Act seeks to provide for the registration and protection of Geographical Indications relating to goods in India.
- The Registrar of Geographical Indication is divided into two parts. Part 'A' consists of particulars relating to registered Geographical indications and Part 'B' consists of particulars of the registered authorized users. The registration process is similar to both for registration of geographical indication and an authorized user which is illustrated below:

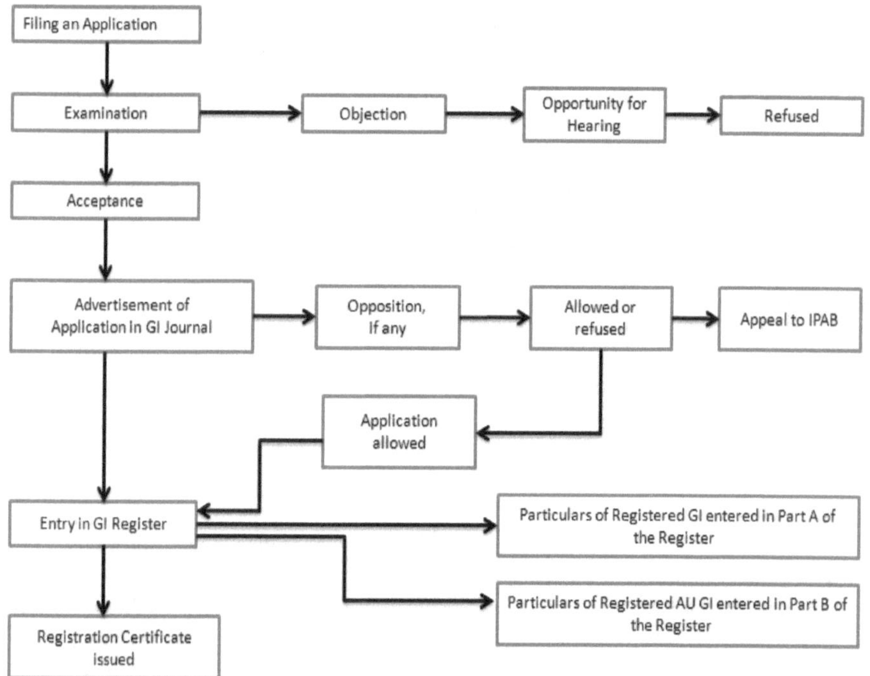

Territorial demarcation of geographical territory :
For Geographical Indications (GIs), territorial demarcation involves defining the specific geographic area where a product's quality, reputation, or other characteristics are essentially attributable to its origin, ensuring the product is linked to that area.

Here's a breakdown of the key aspects of territorial demarcation for GIs:

1. Defining the Geographical Area:

- **Specific Region:**
  GIs are linked to a specific region, locality, or place, not just a country as a whole.
- **Product Link:**
  The area must have a demonstrable link to the product's characteristics, reputation, or quality.
- **Natural and Human Factors:**
  The delimitation should consider the interaction of natural factors (e.g., soil, climate, topography) and human factors (e.g., local practices, production history).
- **Uniqueness:**
  The geographical area should be unique in its ability to produce the product with the specific characteristics that define the GI.

2. Criteria for Delimitation:

- **Physical Criteria:** Soil, climate, topography, water supply, etc.
- **Local Practices:** Conditions of cultivation, varieties, harvesting, processing practices, etc.
- **Local Production History and Reputation:** The history of production in the area and the reputation of the product are important factors.
- **Localization of Producers:** The location of actual or potential producers within the area.

3. Importance of Territorial Demarcation:

- **Protection of GIs:**
  Territorial demarcation is crucial for protecting GIs and preventing their misuse or imitation.
- **Consumer Confidence:**
  It assures consumers that they are purchasing a product with the genuine characteristics and reputation associated with its place of origin.
- **Promotion of Local Products:**
  GIs can promote local products and contribute to the economic development of the region.
- **Intellectual Property:**
  GIs are a form of intellectual property, and territorial demarcation is essential for their legal protection and enforcement.
- **Unfair Competition:**
  It helps prevent unfair competition by ensuring that only products from the designated area can use the GI.
- **TRIPS Agreement:**
  The Trade-Related Aspects of Intellectual Property Rights (TRIPS) Agreement, which is administered by the World Trade Organization (WTO), recognizes the importance of protecting geographical indications to prevent unfair competition.

TRADE SECRETS:

A trade secret is any practice or process of a company that is generally not known outside of the company. Information considered a trade secret gives the company a competitive advantage over its competitors and is often a product of internal research and development.

To be legally considered a trade secret in the United States, a company must make a reasonable effort in concealing the information from the public; the secret must intrinsically have economic value, and the trade secret must contain information. Trade secrets are a part of a company's intellectual property. Unlike a patent, a trade secret is not publicly known.

Trade secrets may take a variety of forms, such as a proprietary process, instrument, pattern, design, formula, recipe, method, or practice that is not evident to others and may be used as a means to create an enterprise that offers an advantage over competitors or provides value to customers.

Trade secrets are defined differently based on jurisdiction, but all have the following characteristics in common:
- They are not public information.
- Their secrecy provides an economic benefit to their holder.
- Their secrecy is actively protected.

Real-World Examples:
- There are many examples of trade secrets that are tangible and intangible. For example, Google's search algorithm exists as intellectual property in code and is regularly updated to improve and protect its operations.

- The secret formula for Coca-Cola, which is locked in a vault, is an example of a trade secret that is a formula or recipe. Since it has not been patented, it has never been revealed.

- The New York Times Bestseller list is an example of a process trade secret. While the list does factor in book sales by compiling chain and independent store sales, as well as wholesaler data, the list is not merely sales numbers (books with lower overall sales may make the list while a book with higher sales may not).

PLANT VARIETY PROTECTION:
Plant variety protection provides legal protection of a plant variety to a breeder in the form of Plant Breeder's Rights (PBRs). PBRs are intellectual property rights that provide exclusive rights to a breeder of the registered variety. In India, the Plant Variety Protection and Farmers Rights (PPVFR) Act, 2001 is a sui generis system that aims to provide for the establishment of an effective system for protection of plant varieties and the rights of plant breeders and farmers. A certificate of registration for a variety issued under this Act confers an exclusive right on the breeder or his successor, his agent or licensee, to produce, sell, market, distribute, import or export the variety. Application for registration of plant varieties can be made in the office of Registrar, PPV & FRA, New Delhi.

Registrable Plant Varieties in India:
The following types of plant varieties can be registered under PPVFR Act, 2001:
- New varieties
- Extant variety
- Farmers' variety
- Essentially derived variety

A new variety shall be registered under PPVFR Act, 2001 if it conforms to the criteria of novelty, distinctiveness, uniformity and stability.

Non- Registrable Plant Varieties in India:

The following types of plant varieties cannot be registered under the PPVFR Act, 2001:
- ➤ Any variety where prevention of commercial exploitation of such variety is necessary to protect public order or public morality or human, animal and plant life and health or to avoid serious prejudice to the environment.
- ➤ Any varieties that involve any technology which is injurious to the life or health of human beings, animals or plants. The expression "any technology" includes genetic use restriction technology and terminator technology.
- ➤ Variety belonging to the species or genera which is not listed in the notification issued by the Central Government.

Duration of Protection for a Registered Variety:
- ➤ Trees and vines – 18 years from the date of registration of the variety.
- ➤ Extant varieties – 15 years from the date of notification of that variety by the Central Government under Seed Act, 1966.
- ➤ Other crops – 15 years fifteen years from the date of registration of the variety.

Services:
- ➤ Advising and assisting clients in determining the availability of a variety for registration, seeking clearance from Plant Variety Registry, searches in the Official Journal of Plant Varieties, denomination clearance, fulfillment of registrability criteria
- ➤ Gene and protein sequence searches
- ➤ Filing notices of opposition/cancellation against any application/registration of infringing varieties on behalf of our clients
- ➤ Assisting clients in enforcement of their rights in their registered plant varieties
- ➤ Assisting clients in research and commercialization of registered plant varieties
- ➤ Advising clients on various matters pertaining to plant variety protection

TOPOGRAPHY OF INTEGRATED CIRCUITS:
- ➤ Layout designs (topographies) of integrated circuits are a three-dimensional arrangement of elements forming an integrated circuit intended for manufacturing. This arrangement and ordering of elements follow from the electronic function that the integrated circuit is to perform.
- ➤ Merriam-Webster defines a circuit as "the complete path of an electric current including usually the source of electric energy" and an integrated circuit as "a tiny complex of electronic components and their connections that is produced in or on a small slice of material (such as silicon)".
- ➤ Integrated circuits are a device with a common surface, on which certain elements with electrical functions are mounted, including transistors, resistors, capacitors, diodes, etc. These components are connected in such a way that the integrated circuit can control the electric current, by adjusting, amplifying, or otherwise modifying it.
- ➤ Depending on the function that they perform, integrated circuits need a special order and arrangement, that is, they require a design of the elements that form the integrated circuit. This is referred to as the layout design (topography) of the integrated circuit.
- ➤ "Layout designs (topographies) of integrated circuits shall be protected by this Law, provided that they are original.

- ➤ Layout designs (topographies) that are the result of the intellectual effort of the creator and are not common knowledge among the creators and manufacturers of layout designs or topographies of integrated circuits, at the time of their creation, shall be considered original.

Duration Period : Layout designs (topographies) of integrated circuits shall be protected for a nonrenewable period of 10 years beginning from the filing date of the application or its first commercial exploitation in any part of the world (Article 78, Law No. 19,039).

Characteristic of granted Rights:

Although the Law establishes, in Article 83, that this right abides by the applicable provisions established in Title III of the Law regarding patents, it also establishes rights proper to layout designs (topographies) of integrated circuits in Article 76 of Law No. 19,039:

The owner of a layout design (topography) of integrated circuits shall have the exclusive right to produce, sell or market in any way the protected object and the right granted to the holder. Consequently, the owner of a layout design (topography) of integrated circuits can prevent any third party, acting without the holder's consent, from:

- Reproducing the protected layout design (topography) of integrated circuits in full or in part for incorporation in an integrated circuit or into any other form, with the exception of reproducing any part of it that does not comply with the originality requirement set out in Article 75 of this Law.
- Selling or distributing in any way, for commercial purposes, the protected layout design (topography) of integrated circuits, or a product that incorporates an integrated circuit that contains an illegally reproduced layout design (topography) of integrated circuits.

The former is complemented by article 77:

The exclusive right of exploitation envisaged under the preceding Article shall not apply to:

- The reproductions of layout designs (topographies) of integrated circuits in which a layout design (topography) of integrated circuits created by third parties has been incorporated, for private purposes or with the sole objective of evaluation, analysis, and research or teaching.
- Commercial exploitation, as defined in said Article, of a layout design (topography) of integrated circuits, that otherwise meets the requirements of Article 75 of this Law, which has been created as a result of analysis and evaluation of a separate protected layout design (topography) of integrated circuits.
- Commercial exploitation, as defined by said Article, of an integrated circuit that incorporates an illegally reproduced layout design (topography) of integrated circuits or in relation to any object that incorporates such an integrated circuit, where the third party who orders or performs such acts did not know or have reasonable grounds to know, upon acquiring the integrated circuit or the object, that he was incorporating an illegally reproduced layout design (topography) of integrated circuits.

TRADITIONAL KNOWLEDGE AND BIOPIRACY:

Bio-piracy refers to the use of biological material and associated traditional knowledge without consent and for commercial gain, often without giving credit or compensation to the communities that developed and maintained that knowledge. In India, bio-piracy has become a significant concern in recent years, particularly in the context of the country's rich biodiversity and traditional knowledge systems. The exploitation of traditional knowledge by corporations and individuals for profit is a significant issue in India. This has resulted in the misappropriation of traditional knowledge associated with plant species, medicinal practices, and other natural resources, which have been used for commercial purposes without permission or recognition of the knowledge holders.

Significance of Traditional Knowledge:
Traditional knowledge means the knowledge, practices, and beliefs that have been passed down from one generation to other generation within a particular community, often through oral transmission. This type of knowledge is often associated with indigenous communities and is considered to be an important part of their culture and identity. There are several significant aspects of traditional knowledge:

A. Preservation of cultural heritage- Traditional knowledge is often deeply rooted in a community's cultural heritage and is considered an important part of their identity. By preserving this knowledge, communities are able to maintain their cultural traditions and pass them down to future generations.

B. Sustainable use of natural Resources-The sustainable use of natural resources is a topic that is frequently covered in traditional knowledge through practices and beliefs. We can make sure that natural resources are used sustainably by incorporating traditional knowledge into current resource management techniques.

C. Contribution to scientific Knowledge-Traditional knowledge has contributed to scientific knowledge in a number of fields, including medicine, agriculture, and ecology. Many modern medicines and agricultural practices are based on traditional knowledge.

D. Promotion of diversity and Inclusivity-Traditional knowledge promotes diversity and inclusivity by acknowledging the contributions of different communities and cultures. By recognizing and valuing traditional knowledge, we can promote greater understanding and respect for different cultures.

Reasons for Bio-Piracy or Misappropriation of Traditional Knowledge :
Bio piracy or misappropriation of traditional knowledge can occur for various reasons, including:

A. Commercial Interests- Companies may seek to exploit traditional knowledge and biodiversity for commercial gain, without providing fair compensation to the communities from which they are taken.

B. Lack of legal Protection-Traditional knowledge and biodiversity are often not protected by intellectual property laws, leaving them vulnerable to exploitation.

C. Inadequate benefit-sharing arrangement- Benefit-sharing arrangements may not be well-defined or may be inadequate, resulting in communities not receiving fair compensation for their contributions.

D. Information Gap-Lack of information or awareness about the value and significance of traditional knowledge and biodiversity can lead to undervaluation and under appreciation of these resources.

E. Power Imbalance- Power imbalances between indigenous communities and external actors can result in the exploitation of traditional knowledge and biodiversity without the consent or benefit of the communities.

F. Lack of Governance-Inadequate governance and enforcement mechanisms can make it difficult to prevent and address bio-piracy and misappropriation of traditional knowledge.

G. Globalization and the expansion of Markets-Globalization and the expansion of markets have increased the demand for natural resources and traditional knowledge, leading to greater pressure to exploit these resources for commercial purposes.

<u>Example of Biopiracy in India :</u>

Sl. No.	Common name	Indigenous use	Pantentee	Action by the Indian Government
1	*Haldi* / turmeric (*Curcuma longa*)	Treatment for sprains, inflammatory conditions and wounds	Two scientists from the University of Mississippi were granted US patent 5,401,504 on the use of turmeric in 1995	The US Patent and Trademark office rejected all patent claims related to turmeric after the Indian government challenged the patent by providing numerous research papers predating the patent, proving that turmeric has long been used to heal wounds in India.
2	Neem (*Azadirachta indica*)	As an air purifier and effective medicine for almost all types of human and animal diseases because of its insect and pest repellant properties	A US timber importer began importing neem seeds to his company headquarter in Wisconsin since 1971 after he studied its curing properties. Using neem extract, he successfully extracted a pesticidal agent called Margosan-O. In 1985, the bio-pesticide derived from neem tree received clearance from the US Environmental Protection Agency (EPA).	In May 2000, a coalition of groups successfully overturned the patent held by the US company, WR Grace and the US Department of Agriculture over the Indian neem tree. The Patent granted to WR Grace & Co. UK and US department of Agriculture was revoked on Challenge.
3	Rice (Basmati)	Unique Aroma and flavour	On 2 September 1997, Texas based RiceTec Inc. was granted patent number 5663484 for a new plant variety that is a cross between American long-grain rice and Basmati rice. RiceTec claimed that the new varieties have the same or better characteristics as the original Basmati rice and can be successfully grown in specified geographical areas in North America.	By mid 2000, the Indian government challenged some of the claims of the RiceTec patent and the world's largest importer of Basmati rice, Saudi Arabia (UK recognized that Basmati rice is unique to Northern India and Pakistan).

02-08: FILING OF IPR

India provides a systematic and comprehensive process for filing and obtaining patents to safeguard intellectual property rights. This legal framework ensures that inventors and innovators have exclusive rights over their inventions. Patent filing procedure in India is a multi-step process, each step of which is regulated by specific rules and formalities to ensure the novelty, utility, and originality of the invention. Knowing this process is important for the successful acquisition of a patent.

Steps for Patent Filing Application in India:
Patent filing application involves a set of processes such as searches, preparing documents, making applications, publishing, examining, and objection response. At each step, originality and the validity of an invention are protected. Filing a patent application in India is a comprehensive process that requires a clear understanding of the legal and procedural requirements. Here's a detailed breakdown of each step:

Step 1: Conduct a Patent Search
Why It's Important: Before filing, conducting a thorough patent search ensures that the invention is novel and does not infringe upon existing patents.
How to do: Search through databases such as Indian Patent Advanced Search System (InPASS) and other international patent databases.
Benefits: Avoids unnecessary rejection due to the existence of prior patents in the same domain.
Step 2: Patent Application Preparation
Provisional Specification: If the invention is still under development, filing a provisional application would help secure an early date for filing.
Timeline: A complete specification must follow within 12 months.
Advantage: Additional time is given to file an improved invention.

Complete Specification: Information about the Invention includes:
- ➢ Title and Abstract.
- ➢ Previous art or weaknesses in available solutions.
- ➢ The Background of the Invention
- ➢ Summary of the Invention
- ➢ Detailed Description and Claims.
- ➢ Drawings, if applicable

Step 3: Lodge the Application
Where To File: Application can be made:
Online: By the website of the Indian Patent Office.
Offline: With the corresponding Patent office located in Delhi, Mumbai, Kolkata and Chennai respectively.

What to Include: All the forms and documents required, which include:
Form 1: Application for grant of patent.
Form 2: Specification-provisional or complete.
Form 3: Statement and undertaking.
Form 5: Declaration of Inventorship.
Power of Attorney if filed through an agent.
Statutory fees.

Step 4: Publication of the Application

When It Occurs: Applications are published in the official patent journal after 18 months from the date of filing.

Early Publication Option: You can apply for early publication by paying extra charges, and the application will get published within a month.

Importance: Publication makes the application public, and any third party can scrutinize it.

Step 5: Application for Examination

How to Apply: File Form 18 for an examination. It must be done within 48 months of the priority date.

Purpose: The application sets in motion the examination process. This is where the Patent Office scrutinizes the application on the aspects of patentability, novelty, and compliance with patent laws.

Step 6: Patent Office Examination

What happens: The Patent Office checks for:

Novelty, inventive step, and industrial applicability.

Legal and technical requirements.

First Examination Report (FER): The examiner raises objections or requires additional information in an FER.

Step 7: Response to Examination Report

Timeline: Overcome FER objections within 12 months.

Amendments: Claims or specifications may be altered, if necessary, to satisfy patentability requirements.

Hearing Opportunity: In case the objections are not overcome, the Controller can provide an opportunity for a hearing to clear up the remaining objections.

Step 8: Pre-Grant Opposition

Who Can Oppose: Any person can oppose the application under Section 25(1) before the patent is granted.

Grounds for Opposition: Novelty, inventive step, or industrial applicability; or non-disclosure of essential information.

Step 9: Grant of Patent

When It Takes Place: After resolving all objections and opposition (if any), the Controller grants the patent under Section 43.

Publication of Grant: Grant published in the official patent journal and public notice of granting such exclusive rights.

Step 10: Post-Grant Opposition

Timeline: Within 12 months from the date of grant. Any person may give notice of opposition.

Objective: Permitting the patentees to challenge the patent with regard to validity, novelty or other grounds.

Documents Required for Patent Filing Procedure in India:

The patent application has to be provided with accurate and detailed documents. The required forms, statements, and technical details have to be submitted to conform with Indian patent laws so as to facilitate the processing. The required forms for submission include:

Form 1: Application for grant of patent

Form 2: Provisional or complete specification

Form 3: Statement and undertaking regarding foreign applications.

Form 5: Declaration as to inventorship.

Form 26: Power of attorney (if filed through a patent agent).

Form 18: Request for examination.

Priority Document: If claiming priority from an earlier application.
Abstract: A brief summary of the invention.
Drawings: If applicable, to illustrate the invention.

Advantages of Obtaining a Patent:

A patent provides exclusive rights, and revenue opportunities through licensing, and strengthens the market position of an innovator. It ensures legal protection against unauthorized use.

Exclusive Rights: The patentee is given exclusive rights to restrain other individuals from using the patented invention without permission.

Commercialization: Patents may be licensed or sold and provide opportunities for revenue generation.

Market Position: It enhances market position because it prevents the competitors from exploiting the invention.

Challenges of Patent Filing in India:

The process of patent filing can be difficult, costly, and very time-consuming. This often requires strategic planning to navigate legal and technical requirements.

Complexity: The process includes complicated legal and technical documentation

Cost: The filing and keeping of the patents can be very expensive.

Time-Consuming: The whole process from filing to issuance of a patent can take years.

1. Patent Flow Chart

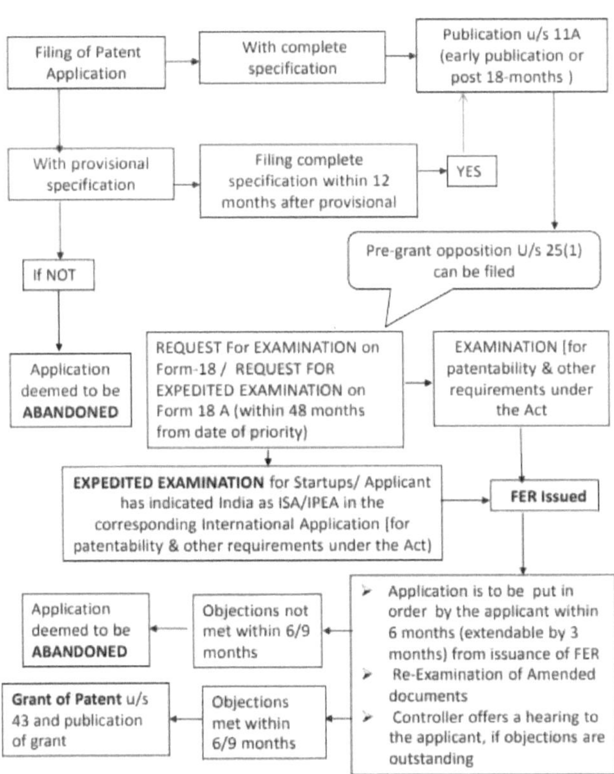

FILING OF TRADEMARKS INCLUDING LEGAL FORMS FILING:

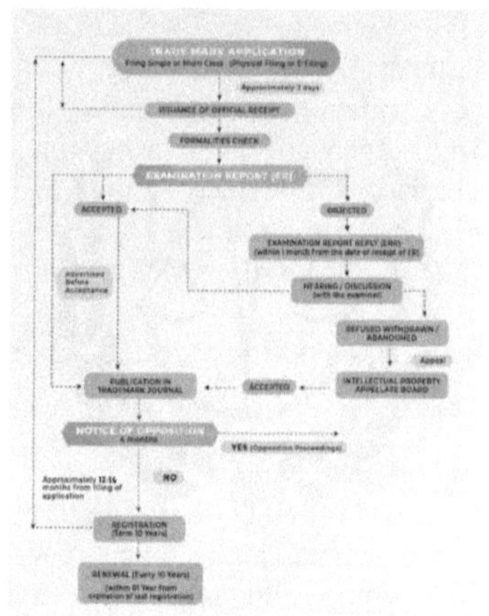

Step-by-Step Guide to Trademark Registration in India:

Trademark registration is a crucial legal process designed to protect unique brand assets and provide exclusive ownership rights to their owners. It involves obtaining legal recognition and safeguards against plagiarism for trademarks such as logos, names, symbols, or phrases, used in connection to specific goods or services. In India, trademark registration is governed by the Trademarks Act, 1999, and administered by the Office of the Controller General of Patents, Designs and Trademarks.

Step 1: Conduct a Trademark Search

Before applying for trademark registration, conduct a comprehensive trademark search to ensure that the proposed trademark is unique and does not conflict with existing trademarks. You can perform a trademark search using the official **IP India Trademark Search** database.

Why is a Trademark Search Important?

- Prevents conflicts with already registered trademarks.
- Reduces the chances of trademark rejection due to similarity.
- Saves time and money by avoiding legal disputes.

Step 2: Filing a Trademark Application

Once a trademark search confirms uniqueness, the next step is to file a trademark application with the Controller General of Patents, Designs, and Trademarks. The application can be submitted **online** through the **Trademark e-Filing Portal** or offline at designated trademark offices.

Required Documents for Trademark Application

- Trademark details (wordmark, logo, or tagline).
- Applicant's identity proof and address proof.
- Business registration certificate (for company applicants).
- Power of Attorney (if filed by a trademark attorney).

- User affidavit (if claiming prior usage of the trademark).

Step 3: Trademark Examination

After submission, the **Trademark Office** examines the application to check for:

- **Compliance with Legal Provisions**: Ensuring the trademark meets registration criteria under the **Trademark Act, 1999**.
- **Similarity with Existing Trademarks**: Checking if the trademark is already registered or closely resembles another.
- **Descriptive or Generic Nature**: Ensuring the mark is not purely descriptive of the product/service.

If the examiner finds any issues, they issue an **examination report** stating objections, which must be responded to within 30 days.

Step 4: Trademark Publication in the Trademark Journal

If the application passes the examination stage, the trademark is **published in the Trademark Journal** for public review. This publication allows third parties to oppose the trademark registration within **4 months**.

Step 5: Opposition Period

During the **opposition period**, third parties can file an opposition if they believe the trademark is similar to theirs or violates existing rights. The process includes:

- Filing a **notice of opposition**.
- Submission of counterstatements and evidence.
- Trademark hearing and final decision by the Registrar.

If no opposition is filed or the opposition is unsuccessful, the application proceeds to the registration stage.

Step 6: Trademark Registration Certificate Issuance

Once the opposition period is cleared, the **Trademark Office issues a Registration Certificate**, granting the owner exclusive rights to use the trademark. The registered trademark remains valid for **10 years** from the date of application.

Step 7: Trademark Renewal (Every 10 Years)

To maintain ownership, the trademark must be renewed every **10 years** by filing a renewal application before the expiration date. Failure to renew may result in the removal of the trademark from the register.

<u>Common Reasons for Trademark Rejections:</u>

Understanding why trademarks get rejected can help applicants avoid delays. Common reasons include:

- **Similarity to Existing Trademarks**: Conflicts with prior-registered marks.
- **Lack of Distinctiveness**: Generic or descriptive marks that fail to differentiate products.
- **Prohibited Words or Symbols**: Usage of government emblems, offensive words, or deceptive terms.
- **Incorrect Trademark Class Selection**: Filing under an incorrect category of goods or services.

Cost of Trademark Registration in India:
The cost of trademark registration in India varies based on the applicant type:

Applicant Type	Government Fees (INR)
Individual/Startup/SME	4,500
Large Companies	9,000

Additional legal fees may apply if hiring a **trademark attorney** for the filing process.

FILING OF DESIGN INCLUDING LEGAL FORMS FILING:

Design registration is a type of intellectual property protection under which a newly created design applied to an article created under an industrial process can be protected from counterfeiting. This registration provides authority to the owner to use the Design for ten years, and the time can be further extended for the next five years. Understanding the importance of design registration ensures that creators protect their intellectual property rights effectively. The present article briefs the Design Registration process in India which helps you to protect your unique designs.

Advantages/Importance of Design Registration in India:
Recognizing the importance of design registration emphasize the significance of securing legal ownership over innovative designs. Following are some advantages that an owner can avail of after completing the design registration process in India:
➢ Exclusive rights over the new and original design
➢ An asset of the proprietor/owner
➢ Can initiate a legal proceeding in case of infringement by a third-party
➢ Serve as prima facie evidence in an infringement suit.
➢ Right to sell, transfer and license the design with ease.

Essentials Requirements :
Under the Design Act, 2000 for a design to be registered and protected under the Act, the following are essential requirements that need to be fulfilled:
➢ A design should be Original and new design. This means that it should not have been used or published previously in any country before the date of application of registration.
➢ A design should be significantly distinguishable from known designs or a combination of known designs.
➢ A design should not comprise or contain scandalous or obscene matter.
➢ A design should not be a mere mechanical contrivance.
➢ A design should be applied to an article and should appeal to the eye.
➢ A design should not be contrary to public order or morality.

Eligibility Criteria:
- Any person or the legal representative or the assignee can apply separately or jointly for the registration.
- The term "person" includes firm, partnership, small entity, and a body corporate.
- In the case of an NRI, his agent or legal representative needs to initiate the Design Registration process in India.
-

Documents Required for Design Registration:
The following documents are to be submitted to get design registration India:
- A certified copy of the original or certified copies of extracts from the disclaimer
- Affidavits
- Declaration
- Other public documents can be made available on payment of a fee.

The affidavit should be in paragraph form and should contain a declaration of truth and verifiability. However, the controller may regulate the cost involved in registration of design in India according to the fourth schedule.

Protection Given to Design Registration:
When a design is registered, copyright is bestowed upon the registered design for a period of 10 years (extendable by 5 years). Through this, the proprietor enjoys an exclusive right over the use of the design in the class in which it's been registered.

What is excluded from the scope of a design registration?
Unlike copyright protection, the registration for design in India doesn't protect any literary or artistic work like books, calendars, stamps, tokens, buildings and structures, and maps. Further, an application cannot be made for designs similar to the national flags, emblems, or signs of any country.

Validity of Design registration:
Design registration in India is valid for a period of 10 years and can be extended for a further term of 5 years with the payment of the necessary fees. The design will lapse if the extension is not done in time but can be restored in the following manner: The application for restoration is to be made within one year from the date of the lapse of the design via Form 4, only in the case of non-payment of the extension fees. Once the application for restoration is approved, the necessary extension fees are to be paid.

Process for Design Registration in India:
The first thing to be noted is that the application to register a design may be applied to five different authorities:
- Controller Designs Patent Office in Kolkata
- The patent office in Delhi
- The patent office in Ahmedabad
- Patent Office in Mumbai
- The patent office in Chennai

The application for design registration must be filed with Form-1 along with the following details:
- Name of applicant
- Address of the applicant

> Nationality of the applicant
> In the case of a company, information regarding the place of incorporation and the legal status of the entity
> The required fee is applicable.
> The class and the sub-class of the article under the Locarno Classification, of the article embodying the design.
> The name of the article to which the design is applied upon.
> Representation of the design

In the case where the design is two-dimensional, two copies of the design are to be submitted.
In the case where the design is three-dimensional, two copies of the design from the viewpoint of the front, back, top, bottom, and the two sides must be submitted.
Further, the applicant must also highlight the unique features of the design that sets it apart from any other existing designs.

If the application is to register the design in more than one class, each class of registration must have a separate application.
> Statement of disclaimer or novelty must be attached to each representation with respect to mechanical processes, trademark, numbers, letters, etc. it should also be endorsed and duly signed and dated on each representation by the applicant or the authorized person on behalf of the applicant.

[THE DESIGNS ACT, 2000]

APPLICATION FOR REGISTRATION OF DESIGNS (See sections 5 and 44)

(For Fee see First Schedule)	
[A] Insert number of class [B] Insert (in full) address and nationality	You are requested to register the accompanying in Class No. [A] .... in the name of [B] .... who claim(s) to be the proprietor(s) thereof
[B1] Category of applicant [Please tick (✓) for the appropriate category]	Natural Person ( ) Start-up ( ) Small Entity ( ) Others ( ) [B1]
[C] State whether drawings, photographs, tracings or specimens	Four exactly similar [C] ....of the design accompany this request.
[D] Insert name of article or articles to which the design is to be applied or state trade description of each of the articles contained in the set	The design is to be applied to [D] ....

[E] Strike out these words if previous registration has been effected.	[E] The design has been previously registered in class(es)...... under No... Details of first application in a convention country or group of countries or inter-governmental organisation. i. Name of the country/inter-governmental organization.... ii. Date of filing................................... iii. Application number........................... iv. Name of the applicant ....
[F] Unless an address for service in India is given, the request may not be considered.	[F] Address for service in India is... .... Email ID: Mobile No:
	Declaration: The applicant claims to be the proprietor(s) of the design and that
[G] To be signed by the applicant or by authorized agent.	to the best of his knowledge and belief the design is new or original. Dated this .... Day of ....20.............. (Signed) [G] ....

TO THE CONTROLLER OF
DESIGNS, THE PATENT
OFFICE, ...

* Strike out the words if no previous registration or priority claim has been effected".

After submission of the application, the patent office will examine the application and raise objections, if any. Upon the clearance or removal of all objections, the design shall be granted a copyright certificate by the patent office.

Cancellation of Design Registration:

Under the provisions of Section 10 of the Design Act, 2000, the registration of design in India registration can be canceled if:

➤ The design is unoriginal and if similar designs already exist.
➤ The design has already been registered in India.
➤ The design has already been published in another country prior to the date of registration.
➤ Does not comply with the characteristics of a design as mentioned under the Design Act.

FILING OF COPYRIGHTS INCLUDING LEGAL FORMS FILING

Copyright is a legal entitlement granted to the owner of intellectual property. As the term implies, it pertains to the right to duplicate or reproduce a creative work. Essentially, copyright signifies that when a person produces a piece of intellectual property, they acquire ownership rights. This means that only the creator or those they authorize have the exclusive right to reproduce or utilize that work. Copyright law provides the original creators of a work with an exclusive right to utilize it or make copies for a designated period. Over time, the copyrighted work may eventually enter the public domain.

Significance of Registration:

Copyright registration is essential as it solidifies your legal ownership of the work. By registering your copyright, you gain control over the dissemination of your work to the public, reproduction rights, and any translations or adaptations of the creative content.

Step-by-Step Copyright Registration Process:

Securing copyright registration involves a systematic process that includes the following key steps:

Step 1: Access the official website.

Visit the Official website of the Copyright Office. Log in with your valid User ID and Password. If you still need to register, click on "New User Registration. Make sure to note down your User ID and Password for future reference.

Step 2: Submission of Application

➤ An application containing all the necessary particulars and a statement of the particulars must be prepared in the prescribed format (FORM XIV).
➤ After logging in, click the "Click for Online Copyright Registration" link. The online "Copyright Registration Form" requires completion in four steps:
➤ Fill out Form XIV, then click "SAVE" to save your entered details, and proceed to Step 2
➤ Prepare a scanned copy of your signature for uploading.
➤ Complete the "Statement of Particulars" and click "SAVE" to save your entered details.
➤ Fill out the "Statement of Further Particulars. This form applies to "LITERARY/DRAMATIC, MUSICAL, ARTISTIC, AND SOFTWARE" works. Click "SAVE" to store your entered details and proceed.
➤ **Make Payment:** This application and the requisite fees outlined in Schedule 2 of the Copyright Act are then forwarded to the copyright registrar. Use the Internet Payment Gateway to make the required payment.

It's important to note that a separate application is necessary for each distinct work. Additionally, the applicant and an Advocate holding a Vakalatnama, or a Power of Attorney (POA) must sign every application.

Step 3: Dairy Number Issuance:
Upon receiving the application, the registrar will issue a Dairy Number, marking the initiation of the copyright registration process. Subsequently, there is a mandatory 30-day waiting period for any potential objections to be submitted. Finally, print one hard copy of each of the "Acknowledgement Slip" and the "Copyright Registration Form" and send them by post to the following address:
- Copyright Division
- Department For Promotion of Industry and Internal Trade
- Ministry of Commerce and Industry
- Boudhik Sampada Bhawan,
- Plot No. 32, Sector 14, Dwarka, New Delhi-110078
- Email Address: copyright[at]nic[dot]in
- Telephone No.: 011-28032496

Step 4: Copy Right Objection Handling:
If no objections are raised within 30 days, a scrutinizer will assess the application for any discrepancies. If no differences are found, the registration will proceed, and an extract will be provided to the registrar for entry into the Register of Copyright.

Step 5: Objection Resolution:
If objections are received, both parties will receive a notification from the examiner outlining the objections. A hearing will be arranged to address these objections.

Step 6: Application Scrutiny:
Following the hearing and the resolution of objections, the scrutinizer will meticulously review the application if applicable. Subsequently, they will either approve or reject the application, depending on the specific circumstances.

Step 7: Get a Copyright Registration Certificate:
Once the application is approved, the relevant authority will issue the copyright registration certificate. In the usual course of events, the entire process typically takes approximately 2 to 3 months to complete.

Checking the Status of Copyright Registration Application:
- To verify the status of your Copyright registration application, follow these simple steps:
- Visit the website of the Copyright registrar and locate the "Status of Application" section.
- Provide the diary number you received upon submission, which is also referred to as the acknowledgment number.
- Submit this information, and you will receive the current status of your application.

Copyright Registration Workflow

Copyright Registration Workflow

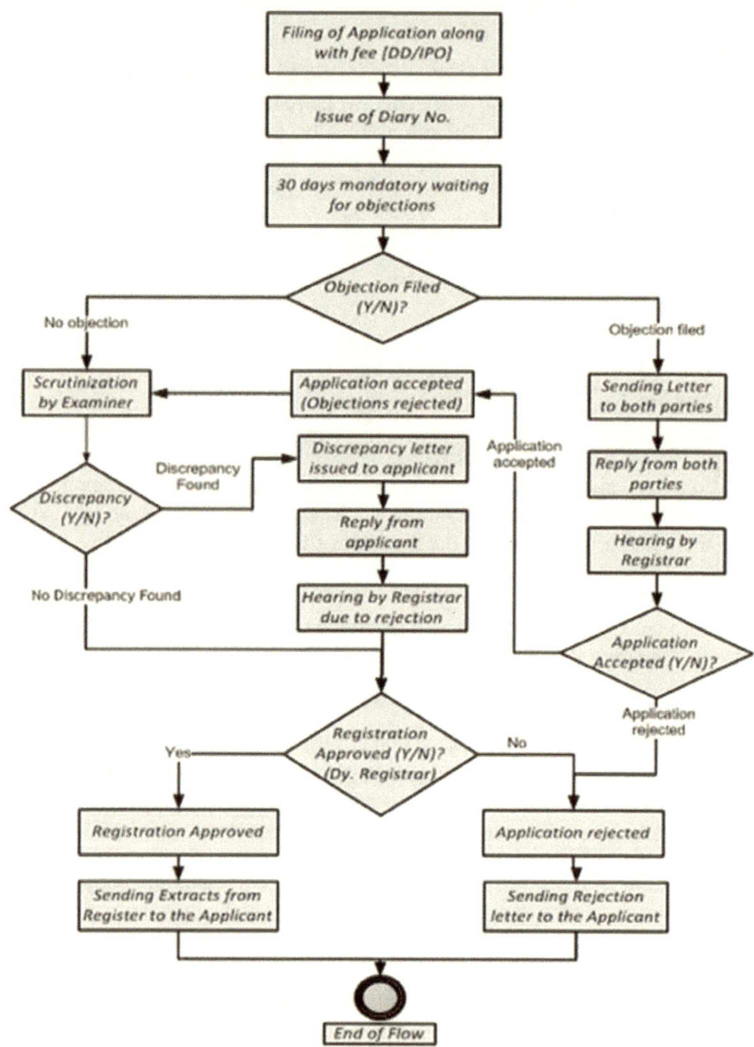

03-09: INTRODUCTION TO IPR COMMERCIALIZATION

Introduction:
Commercialization in simple words refers to introducing new products or services in the market. Around the world, several rules and regulations are made to ensure that Intellectual Property is commercialized and protected. The main motive of the commercialization of IPR is to encourage people to bring new ideas and creations into the market and make it marketable and profitable.

Objective of IPR Commercialization:
The objectives of Intellectual Property Rights (IPR) commercialization are to incentivize innovation and creativity, protect intellectual assets, drive economic growth, and foster a culture of continuous advancement by making inventions and creations marketable and profitable. Here's a more detailed breakdown of the objectives:

- **Incentivize Innovation and Creativity:**
IPR commercialization aims to encourage individuals and organizations to invest in innovative and creative works by granting exclusive rights to prevent others from using their ideas, designs, and inventions. This allows creators and inventors to profit from their work, fostering a culture of continuous innovation and creativity.

- **Protect Intellectual Assets:**
IPR commercialization provides legal protection for intellectual property, ensuring that creators and inventors can benefit from their work and prevent unauthorized use or imitation. This protection is crucial for attracting investment and promoting economic growth.

- **Drive Economic Growth:**
By protecting intellectual assets and facilitating their commercialization, IPR plays a vital role in driving economic growth. It attracts investments, boosts market opportunities, and creates new jobs and industries.

- **Promote a Culture of Continuous Advancement:**
IPR commercialization encourages the development and deployment of new technologies, products, and artistic works, leading to continuous advancements and improvements in various fields.

- **Make IPRs Marketable and Profitable:**
The primary goal is to transform IPRs into tradable financial assets, enabling businesses to generate revenue and profits from their intellectual property.

- **Encourage Entrepreneurship:**
Commercialization of IPRs fosters entrepreneurship by providing opportunities for individuals and businesses to develop and commercialize new ideas and inventions.

- **Connect Inventors and Investors:**
IPR commercialization aims to facilitate the connection between inventors and potential investors, ensuring that innovative ideas and inventions can be brought to market.

- **Protect Traditional Knowledge:**
IPRs also aim to protect traditional knowledge, ensuring that indigenous communities and cultures benefit from their intellectual heritage.

Methods of Commercializing Intellectual Property:

The strategy adopted for commercialization plays a crucial role in yielding returns. An inappropriate strategy may lead to botched results. However, the formulation of a strategy depends heavily on the method of commercialization of intellectual property to be adopted. Hence, below entails a discussion of the different methods of commercializing intellectual property along with a brief outline of some key decisions required to be taken when building strategy. There are five primary ways of commercializing one's intellectual property. These are as follows:

- commercialization by the Owner.
- commercialization through Assignment.
- commercialization through Licensing.
- commercialization through Franchising.
- commercialization through Joint Ventures.
- commercialization through Spin-offs.

1.Commercialization by the Owner:

Oftentimes, owners of intellectual property, whether individuals or companies, decide to take forward the commercialization of their intellectual property by themselves. It may be because the owner has enough capabilities for carrying out the marketing themselves or does not have enough resources for entering into a partnership for the same or simply because the owner is hesitant to share their data with third parties. However, commercialization by the owner themself involves considerable risk for the sole reason that owners of intellectual property are businessmen or companies run by businessmen, who may not be experts in intellectual property and the laws applicable thereof.

Things to Keep in Mind :

1. <u>Maintaining Secrecy</u> – Only inventions and designs which are not previously disclosed can be registered for patents and industrial designs. Furthermore, trademarks and domain names are registered on a first to file basis. Therefore, it is important to make sure such confidential information is not publicised unauthorizedly.

2. <u>Using Intellectual Property Databases and Conducting Freedom to Operate Analyses</u> – Checking intellectual property databases helps to ensure that one's idea is new, original and worth pursuing. Further, FTO analyses are aimed at evaluating whether a particular intellectual property, specifically patents, can be exploited commercially without infringing any third-party rights, thereby helping in avoiding infringement allegations.

3. <u>Keeping Records</u> – Records form a valuable source when drafting patent applications and keeping records of one's inventions help in proving the date and ownership of the said invention if and when needed.

4. <u>Protect Intellectual Property and Enforcing Intellectual Property Rights</u> – Diligently protecting one's intellectual property allows for their full utilization as well as aids in their proper management. Enforcing intellectual property rights is a cost-effective preventive measure for deterring infringing conducts.

2.Commercialization Through Assignment:

Assignment refers to the transfer of the ownership of an intellectual property, such as copyright or trademarks, and the rights therein to another party. It becomes a useful tool for commercialization when the owner of the intellectual property lacks the capabilities and resources to profitably commercialize their intellectual property. It is an outright sale of the intellectual property, the result of which is that the owner is absolutely relieved from the risks, obligations and responsibilities of maintenance associated with concerned intellectual property and nor is the buying party burdened with the covenant to pay regular royalties. However, because of this very nature of sale, negotiations with regard to the consideration amount may become difficult since intellectual properties such as patents and industrial designs are in and of themselves complex. Further, such sale may also conflict with the existing licensing agreements with regard to the concerned intellectual property, should there be any.

Things to Keep in Mind:
1. Non-Disclosure Agreements – The process of assignment involves detailed negotiations and requires exclusive information to be shared between the parties, although the same might not always result in a successful assignment. Therefore, it is prudent to sign NDAs in an effort to guarantee that any shared confidential information is not to be disclosed or used for purposes other than such negotiations by either party.
2. Conducting Due Diligence – Conducting due diligence with regard to the intellectual property to be assigned reveals assets and liabilities attached to it and aids in crystallizing its value. Therefore, it also functions as a risk management tool by revealing sensitive information with regard to the concerned intellectual property.
3. Understanding Key Terms – Knowing the relevant issues with regard to the intellectual property to be assigned and the important clauses to be deliberated on go a long way in maximizing the efficiency of an assignment agreement. Some of such important clauses are as below:
    o The form of agreement should be in a written form.
    o The intellectual property and the accompanying rights to be assigned must be clearly mentioned and elaborate.
    o The consideration amount, mode of payment and time for payment must be clearly stated.
    o Contractual assurances taken by both the parties concerning specific facts must be precisely elaborated.
    o The parties must clearly agree to the law and form of dispute resolution to be employed in case of conflict.

3.Commercialization Through Licensing:
A licensing contract is one where the owner of an intellectual property grants permission to use it for some form of regular payment generally called royalty. The ownership is not transferred. It can be understood as renting out one's intellectual property. Such agreements are generally restricted in terms of time period, purpose of use or the geographical area of applicability. Such agreements are beneficial in the sense that the licensor can avail new revenue streams without giving up the ownership of the intellectual property while also helping in widening their customer base. It also reduces the distribution and marketing expenses to an extent. The licensee benefits from avoiding the research and development costs and the risks associated therein. It also helps in widening their product portfolio. However, it is a double-edged sword because the licensee may become a competitor of or technologically dependent on the licensor. Furthermore, the licensee will be obligated to bear the burden of royalties even when the

licensed intellectual property is not generating revenue. Licensing of patents is more complex owing to the technical information involved.

Things to Keep in Mind:
1. Defining the Type of Licence – The contract should clearly define the type of licence to be granted, whether sole, exclusive or non-exclusive, based on the requirements and goals of the licensor.
2. Preparing for Negotiations – Licensing agreements are usually long-term business arrangements; they generally entail long negotiations in order to unequivocally define the rights and liabilities of the parties. Some important topics of negotiation are the right to sublicense, improvements, payment, warranties, infringement acts, and governing law and settlement of disputes.
3. Understanding Key Terms – Knowing the relevant issues with regard to the intellectual property to be assigned and the important clauses to be deliberated on, go a long way in maximizing the efficiency of a licensing agreement. Some of such important clauses are as below:
    o The agreement should be in written form.
    o The commencement, duration and termination of the agreement must be clearly laid down.
    o The intellectual property and the rights therein to be licensed should be clearly defined and elaborated.
    o The type of licence, whether exclusive or non-exclusive, should be clearly stated.
    o The geographical scope and field of use of the licence should be unequivocally stated and defined.
    o The parties must clearly agree to the law and form of dispute resolution to be employed in case of conflict.

The second part of this article will further explore commercialization through Joint Ventures and Spin-Offs along with a deep dive into the important steps to keep in mind when strategizing commercialization.

4.Commercialization Through Franchising:

Franchising is essentially a subset of licensing whereby the owner of an intellectual property grants the franchisee to replicate the entire business concept in a different location. The franchiser (owner) provides continued support and training in order to ensure the maintenance of the sanctity of their business concept. Franchising is commonly adopted to commercialize trademarks.

Things to Keep in Mind
1. Conducting Feasibility Study – This helps in forming an outlook for the adoption of a franchise. It elaborates the viability of a franchise in the target business and location while also aiding in planning the setting up of a franchise.
2. Testing the System – Applying the developed franchising system in at least one pilot unit in the same or similar market can help in testing the operational aspects of the business and in perceiving the possible defects before the launch of franchising.

Commercialization Through Joint Ventures:

A joint venture can be understood as a collaboration of two or more parties to achieve a specified goal or fulfil a specified project by sharing risks and resources. Since parties generally bring their intellectual property to such joint ventures, commercialization of their existing intellectual property often becomes one of the ends of a joint venture. Such an arrangement is advantageous because it allows for the exploitation and development of intellectual property by reducing the burden of investment and risks due to the same being generally shared between the parties. However, unequal expertise between the parties may result in an imbalance in the intellectual property assets and investments brought in by all the parties. Further, adapting intellectual property management to different management structures as required by a joint venture may also result in hindrances in the efficient commercialization of intellectual property.

Things to Keep in Mind
1. Pre-contractual Considerations – Executing non-disclosure agreements to protect one's own intellectual property while also conducting due diligence with regard to the intellectual property of the other party(s) is important to ensure that the negotiations do not become detrimental to any of the parties.
2. Contractual Considerations – Knowing the relevant issues with regard to the intellectual property to be assigned and the important clauses to be deliberated on go a long way in maximizing the efficiency of a joint venture.
   o Explicitly outline the extent of access to the rights of background intellectual property of all the parties.
   o The financial contribution of each party to the joint venture with regard to intangibles should be clearly demarcated.
   o The management structure of the joint venture should be precisely defined.
   o The effect of termination on the background intellectual property that was developed during the joint venture and the rights therein should be clearly accommodated.
   o The effect of exit of existing partners or entry of new partners on the background intellectual property that was developed during the joint venture and the rights therein should be delimited in express terms.
3. Consideration during implementation of the Joint Venture – Bring the ownership regime of intellectual property as determined in the joint venture agreement into effect, demarcate the ownership of all the improvements made or to be made to the background intellectual property and decide the extent of the commercializing activities allowed to all the parties.
4. Considerations when Terminating the Joint Venture – The consequences of termination of the joint venture or exit of a partner on intellectual property and the rights therein as mentioned in the agreement should be given effect.

5.Commercialization Through Spin-Offs:
Spin-offs are separate legal entities created by the owner of an intellectual property with the primary aim of commercializing the said intellectual property. They generally act as a bridge between the market and the owner by converting the subject of the intellectual property into a marketable product and releasing them into the commercial market. Thus, spin-offs often function as an important means of technology transfers within the market.

Things to Keep in Mind

1. Transferring Intellectual Property – Generally, the capital of the spin-off consists predominantly of the intellectual property. Therefore, it is important to decide the mode of such transfer, in essence, by assignment or license, in accordance with the requirements of the owner of the intellectual property.
2. Conducting Due Diligence – Conducting due diligence of the intellectual property allows investors to ascertain the significance of different methods of transferring intellectual property and the resultant consequences on the owner and the spin-off.
3. Necessary Agreements – Executing comprehensive non-disclosure and non-solicitation agreements with the investors, key managerial personnel and the employees of the spin-off along with detailed licensing or assignment agreements are crucial to protect the intellectual property.

Important Steps When Strategizing Commercialization:
The commercialization of intellectual property involves a detailed strategy mapping out the different stages involved in the process. The strategy varies greatly on the basis of different kinds of businesses, different business philosophies, etc. Two key influential factors are the methods chosen to commercialize the intellectual property and the extent to which the intellectual property is to be commercialized. On the other hand, the strategy and its implementation influence the outcome, that is, the economic gain from such commercialization. Thus, the importance of choosing a suitable strategy cannot be downplayed. While the formulation of a strategy depends largely on the owner, their business and economic experts, there are some things which are recommended when deciding on a strategy to commercialize intellectual property. These are as follows:

- Market Analysis
- Intellectual Property Audit
- Intellectual Property Valuation

1. **Market Analysis:**
A market analysis is basically a thorough study of the target market in order to gauge its strengths, weaknesses, opportunities and risks with regard to a product or service. It is crucial to conduct a comprehensive market analysis in all the markets where the intellectual property is sought to be commercialized in order to analyze the probability and extent of success. A good market analysis entails an evaluation of the following:

- The economic value of the intellectual property and the rights therein sought to be commercialized via a product or service.
- The size of the potential market.
- The actual and potential demand for the product in the target market.
- The purchasing power of the potential customers.
- Whether similar products or services are already available or will be available in the near future in the target market.
- The size and potential of the competitors in the target market.
- The size and capacity of potential business partners.
- The logistical issues which may arise in the physical delivery of the product or service.
- Domestic legal framework affecting the business in the target market.

2. **Intellectual Property Audit:**

Like the phrase suggests, the intellectual property audit is the process of reviewing all the intellectual property that one owns or uses. It includes both registered and unregistered intellectual property. The intellectual property acquired from a third party should also be included in such an audit. Generally, it should be done once every year, but it becomes crucial when strategizing the course of action for the commercialization of one's intellectual property since it helps in:

- Cataloguing one's intellectual property and the rights therein, which in turn also aids in using them as collateral for loans and borrowings.
- Determining the aggregate economic value of one's venture including one's intangible assets.
- Assessing potential risks to one's venture and accordingly establishing counter measures and corrective plans to mitigate the same.
- Incorporating best practices and effective strategies to better protect and manage one's intellectual property.
- Monitoring compliance with contractual duties and obligations.
- Ensuring timely registration and renewal of all intellectual property, which will accord better protection to such assets by facilitating their enforcement.

3.   **Intellectual Property Valuation:**

The next step after conducting an audit of one's intellectual property is their valuation, which includes assessing and quantifying the economic value of such intellectual property including their current and potential economic benefits. Its importance can be realized from the following:

- It provides full awareness of all the required information interacting with the value of one's intellectual property.
- It outlines the financial outlook of the consequences of potential risks posed in the commercialization of intellectual property and thereby aids in the formation of counter measures and corrective plans.
- It aids in acquiring an economic understanding of the concerned industry, the target market and the specific business sector which may influence the valuation of one's intellectual property.

TACTICS AND ACTIONS FOR IPR COMMERCIALIZATION:

IPR commercialization involves turning intellectual property into a profitable product or service, which can be achieved through tactics like direct commercialization, assignment, licensing, joint ventures, and partnerships, requiring strategic planning and market analysis.

Tactics and Actions for IPR Commercialization:

- **1. Understanding Your IPR:**
  - **IP Audit:** Conduct a thorough audit of your intellectual property assets to identify what you own and its potential value.
  - **IP Valuation:** Determine the market value of your intellectual property to inform commercialization decisions.
  - **Market Analysis:** Research the target market for your product or service, including demand, competition, and potential partners.
- **2. Choosing a Commercialization Strategy:**
  - **Direct Commercialization:** Develop and market products or services based on your own intellectual property.

- **Assignment:** Transfer ownership of your intellectual property to another party in exchange for a payment.
- **Licensing:** Grant others the right to use your intellectual property in exchange for royalties or other payments.
- **Joint Ventures:** Collaborate with other companies to develop and market products or services based on your intellectual property.
- **Franchising:** Grant others the right to use your brand and business model in exchange for fees and royalties.
- **Spin-offs:** Create a new company to focus on a specific intellectual property asset.

- **3. Implementing Your Strategy:**
  - **Develop a Business Plan:** Outline your commercialization strategy, including target market, product/service development, marketing plan, and financial projections.
  - **Protect Your IP:** Secure your intellectual property rights through registration and enforcement to prevent infringement.
  - **Negotiate Agreements:** Carefully negotiate licensing, assignment, or joint venture agreements to protect your interests.
  - **Build Partnerships:** Identify and collaborate with potential partners who can help you commercialize your intellectual property.
  - **Monitor and Enforce:** Continuously monitor the market and enforce your intellectual property rights to protect your commercialization efforts.

- **4. Key Considerations:**
  - **Legal Compliance:** Ensure that your commercialization activities comply with all relevant laws and regulations.
  - **Due Diligence:** Conduct thorough due diligence on potential partners or licensees to assess their capabilities and financial stability.
  - **Intellectual Property Protection:** Protect your intellectual property through patents, trademarks, copyrights, and trade secrets.
  - **Intellectual Property Strategy:** Develop a comprehensive intellectual property strategy to manage and leverage your assets effectively.

03-10:IPR PORTFOLIO MANAGEMENT

Patent Portfolio Management:

In today's knowledge-driven economy, intellectual property plays a vital role in creating and sustaining competitive advantages for businesses. Among various forms of intellectual property, patents hold significant value as they protect novel inventions and grant exclusive rights to the patent holder. Effective patent portfolio management is essential for companies to optimize their intellectual property assets, align their patent strategy with business objectives, and maximize their return on investment.

Importance of Patent Portfolio Management:

- **Strategic Alignment:**
  It ensures that patenting activities are aligned with business objectives and market opportunities.
- **Resource Optimization:**
  It helps companies make informed decisions about which patents to pursue, maintain, and enforce, optimizing resource allocation.
- **Competitive Advantage:**
  A well-managed patent portfolio can provide a competitive edge by protecting innovations and deterring competitors.
- **Revenue Generation:**
  It can help companies monetize their patents through licensing, sales, or other means.
- **Risk Mitigation:**
  It helps identify and address potential risks related to patent infringement or obsolescence.

Key Activities in Patent Portfolio Management:

- **Patent Acquisition and Evaluation:**
  The first step in patent portfolio management is identifying inventions within the company that have commercial potential. This involves evaluating the novelty and marketability of inventions, considering factors such as market demand, technological advancements, and competitive landscape. A comprehensive evaluation helps determine which inventions should be patented to protect valuable intellectual property.
- **Strategic Patent Filing:**
  Once an invention is deemed patent-worthy, strategic patent filing becomes crucial. Companies must consider the jurisdictions where protection is needed, taking into account factors such as target markets, potential competitors, and the cost of filing and maintenance. A well-planned patent filing strategy ensures broader protection, reduces the risk of infringement, and strengthens the company's competitive position.
- **Patent Prosecution and Enforcement:**
  Patent prosecution involves interacting with patent offices during the examination process to secure the grant of patents. Collaboration with patent attorneys is vital to respond effectively to office actions, address objections, and present compelling

arguments for patentability. By actively participating in the prosecution process, companies can ensure the issuance of robust, enforceable patents.

Enforcement of granted patents is another critical aspect of patent portfolio management. Companies should monitor potential infringements, evaluate their strategic significance, and take appropriate actions to protect their rights. This may involve negotiating licensing agreements, initiating litigation, or engaging in alternative dispute resolution methods to safeguard the value of their patent portfolio.

➢ **Patent Maintenance and Optimization:**
Maintaining a patent portfolio requires ongoing vigilance. Patents have maintenance fees and renewal deadlines that vary across jurisdictions. Patent portfolio managers must stay organized and track these deadlines to avoid inadvertent abandonment of valuable patents. Regular portfolio audits and analysis help identify low-value patents that can be pruned, freeing resources for more impactful filings.

Optimization of the patent portfolio involves evaluating the strength, relevance, and strategic alignment of existing patents. By identifying gaps or areas for improvement, companies can strategically file new patents or modify existing ones to enhance their coverage and competitiveness.

➢ **Monetization and Licensing:**
A well-managed patent portfolio can be monetized to generate additional revenue streams. Companies can license their patents to other organizations, granting them the right to use the protected technology in exchange for licensing fees or royalties. This approach allows companies to leverage their intellectual property assets without the need for extensive manufacturing or marketing efforts.

Alternatively, companies may choose to sell their patents outright, especially if they are not aligned with their core business or if there is a market demand for those patents. Patent auctions and transactions provide opportunities to realize immediate value from dormant or non-strategic patents.

➢ **Portfolio Analysis and Strategy:**
Regular analysis of the patent portfolio is essential to ensure its alignment with business goals and industry dynamics. By conducting a comprehensive assessment, companies can identify strengths, weaknesses, and potential risks within the portfolio. This analysis can inform decisions regarding patent acquisition, divestment, or strategic collaborations with other entities.

Furthermore, staying informed about emerging technologies, competitive landscapes, and regulatory changes helps companies adapt their patent strategies accordingly. By continuously monitoring market trends and technological advancements, companies can proactively position their patent portfolio to capture emerging opportunities and address potential threats.

<u>Trademark Portfolio Management:</u>
Trademark Portfolio Management (TPM) is the efficient and strategic management of the registration, infringement, litigation etc. types of services related to the trademark or service mark. This type of management enables a company to keep the business related to its trademark secure and profitable. This type of trademark portfolio management service usually involves responsibilities at a strategic, legal, financial level. The trademark portfolio service consists of, not only the monitoring of the maintenance strategy and advice on the internationalization of those trademarks. It also enlists the measures to provide trademarks with maximum protection.

Importance of Portfolio Management

- The trademark must be **renewed punctually and protected rigorously** in the relevant jurisdiction. Thus, by maintaining a portfolio it is easier to keep a record and maintain trademarks which also help in protecting them from prospective infringement. Furthermore, TPM creates a barrier to entrance for competitors.
- Trademark portfolio management allows an **effective consultation and maintenance** of all the trademarks.
- By centralizing the resources, company can take **informed decisions** regarding the portfolio and have the opportunity to be proactive rather than reactive.

Building a Trademark Portfolio:

It is essential to build trademark portfolio as it is crucial for maximizing and protecting the company's most valuable asset that is its brand. If a trademark portfolio is not properly built, the company may face an increased risk of infringement claims and many other issues. There are crucial steps to build a trademark portfolio which are as follows-

- **Conducting a trademark search of legally protectable mark:**

There are certain steps to follow for choosing a strong trademark to legally register. The company should choose a trademark which is easy to speak, spell, read and remember and at the same time non identical, non-descriptive, non-geographical, non-scandalous. After choosing a trademark the proprietor should check the availability of the mark at the IP portal of government, if it's available, the company should proceed to the next step.

- **Registering legally available trademark:** To proceed with this step the applicant should collect the documents such as logo or brand name that is to register along with the details about the classes in which the trademark will be registered. The company should also present the power of attorney to authorise a trademark attorney to file for registration applicant's behalf. The applicant is required to file these documents with trademark registry office (TRO) either by physical filing or e-filing.
- **Monitoring legally protected trademark:** This stage comes after the business has acquired the right to use the registered trademark. The monitoring includes-
- Licensing marks to third parties in exchange for royalties or other considerations.
- Monitoring the marketplace for infringement and misuse. (Investigating, action, cyber-piracy, counterfeiting).
- Conducting Trademark audits.
- Expanding or modifying use of existing mark.
- Ensuring that marks are properly used in commerce.

Portfolio Review:

Portfolio review is similar to the health check-up of business. Companies of all size can benefit from annual trademark review. Portfolio review involves a review of the company's business and the way it uses its trademark, compared to a review of the company's trademark registrations. The trademark which is no longer in need is required to be removed. It is **important** to conduct a portfolio review for reasons such as, to check geographic scope of use against domestic/foreign registration coverage and to prepare for future expansions. It is also necessary as it helps to confirm compliance with third party licenses, settlement agreements and other agreements. Further, the review helps in identifying the abandoned trademarks and taking necessary action to either pursue them or to remove them. Conducting periodic audits is also essential in managing the portfolio as it helps in ensuring that the trademark owner's compliance with requirements and deadlines for acquiring and maintaining rights.

Trademark Enforcement:
Trademark protection grants exclusive rights and prevents unlawful and unauthorized use of mark by any third party. Trademark enforcement is important so as to effectively enforce company's trademark against the deceptively similar or infringing marks. A tailored enforcement strategy is essential to maintain the profitability of a brand. The attorney's hired for trademark portfolio management should actively look for competitor's behaviour and efficiently enforce client's trademark strategy through a variety of means, beginning with the development of a comprehensive and strategic enforcement policy. Role of trademark portfolio management is that it helps in identifying the infringer with regular checks and helps in taking timely action against them.

Benefits of Working with Trademark Attorney:
The benefits of working with trademark attorney for trademark portfolio management is that the company can totally trust the knowledge of the attorney regarding the laws, changing trends and quick response towards any problems that may arise in the future. Further, there are a lot of things that can easily be handled by an attorney like filing and prosecution of trademarks, renewals of trademarks, docketing, portfolio audit and effective enforcement of the trademark rights. The attorney keeps themselves updated with changing pattern of intellectual property which allows the proprietor to benefit from them.

Challenges of Managing the Portfolio:
- It can be challenging to hire or train managers who are well adjusted to trademark management strategy. They should have knowledge of trademarks but as well as should be conversant with the IP strategies of the organization.
- With the advent of technological era the problems like counterfeiting on online platforms and changing laws can pose serious challenges towards portfolio management. One should remain up to date with these changes to adapt their strategies for managing trademarks.
- There should be a robust and effective trademark watching solution in place to regularly monitor the registries for threatening applications.
- Educating other stakeholders in the business, as well as licensing partners, manufacturers and suppliers on what to look out for is crucial, as is taking quick enforcement action to protect the integrity of trademark portfolio when required.

<u>**Copyright Portfolio Management:**</u>

Copyright portfolio management is the strategic process of overseeing and optimizing a collection of copyrights owned by an individual or organization to maximize their value and business goals. This includes identifying, acquiring, renewing, monitoring, and enforcing these rights.

Importance of Effective Copyright Portfolio Management:

- **Protection of Creative Works:** Safeguarding original works from unauthorized use.

- **Maximizing Value:** Increasing the commercial potential of copyrighted assets.
- **Competitive Advantage:** Establishing a stronger brand and market position.
- **Revenue Generation:** Licensing and selling rights to copyrighted works can generate income.
- **Risk Mitigation:** Identifying and addressing potential copyright infringements to minimize legal risks.

Key Aspects of Copyright Portfolio Management:

1. Copyright Registration and Maintenance:
- Understanding the importance of registering copyrights to strengthen legal protections.
- Steps for registering various types of creative works (e.g., literary, musical, artistic, etc.).
- Maintaining copyright registrations and renewals to ensure ongoing protection.

2. Copyright Enforcement:
- Strategies for identifying and addressing copyright infringement.
- Legal procedures for issuing cease-and-desist notices, pursuing lawsuits, and negotiating settlements.
- Building a strong legal team to handle copyright disputes.

3. Licensing and Commercialization:
- Developing licensing agreements for different uses of copyrighted works (e.g., distribution, reproduction, adaptation).
- Negotiating favorable licensing terms to maximize revenue and control.
- Exploring different licensing models (e.g., exclusive, non-exclusive, royalty-based).

4. Portfolio Optimization:
- Evaluating the value and potential of individual copyright assets.
- Identifying opportunities for licensing, resale, or other monetization strategies.
- Developing strategies for managing copyright portfolios efficiently, including inventory tracking and risk assessment.

5. Industry-Specific Considerations:
- Understanding copyright laws and regulations in different industries and countries.
- Adapting copyright management practices to the specific needs of the industry (e.g., publishing, music, film, software).
- Staying informed about changes in copyright laws and regulations.

Industrial Design(ID)Portfolio Management

Industrial Design (ID) Portfolio Management refers to the process of organizing, curating, and presenting a collection of design projects that showcase an individual's or company's design expertise. An ID portfolio is crucial for designers when seeking job opportunities, pitching to clients, or applying for design awards. Portfolio management is the strategic approach to ensure the portfolio is relevant, cohesive, and effective in communicating design skills and methodologies.

key considerations in Industrial Design Portfolio Management:

1. Purpose and Goals of the Portfolio:

- **Personal Branding:** The portfolio serves as a personal brand tool, showing your design philosophy, style, and process.
- **Target Audience:** The portfolio should be tailored to the audience you are trying to impress (e.g., potential employers, clients, or educational institutions).
- **Showcasing Skill Sets:** The portfolio should effectively demonstrate a range of design skills, from conceptualization to prototyping, material selection, ergonomics, and sustainability.

2. Content of the Portfolio:

- **Project Selection:** Include a diverse range of projects that demonstrate versatility and specialization. It's important to show different aspects of industrial design:
  - Product design
  - Conceptual sketches
  - CAD models and renderings
  - Prototypes and real-world applications
  - Research and development processes
  - User experience (UX) and human-centered design
- **Case Studies:** Each project should tell a story. Focus on the design challenge, the process, the solutions, and the impact of the project. A good case study includes:
  - Problem Definition
  - Ideation and Sketching
  - Prototyping and Testing
  - Final Product and Real-World Application
  - Reflection on Lessons Learned
- **Process Documentation:** Employers value how you solve problems. Document the steps from concept development to the final product. This could include wireframes, sketches, 3D models, and prototypes.
- **Photography & Presentation:** High-quality photos of physical prototypes, models, and renderings are essential. Good lighting, context, and high-resolution images enhance the presentation.

3. Cohesion and Structure

- **Flow and Order:** Organize your portfolio logically. Start with the most impactful or diverse projects. Group projects by type or by complexity (simple to more intricate).
- **Consistency in Design:** Ensure your portfolio follows a consistent layout and design style. This includes typography, color schemes, and margins. A cluttered portfolio distracts from the content.
- **Introduction & About Section:** Include an introductory page with your personal statement, design philosophy, and background. Your portfolio should reflect who you are as a designer, so this is a chance to showcase your personality and approach.

4. Digital vs. Physical Portfolio

- **Digital Portfolio:** Most designers today need a digital portfolio. It's easier to share, update, and make accessible worldwide.
  - Create a personal website or use platforms like Bedance, Dribbble, or LinkedIn.
  - Ensure it's mobile-responsive and easy to navigate.

o   Optimize images and videos for faster loading times.
    o   Consider adding an interactive aspect to showcase animations, 3D models,
        or videos of prototypes in use.
- **Physical Portfolio:** Although digital is essential, a physical portfolio might still be
  needed for interviews, design exhibitions, or client meetings.
    o   Focus on high-quality printed images of key projects.
    o   Keep it compact and organized and use a premium binder or portfolio case.

5. Tailoring the Portfolio

- **Customization:** Tailor your portfolio to specific industries or job roles. For example,
  a portfolio for a tech-focused design firm should highlight innovative product designs
  and tech-savvy projects, while a portfolio for a sustainability-driven company may
  emphasize eco-friendly designs.
- **Highlight Key Projects:** Always choose the most impressive and relevant work to
  showcase. If you're applying for a particular job or client, make sure the projects
  resonate with the employer's needs.

6. Managing the Portfolio Over Time

- **Update Regularly:** Design is an evolving field. Regularly update your portfolio to
  include your latest projects, whether freelance work, collaborations, or personal
  projects.
- **Track Achievements:** Include any relevant awards, recognitions, or publications
  where your work has been featured. This helps to boost credibility.
- **Gather Feedback:** Always ask for feedback from peers, mentors, or industry
  professionals. They may provide useful insights on areas for improvement or
  different perspectives on your design process.

7. Presentation and Delivery

- **Interviews and Presentations:** When presenting your portfolio in person or online,
  practice explaining your design process and how your work addresses the needs of
  the project.
    o   Focus on storytelling: Explain the challenge, the approach, and the
        outcome.
    o   Keep it interactive: Invite questions from the audience and be open to
        feedback.

8. Key Tools for Portfolio Creation

- **Software for Portfolio Creation:**
    o   **Adobe InDesign:** Perfect for layout design and creating print-ready
        portfolios.
    o   **Adobe Photoshop & Illustrator:** For image editing and creating visual
        elements.
    o   **SketchUp, Rhino, Fusion 360:** Useful for showcasing 3D models and
        design renderings.
    o   **Behance** or **Dribbble:** Ideal for creating and displaying an online portfolio.
    o   **PowerPoint or Keynote:** Often used for quick presentations or interviews.

9. Additional Considerations

- **Diversity in Projects**: Show that you can work with a variety of materials, processes, and industries.
- **Communication**: Industrial designers need to be excellent communicators. Ensure your portfolio tells a clear, concise story about each project.
- **Reflection and Growth**: Show that you've learned from each project. It's important to reflect on how each experience improved your design approach.

<u>Demise of patent Owner and transfer rights:</u>

A patent is an exclusive right awarded for an invention. An invention is a product or a technique that, in general, offers a new way of doing something or presents a new technical solution to a problem. A patent is like an investment for an inventor to use the invention solely or earn through licensing it.

<u>In India, patent protection can be achieved by the following:</u>

- ➤ Filling up and submitting a patent application to the patent office.
- ➤ Inspecting the application and conducting thorough search of all reports available by the patent office
- ➤ The application for the grant will be placed for grant once all patent conditions have been satisfied. The Patent Journal, which is released periodically, publishes notification of the grant of a patent.

A patentee has the choice to prevent others from producing, using, practicing, or selling the invention without his permission after receiving a patent.

A patentee can transfer the ownership of the patent to another to use the invention by way of:

1. Assignment
2. Licenses
3. By activity of law

1.ASSIGNMENT:

Assignment is not defined in Indian Patents Act. The patentee transfers all or a part of his patent rights to the appointee who obtains the right to prevent others from creating, utilizing, Practising, or disseminating the invention. Section 50(3) of the Patents Act, 1970 states that in case a patent is co-owned by two or more individuals, any share of the patent cannot be assigned to anyone else without the consent of all co-owners.

Types of Assignment:

There are three types of assignments.

1.Legal assignment:

An assignment (or consent to appoint) under a valid patent is one in which the trustee may identify himself as the patent owner. A deed must be used to allot a patent that was created through one. All patent rights are granted to a duly appointed person who is qualified to be its owner.

2.Equitable assignment

Any form or agreement including a letter in which the proprietor agrees to share a certain share of the patent with another individual is referred to as the equitable assignment of the patent. In any case, an appointee in such a situation is not eligible to have his name listed as the patent owner in the register. However, they can notify the register of their interest in the patent.

3.Mortgages:

Mortgages are assignments in which the owner transfers all or a portion of their rights to the assignee in return for a fixed sum of money. The owner regains full ownership of the mortgaged property once the debt has been settled. The lender must have their name listed in the register as a mortgagee rather than registering themselves as the proprietor.

Requirements for Patent Assignment:

- ➢ As mentioned before, patent assignment can only be considered a valid assignment if it has been drafted in writing and duly executed through the legal process.
- ➢ The written draft must define all the rights and obligations of both the parties with respect to the patent.
- ➢ The assignee shall apply in writing to the Controller of Patents to enter their name into the register of patents. Once the Controller of Patents is satisfied that the assignee has a genuine interest in the patent, they shall enter the details of assignment into their register.
- ➢ Form-16 must be duly filled and filed before the Controller General of Patents, Designs and Trademarks. It records the necessary details that must be mentioned for assignment, such as name of the applicant, details of all parties involved, description of the draft through which assignment is being sought.
- ➢ Two copies of the deed must be attached to the application as well.
- ➢ Fees for the process varies for different individuals and entities and is different when applied physically and through the Internet. A detailed breakdown of the official fees for the process is mentioned in the First Schedule of the Patent Act.

Amending Patent Assignment Agreement:

The parties to the assignment may agree to change certain provisions of the agreement in the event of an infringement or mutual concession. The equitable assignment deed can primarily be used to process amendments to patent assignments. If the deed needs to be changed, it must be registered with the Controller of Patents before the assignment process is complete.

Termination of Patent Assignment Agreement:

Since a deed is permanent and irrevocable, it cannot genuinely be terminated. A patent assignment pretty essentially constitutes a choice that cannot be undone. If it is a mortgage assignment deed, it can only be terminated.

2.LICENSING:

Patent licensing is a process of granting permission to a third party to extract benefits by selling and using the licensed product. The patent owner gives license to a third party to use his patented invention based on the agreement and royalty. The license can be given for a period of time as per the mutual understanding between patent owner and licensee. During this time period, the licensee can use patented invention and can take financial benefits.

Licensing is a contract between two parties where licensor agrees the terms and conditions of patent owner. Since it is a contract or agreement, it must follow the Sections 10 and 11 of Indian Patent Act 1970. As per Section 68 of the Patent Act 1970, the agreement must be in writing.

Types of Licenses:
There are eight types of patent licensing as follows:

1.Exclusive license:
Exclusive licencing grants the licensee all rights, excluding the title to the innovation. Patent ownership is transferred from the patent owner to the licensee. Only the invention's title belongs to the patent holder. As a result, the licensee takes on all of the invention's obligations. The patent cannot, however, be licensed to another party by the licensee. It is given solely to him/her. As a result, the only individual with permission to exploit the patented invention is the licensee.

2.Non-exclusive license:
In Non-Exclusive Licensing, the license of the patent can be granted to more than one party and all of them can commercialize the patent into the market. Thus, patent owner has rights to license his patented invention to more than one party.

Sub license:
Licensee has rights to issue Sub license to different organizations for making the product of patented invention. Patent owners give rights to licensee and the licensee has the right to issue the license further to a third party that can use patented invention. The financial benefits will depend on the contract between the primary licensee and third party.

Cross-license:
Cross-Licensing is the exchange of licenses between different organizations and creators. When invention requires the support of other products to make its place in the market, Cross-Licensing process is used.

Voluntary licensing:
Licencing on a voluntary basis is a gesture of goodwill towards the community. It also applies to patents for medicines. With voluntary licencing, the owner of a patent can grant the right to produce, import, or distribute a pharmaceutical product to other parties on an exclusive or non-exclusive basis. The licensee is allowed to sell and distribute the goods in a market, according to the agreement. According to the terms and conditions outlined in the contract, the patent owner receives their royalty.

Compulsory licensing:
In Compulsory Licensing, the authorization is given to a third party to make, use or sell a patented invention without the consent of patent owner. According to the Sections 84 and 92 of Indian Patent Act 1970, if the specified conditions are satisfied, license can be granted to a third party without permission of patent owner. According to Section 84 of IPA 1970, any person who is interested or already the holder of the license under the patent can request to the Controller for grant of Compulsory License after three years from the date of grant of that patent. The patent office considers the nature of the invention, ability of the applicant to use the invention for the public interest, any measures already taken by the patentees or any licensee to make full use of the invention and time elapsed from grant of the patent. Compulsory Licensing is usually reserved for pharmaceutical patents. Government allows someone to practice

patented invention to make, use or sell patented invention without taking permission of patent owner for the public benefits.

Carrot licensing:
This strategy is appropriate when the potential licensee is not using the patented innovation and is not obligated to obtain a licence. In this situation, the patent holder must persuade the party to use his product and explain how licencing it can be advantageous for them. In a marketing strategy known as carrot licencing, the owner of the patent tries to demonstrate to the licensee what may be accomplished by purchasing a licence for it.

Stick licensing:
Stick Licensing is another approach of licensing which is totally contrast of the carrot licensing. In Stick Licensing approach, prospective licensee is already using the patented technology and thus infringing the patent. The patent owner can file a suit against the infringer or settle with the infringer agreeing to license his patent.

Difference between Assignment and Licenses:

Assignment	License
Assignment refers to the transfer of ownership and of the patent to the assignee.	A license grants you the permission to use any patented invention, which would otherwise be referred to as infringement.
Assignments must be executed in writing.	Licenses can be granted without any written documentation.
Assignees don't need to pay any royalties to the original owner.	Licensees may be expected to pay certain royalties in exchange of using the inventor's product.
As you become a proprietor of the patent, it may be a bit expensive to get an assignment.	Licenses are much cheaper than assignments as you will also be paying some royalty in exchange of using the patent.

3. TRANSMISSION OF PATENT BY OPERATION OF LAW:

When a patentee passes away, the patent's premium passes to his legal representative. If an organization dissolves, goes out of business, or is liquidated, the patent is transferred by legal means.

Conclusion:
A licence is the right granted to use the creation while keeping the exclusive rights with the patentee, whereas an assignment is the exchange of a variety of restriction rights by the patentee to the appointee. As a result, an appointee may transfer his privileges to third parties, whereas a licensee is not permitted to do so or to modify the title of his position.
An appointee is given all of the rights that the patent owner can enjoy, whereas a licensee is not permitted to do so. Additionally, an appointee has the right to file a lawsuit against the infringer while the licensee is not permitted to do so for the infringement of the patent in his name. The patentee can select the best strategy for commercializing his or her discovery after learning the difference between assignment and licence from the aforementioned information.

03-11: TECHNO-LEGAL LICENSING

Techno-legal licensing refers to the legal framework and agreements that govern the transfer of intellectual property (IP) or technology between parties. It involves the licensor granting permission to the licensee to use their IP, often in exchange for payment or other considerations. This process ensures that the technology is used responsibly and ethically, while also protecting the licensor's rights.

PATENT LICENSING:
Patent licensing is a process of granting permission to a third party to extract benefits by selling and using the licensed product. The patent owner gives license to a third party to use his patented invention based on the agreement and royalty. The license can be given for a period of time asper the mutual understanding between patent owner and licensee. During this time period, the licensee can use patented invention and can take financial benefits. Licensing is a contract between two parties where licensor agrees the terms and conditions of patent owner. Since it is a contract or agreement, it must follow the Sections 10 and 11 of Indian Patent Act 1970. As per Section 68 of the Patent Act 1970, the agreement must be in writing.

Advantages/Disadvantages of Patent Licensing:
Once patent license procedure is completed, both licensee and licensor have few advantages and disadvantages. The patent owner can transfer risk of manufacturing /production of a design or a product to licensee. The patent owner need not worry about mass production and global market. If the patent is licensed to a well-established company having a large customer base, then patent product will have a large market and patent owner can get good financial benefit. However, lots of efforts are required to find the appropriate licensee for the invention. It is very important to get a potential licensee and have a written agreement so that chances of success will be more. The main disadvantage of patent owner is that he loses his own control partially of fully on his own invention for the period of license. It is always a risk for patent owner as he has to believe on licensee, his strategy, quality management and commercialization the patent product to get more financial benefits. The licensee may have to pay more royalties if he wanted to expand the production/sale of patent product into other markets. The patent owner gets his exclusive rights over his invention once the license duration expires.

Types of Patent Licensing:
There are eight types of patent licensing as described below.

1. Exclusive License:
In Exclusive licensing, all the rights except title of the invention are given to the licensee. Patent owner transfers the ownership of the patent to the licensee. Patent owner has only the title of the invention. Thus, licensee acquires all the responsibilities related to the invention. However, licensee cannot license the patent to anyone else. It is exclusively granted to him/her. Thus, licensee is only the authorized person to use the patented invention.

2. Non-Exclusive License:
In Non-Exclusive Licensing, the license of the patent can be granted to more than one party and all of them can commercialize the patent into the market. Thus, patent owner has rights to license his patented invention to more than one party.

3. Sub License:

Licensee has rights to issue Sub license to different organizations for making the product of patented invention. Patent owners give rights to licensee and the licensee has the right to issue the license further to a third party that can use patented invention. The financial benefits will depend on the contract between the primary licensee and third party.

4. Cross-Licensing:

Cross-Licensing is the exchange of licenses between different organizations and creators. When invention requires the support of other products to make its place in the market, Cross-Licensing process is used.

5. Voluntary Licensing:

Voluntary licensing is an act of goodwill towards the society. It is also applicable for pharmaceutical patents. In Voluntary Licensing, patent owner can license his patented invention to other parties on exclusive or non-exclusive basis and give right to manufacture, import or distribute a pharmaceutical product. According to the agreement, licensee can sale and distribute the product in a market. Patent owner gets its royalty as per the terms and conditions mentioned in the agreement.

6. Compulsory Licensing:

In Compulsory Licensing, the authorization is given to a third party to make, use or sell a patented invention without the consent of patent owner. According to the Sections 84 and 92 of Indian Patent Act 1970, if the specified conditions are satisfied, license can be granted to a third party without permission of patent owner. According to Section 84 of IPA 1970, any person who is interested or already the holder of the license under the patent can request to the Controller for grant of Compulsory License after three years from the date of grant of that patent. The patent office considers the nature of the invention, ability of the applicant to use the invention for the public interest, any measures already taken by the patentees or any licensee to make full use of the invention and time elapsed from grant of the patent. Compulsory Licensing is usually reserved for pharmaceutical patents. Government allows someone to practice patented invention to make, use or sell patented invention without taking permission of patent owner for the public benefits.

7. Carrot Licensing:

Carrot Licensing is one of the approaches of patent licensing. This approach is suitable when prospective licensee is not in the practice of the patented invention and not falls under any obligation to take a license. In this case, patent owner has to convince the party to use his product and how licensing the product can be beneficial for them. Carrot Licensing is a marketing policy where the patent owner tries to show the licensee what could be achieved by taking a license for his patent.

8. Stick Licensing:

Stick Licensing is another approach of licensing which is totally contrast of the carrot licensing. In Stick Licensing approach, prospective licensee is already using the patented technology and thus infringing the patent. The patent owner can file a suit against the infringer or settle with the infringer agreeing to license his patent.

Licensing under Indian Patent Act 1970
Sections 84-92 of IPA 1970 are related to Licensing of a patent. According to the IPA 1970, patent licensing should be in writing between the licensor and the licensee. Section 84 of IPA 1970 states the terms and conditions required for issuing Compulsory Licensing. The Act has the provision and empowers the Controller to issue the Compulsory Licensing to a third party. Compulsory Licensing is possible only if the patented invention is useful to public health or in National Emergencies or health crisis. According to the 84 Section of IPA 1970, after three years from the grant of the patent, any interested person can write an application to the Controller for grant of Compulsory License on the following grounds:
- The reasonable requirements of the public for the patented invention have not been satisfied.
- Patented invention is not available to the public in affordable price.
- Patented invention is not worked within the territory of India.

After receiving the application, the Controller can grant a Compulsory License to that party/person.

However, before granting the Compulsory License, the Controller has to consider several factors such as:

- Royalty/remuneration for the patentee are reasonable.
- Licensee will use patented invention properly.
- Patented invention will be available to the public at reasonable prices.
- The license is non-exclusive and non-assignable.
- The license will not be longer than the term of the patent.
- Licensing the patented invention is for the better supply in Indian market.
- If patented invention is for semiconductor technology, the license granted is for non-commercial public use.

Compulsory Licenses can be granted to a pharmaceutical products and export of certain pharmaceutical products that are necessary for public health of a country having weak capacity of pharmaceutical industry can be allowed.

Patent License and Patent Assignment:
In Patent License, patent owner grants permission to a third party to extract benefits on the patents for limited period of time. Transfers of rights are temporary in nature. In Patent License, the licensee has to pay the royalty to the patent owner for the entire duration of the license period. In Patent Licensing, patent owner still holds the rights on his patented invention.
In Patent Assignment, patent owner transfers exclusive rights of the patent to a third party permanently. Such a transfer is recorded in the official patent record. In Patent Assignment, the assignee has to pay the lump-sum amount to the patent owner/assignee in the beginning and later can receive profits from the patented invention.

Imperative tips for Patent Owner:
Patent owner should think before licensing his patented invention and should thoroughly study on following points before licensing his patent:
- Whether to invest capital amount or licensing can be better option

- ➢ If licensing option is selected, then whether an individual or a company can be better option
- ➢ If selling patent is chosen, then whether keeping rights on patent is important to or not.
- ➢ Market Research is very important before licensing, companies who are manufacturing a similar kind of product can be checked.
- ➢ Showcasing the patented invention is also very important to get the best company as a licensee.

Considering above points, patent owner can decide the options of licensing, selling or manufacturing his patented invention. In licensing the patent, the patent owner should choose licensee carefully and thinks about royalty. A big company can offer good royalty. The royalty rate can vary from five to twenty percent depending on the licensee.

Limitations of Patent Licensing:
Licensing is very convenient way for the patent owner to take financial benefits from his patented invention.

However, licensing has few limitations and risks as follows:

- ➢ Licensing could be less profitable. It may happen that if patent owner make the invention available in market can achieve more profit than licensee. Though investing capital is a risk, but profits can be more than expectations.
- ➢ Patent owner has to depend on the licensee for profits. Patent owner is totally dependent on the licensee, his sources, his skills and the efforts for marketing the patented invention and further for financial benefits. Thus, if proper licensee is not selected then the product may fail in market.
- ➢ An agreement of licensing should be drafted very carefully. All the terms and conditions related to royalty and further processing should be stated clearly in the agreement. Also agreement should clearly states all the clauses related to investment and data related to patented invention.
- ➢ The licensee has to pay fixed royalties to the patent owner irrespective of the status of the product in the market.

Trademark Licensing:
Trademark Licensing refers to the contractual agreement between a trademark owner (the licensor) and another party (the licensee), whereby the owner allows the licensee to utilise the registered trademark in specific ways, under specific terms, and for a specific duration.

Trademark licensing is a process by which the owner of a registered trademark, also called the licensor, grants the right to use his trademark, either fully or partially, to a third party, also called the licensee under a mutually agreed licensing agreement. This agreement is signed by both the parties, and the usership rights granted as a result is limited to a defined period, restricted to specific products /services and specific geographic boundaries only. The rights typically encompass the usage of the trademark on products, services, marketing materials, packaging, and other designated areas.

The advantages of trademark licensing are significant for both parties involved- the licensor and the licensee. For the licensor, it offers an opportunity to expand the reach of their brand beyond its core operations and generate additional revenue through licensing fees and royalties. It also allows them to capitalize on the licensee's expertise in manufacturing, distribution, or marketing, enabling a broader market presence without diverting resources from their primary business activities.

Types of Trademark Licensing:

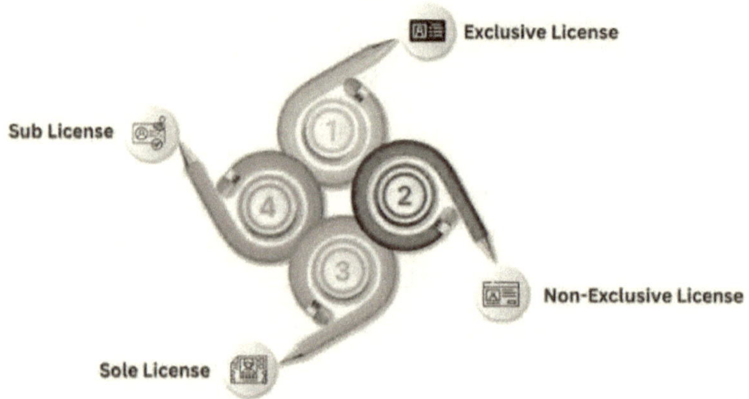

1. Exclusive License:

The licensee is the only user of the trademark. The licensor neither retains his right to use nor to grant further Licenses. However, he retains the right to exclusively own the trademark.

2. Non-Exclusive License:

The licensee is just one of the users of the trademark. The licensor retains his right to use and grant further Licenses as well. Even in this case, the exclusive right to own the trademark lies with the Licensor only.

3. Sole License:

The Licensee is the only other user of the trademark besides the licensor. The licensor does not retain his right to grant further Licenses but retains his right to use and exclusively own the License.

4. Sub License:

The licensor and the licensee both have the right to use and grant further Licenses of the trademark to third parties. The Licensor, however, is the sole and exclusive owner of the trademark.

Legal Framework of Trademark Licensing in India:
We can explore the legal framework for Trademark Licensing in the all-encompassing Trademark Act of 1999. Although the Act does not exclusively use the term "Trademark Licensing", the provisions for the same are made using the term "permitted use". The licensee, as per the act, is termed as the "registered user" and the licensor, as the "registered proprietor". Let's go through the specific provisions for a better understanding!

1. Section 2, Trademark Act, 1999:

Section 2 of the Trademark Act, 1999, grants "permitted use" of the trademark to a "registered user" for goods or services he deals with in his normal course of trade, and for which the trademark is originally registered.

2. Section 48, Trademark Act, 1999:

Section 48 of the Trademark Act, 1999, defines a "registered user" as a person other than its registered proprietor, who has been granted the "permitted use" of the trademark, subject to his registration under Section 49 of the Act, and limited to scope of goods/services for which the trademark is registered.

3. Section 49, Trademark Act, 1999:

Section 49 of the Trademark Act provides for Registration of the person who has been granted the right to "permitted use" of the Trademark by its registered proprietor. The section mentions all the procedures and requirements for such registration in detail. After the registration, the concerned person becomes a "registered user" of the mark under the Act.

4. Section 50, Trademark Act, 1999:

Section 50 of the Trademark Act, 1999, provides for the cancellation of the "Registered User" by the Registrar based on certain valid grounds. These grounds for cancellation, along with its procedure, are also mentioned in Section 50 itself. We have discussed this section in detail further in this blog.

5. Section 52, Trademark Act, 1999:

Section 52 of the Trademark Act, 1999, lays down the provisions related to Infringement of the Trademark License. The "registered user" of the Trademark has the right to institute a legal proceeding against the "registered proprietor" in case he infringes the agreement of Trademark Licensing signed between the two.

Trademark Licensing Agreement: Its Importance & Contents:

A Trademark License Agreement is a legally binding document that establishes the rights and obligations between the proprietor of a registered trademark (licensor) and a third party (licensee). The agreement grants authorization to the licensee to manufacture, sell, or distribute products or provide services using the licensed trademark. This agreement ensures that the licensor retains the ownership of the licensed trademark and maintains control over the quality of the products it is being used for, while allowing the licensee to utilize it for commercial purposes.

A well-drafted Trademark License Agreement should include the following key elements:

1. **Parties:** The agreement should clearly identify and include the names and details of the licensor (trademark owner) and the licensee (the party obtaining the License).
2. **Description of the Trademark:** The agreement should provide a clear and precise description of the trademark being licensed. This includes specifying the registered trademark's details, such as the registration number and the specific classes of goods or services it covers.
3. **Grant of License:** The agreement should explicitly state the scope of the License being granted, including the specific products, services, or activities covered under

the License. It should define the territory or geographic area in which the licensee has the right to use the trademark.

4. **Quality Control:** The agreement should outline the licensor's right to maintain quality control over the products or services offered by the licensee under the licensed trademark. It should establish the standards and procedures for quality control to preserve the reputation and goodwill associated with the trademark.

5. **Consideration:** The agreement should specify the consideration or financial arrangement between the licensor and the licensee. This includes any upfront fees, ongoing royalties, or other monetary obligations that the licensee must fulfill.

6. **Term and Termination:** The agreement should clearly state the duration or term of the License. It should also outline the conditions under which either party can terminate the agreement, including provisions for breach, non-performance, or expiration of the agreement.

7. **Rights and Obligations:** The agreement should outline the rights and obligations of both the licensor and the licensee. This includes their respective duties in maintaining the trademark's integrity, protecting its rights, and complying with applicable laws and regulations.

8. **Indemnification:** The agreement should include an indemnification clause, specifying the responsibilities of each party in case of any losses, damages, or legal claims arising from the use of the licensed trademark.

9. **Non-transferability:** The agreement should clarify that the License is non-transferable, meaning the licensee cannot transfer or sublicense the rights granted without the licensor's prior written consent.

10. **Governing Law and Dispute Resolution:** The agreement should mention the governing law that applies to the interpretation and enforcement of the agreement. It should also specify the mechanism for resolving any disputes, such as through arbitration or litigation.

To ensure the validity and enforceability of the Trademark License Agreement, it is essential to have a written agreement signed by both the licensor and the licensee. Seeking legal advice during the drafting and negotiation of the agreement is recommended to ensure compliance with the relevant laws and to protect the interests of both parties involved.

Trademark License Registration: Requirement & Procedure:
Section 49 of the Trademark Act, 1999, makes it mandatory for the registration of the licensed user of a trademark with the Indian Trademark Registry. For this a joint application must be filed to the Registrar by the proprietor of the trademark and its proposed registered user in the TM-U form on the **IP India website**.

The form must be accompanied by certain documents required for Trademark License Registration, including:
1. A copy of the Trademark License Agreement
2. Affidavit by the Registered Proprietor of the Trademark, mentioning the terms of agreement, its duration, scope of goods or services, and any other limitations in use imposed by the agreement.

Upon submission, the form is examined by the Trademark Registry Office, and if it is found to be correct, the Office registered the proposed user as the "registered user" of the trademark.

Cancellation of Trademark License Registration:

Once the registration of the proposed user is complete, it stays valid unless cancelled by the Registrar. The Registrar has the power to make changes or cancel the registration of a person as a registered user of a trademark, under Section 50 of the Trademark Act. This can occur due to applications made either by the registered user or the registered proprietor of the Trademark. Additionally, even the Registrar is entitled to initiate the cancellation in his capacity. The grounds for cancellation and its procedure are mentioned in Section 50 of the Act itself. Here is a detailed explanation-

Variation by the Registrar:

The Registrar can change the registration of a person as a registered user for specific goods or services upon the written request of the trademark owner.

Cancellation by the Registrar on the Request of owner/registered user

- The Registrar can cancel the registration of a person as a registered user upon written application by the trademark owner, registered user, or another registered user who is affected by such registration.
- The specific grounds for cancellation may include:
    1. The registered user using the trademark in a way that causes confusion or deception or goes against the agreement with the trademark owner.
    2. The proprietor or registered user hiding or misrepresenting important information during the registration process.
    3. Changes in circumstances that would have affected the decision to register the user.

Cancellation by the Registrar in His Own Capacity

- The Registrar can cancel the registration if there is a failure to enforce or comply with the agreement between the trademark owner and the registered user regarding the quality of goods or services associated with the trademark.
- The Registrar can cancel the registration if the trademark is no longer registered for specific goods or services.

Notice and Procedure for Cancellation

- The Registrar must provide notice to the registered proprietor (trademark owner) and other registered users (excluding the applicant) regarding any application for variation or cancellation.
- Before cancelling the registration, the registered proprietor and the registered User must be given a reasonable opportunity to be heard.

Copyright Licensing:

Copyright licensing is a legal agreement where a copyright owner grants permission to others to use their copyrighted work, specifying the terms and conditions of that use, such as scope, duration, and territory.

Importance of Copyright Licensing in India

Copyright licensing doesn't mean passing on ownership of the creation; it is just a transfer of interest that the licensee can use to modify the work without the fear of infringement. Thus, it protects the original creation and the creator which makes it important because it fosters creativity, encourages innovation, and promotes the dissemination of knowledge. It is more like a legal way that copyright owners can take to monetize their works while enabling others to legally utilize their copyrighted materials for various purposes.

So, to sum up, copyright licensing is important because:

> ➢ It prevents unauthorized copying or infringement by giving copyright owners the exclusive right to control their works' use and distribution.
> ➢ Allows copyright owners to earn royalties by licensing their works via a licensing agreement.
> ➢ It benefits the licensees, such as individuals, businesses, or organizations to use copyrighted materials while avoiding potential infringement claims and legal disputes and ensuring compliance with copyright laws.
> ➢ Facilitates access to a wide range of creative works such as publishing, translation, performance, adaptation, distribution, or display, based on the specific rights granted in the license agreement.
> ➢ Fosters collaboration and innovation by allowing creators to share their works with others. Licensees can build upon existing copyrighted materials, create new works, and contribute to the growth of various creative industries.
> ➢ It prevents unnecessary disputes from arising as copyright licensing agreements often include provisions for resolving disputes and parties can agree on mechanisms such as arbitration, mediation, or referral to the Copyright Board in case of conflicts arising from the license agreement.

Types of Licenses in Indian Copyright Licensing Law

In Indian copyright law, copyright licensing is classified into two different types i.e., Voluntary licenses and Compulsory licenses.

1. Voluntary License -
The voluntary license, as defined in Section 30 of the Indian Copyright Act, allows the copyright owner to grant another person the right to make exclusive or nonexclusive use of a copyrighted work. The license is deemed voluntary because the copyright owner granted it willingly.
Under voluntary licensing, ownership remains with the copyright owner and only specific rights such as reproduction, distribution, adaptation, performance, or display, among others, are transferred to the licensee. It can be given for both an existing work and future work, but the license will only become effective in future work once the work comes into existence.
Voluntary licensing can take various forms, including -

> ➢ **Exclusive License -**

Which grants exclusive rights only to the licensee, and no other person or entity, including the copyright owner, can use the copyrighted work during the license period.

> **Non-Exclusive License -**
> Where the copyright owner allows multiple licensees to use the copyrighted work simultaneously and the owner can also continue to use the work and grant licenses to others.

> **Co-Exclusive License -**
> That allows multiple licensees to use the copyrighted work but restricts the number of licensees.

> **Sole License -**
> That grants exclusive rights to the licensee, but the copyright owner retains the right to use the work as well. However, the copyright owner cannot grant licenses to any other parties.

> **Implied License -**
> Not explicitly granted through a written agreement but is instead implied by the conduct or circumstances of the parties involved.

2. Compulsory License -

According to Section 31 of the Indian Copyright Act, a compulsory license is a statutory license that permits the government to grant a license for the use of copyrighted works without seeking the consent of the rights holder.

The Copyright Board in India can grant compulsory licenses for copyrighted "Indian works" in certain situations, including, Refusal to republish or allow republication of the work. Refusal to allow the performance of the work in public, resulting in its withholding from the public.

Refusal to allow communication of the work to the public by broadcast or, in the case of sound recordings, the work recorded in such record on reasonable terms.
Certain types of works are eligible for compulsory licenses which include artistic works authored by Indian citizens and cinematographic films or sound recordings made or manufactured in India. The concept of compulsory licensing in copyright law is addressed in various international agreements, such as the Trade-Related Aspects of Intellectual Property Rights (TRIPS) Agreement, which sets out minimum standards for copyright protection. The specific provisions and procedures for compulsory licensing may vary between countries, as they are determined by national copyright laws.

Key Considerations in a Copyright Licensing Agreement

> For a license agreement to be valid, as per Section 19, it must be in written form and should be signed by the copyright owner or any other agent authorized by the owner, and must also contain the following details:
> Identification of the work and rights licensed.
> A license's duration and the geographical territories where it can be exercised.
> Royalties or other monetary arrangements that the licensee must provide to the copyright owner if the license is granted.
> Specific conditions relating to revisions, extensions, and terminations of licenses.

➤ Dispute resolution mechanisms mutually agreed upon by the parties, which may involve arbitration, mediation, or referral to the Copyright Board.

Copyright Licensing Procedure in India:

➤ Although due to digital advancement, anyone can follow the licensing procedure on their own, it is advisable to seek the help of a professional copyright protection service provider to prevent any kind of errors or complications. The following is the procedure to obtain copyright licensing in India:

➤ Copyright owners or prospective owners can initiate licensing processes by drafting and submitting a license agreement (crafted by copyright experts) to potential licensees.

➤ The Copyright Board then settles disputes related to copyright licensing if any and even grants compulsory licenses under specific circumstances.

➤ In the case of unpublished Indian works where the author is deceased, unknown, or cannot be traced, anyone can apply to the Copyright Board for a license to publish or translate the work. The Board may conduct inquiries and investigations before granting the license, subject to the payment of royalties and other conditions.

Benefits and Challenges of Copyright Licensing

➤ Copyright licensing benefits both - copyright owners and licensees. While copyright owners can generate revenue and royalties from licensing their works, licensees gain legal permission to use copyrighted materials, avoiding potential infringement claims. However, determining fair and reasonable royalty rates and ensuring compliance with license terms, and preventing unauthorized use can be challenging.

➤ Also, the digital environment presents unique challenges in copyright licensing due to issues like online piracy, global reach, and new modes of content distribution. However, it also opens up opportunities for innovative licensing models and wider accessibility. Various digital rights management (DRM) technologies and licensing platforms have emerged to facilitate the licensing, distribution, and protection of digital content in India.

Industrial Design Licensing:

Industrial design registration is a legal process that grants the owner exclusive rights to the design. It prevents others from using, copying, or imitating the registered design without permission. This protection is essential for designers and businesses to maintain a competitive edge and leverage the commercial value of their designs.

Benefits of Industrial Design Registration:

1. Legal Protection Registering an industrial design provides legal protection against infringement. It grants the designer exclusive rights to use, license, or sell the design, and provides the basis for legal action if others infringe on these rights.

2. Competitive Advantage A registered design can enhance a product's marketability and differentiate it from competitors. By protecting the unique appearance of a product, businesses can maintain a distinct brand identity and attract customers.

3. Increased Value Registered industrial designs can add value to a business's intellectual property portfolio. They can be licensed, sold, or used as collateral for financing, contributing to the overall value of the business.

4. Deterrence of Infringement The registration of a design serves as a public notice of ownership, which can deter potential infringers from copying or imitating the design. It also provides a clear record of ownership that can be used in legal disputes.

5. Global Protection Design registration can be extended to multiple jurisdictions through international treaties, providing protection in various countries. This is particularly valuable for businesses operating in global markets.

THE REGISTRATION PROCESS

Eligibility Criteria:

a. Originality The design must be original and not copied from existing designs. It should represent a new and unique aesthetic that distinguishes it from other designs.

b. Novelty The design should be novel and not publicly disclosed before the filing date. Prior publication, use, or disclosure can impact the design's eligibility for registration.

c. Non-Functionality The design must be purely ornamental and not dictated by the technical function of the product. Functional aspects of a product are typically covered by patents, not design registration.

Preparing for Registration:

a. Design Search Conduct a design search to ensure that the design is not already registered or publicly disclosed. This can help avoid potential conflicts and improve the chances of successful registration.

b. Documentation Prepare detailed drawings or photographs of the design from different angles. These visual representations should clearly depict the design's unique features. You may also need to provide a brief description of the design.

c. Application Form Complete the application form provided by the relevant design office. This form typically includes information about the designer, the design, and the product in which the design will be applied.

Filing the Application

a. National Registration File the application with the national design office in the country where protection is sought. Each country has its own design registration system and requirements.

b. International Registration For broader protection, consider filing under international treaties such as the Hague System. The Hague System allows for the registration of designs in multiple countries through a single application.

c. Fees Pay the required filing fees, which vary depending on the jurisdiction and the number of designs included in the application. Ensure that all fees are paid in full to avoid delays in the registration process.

Examination and Publication

a. Formal Examination The design office will conduct a formal examination to ensure that the application meets all legal requirements. This includes checking for compliance with eligibility criteria and verifying the completeness of the application.

b. Substantive Examination In some jurisdictions, a substantive examination may be conducted to assess the design's novelty and originality. This examination ensures that the design meets the criteria for registration.

c. Publication Once the design is accepted, it will be published in the official design register. Publication serves as a public notice of the design's registration and provides an opportunity for third parties to file objections or oppositions.

Registration and Enforcement

a. Certificate of Registration Upon successful registration, the designer will receive a certificate of registration. This certificate serves as evidence of ownership and provides the legal basis for enforcing the design rights.

b. Enforcement of Rights Monitor the marketplace for potential infringements of the registered design. If an infringement occurs, the designer can take legal action to enforce their rights, including filing cease-and-desist notices, seeking damages, or pursuing legal remedies through the courts.

c. Renewal Design registrations are typically valid for a limited period, such as 5 to 10 years, depending on the jurisdiction. Renew the registration before it expires to maintain protection.

Key Considerations for Industrial Design Registration

> **International Protection:**
> If you plan to market your design internationally, consider filing for protection in other countries. The Hague System provides a streamlined process for obtaining protection in multiple jurisdictions, simplifying the registration process and reducing administrative burdens.

> **Design Maintenance:**
> Regularly review and update your design portfolio to ensure that all designs are protected and registered. Keep track of renewal deadlines and maintain accurate records of your design registrations.

> **Collaborations and Assignments:**
> If your design was created in collaboration with others or assigned to a different party, ensure that all agreements are documented and that the appropriate rights are assigned or transferred. Clear agreements help avoid disputes and clarify ownership.

> **Legal Advice:**
> Consult with intellectual property attorneys or experts to navigate the complexities of industrial design registration. Legal professionals can provide guidance on the registration process, assist with drafting applications, and offer advice on enforcement and protection strategies.

Techno-Legal Assignment:

A techno-legal assignment in IPR (Intellectual Property Rights) refers to the transfer of ownership or certain rights related to a specific technology or invention, typically covered by patents, copyrights, trademarks, or trade secrets. This transfer is formalized through a written agreement, known as an assignment agreement, and involves the assignor (the original owner) transferring their rights to the assignee (the new owner).

Patent Assignment:

A patent assignment is a legal document that transfers ownership of a patent from one party (the assignor) to another (the assignee), allowing the assignee to exercise all rights associated with the patent. It's crucial for anyone involved in hiring engineers, buying patents, or licensing patents to understand the basics of patent assignments.

Section 70 of the Patent Act grants power to the proprietor (assignor) to assign, grant license, etc. to other individuals (assignee) with respect to the patent. This grant of power must be in written and duly executed for it to be a legally acceptable transfer of rights.

Assignor: Owner of the patent (proprietor)

Assignee: Individual to whom the rights are being assigned to

Types of Patent Assignments:
Although the main aim of the patent is preventing others from using the inventor's invention, on the flip side, patent assignment allows them to share their rights with someone they consider worthy.

There exist three types of patent assignments. They are:

- **Equitable Assignment:** An agreement along with a letter wherein the inventor agrees to share a certain portion of the patent with another person is considered as equitable assignment of the patent. Although the assignee is unable to enter his/her name as one of the owners, they can inform the register of their interest in the patent.

- **Legal Assignment:** An agreement wherein the assignee enter their name as the owner of the patent in the government records is referred as a legal assignment. The assigning of the patent that is created through a deed can only be done through a deed. Once the process is done by the assignor, the assignee is able to acquire all the rights of the patent.

- **Mortgages:** An assignment wherein complete or partial right is given to the assignee by the owner in exchange of money. After the amount is repaid all the rights of the mortgaged property goes back to the owner. The lender can only enter their name as the mortgagee in the register but cannot register themselves as the proprietor.

Requirements for Patent Assignment:
- As mentioned above, a patent assignment can only be deemed valid if it is duly executed through the legal process has been drafted in writing.
- The draft must elucidate all the obligations and rights of both the parties w.r.t the patent.
- Form-16 must be filled and filed to the Controller General of Patents, Designs and Trademarks. All the necessary details that must be mentioned for assignment are recorded in it that includes details of the parties, applicant's name, description of the draft through which assignment is being sought.
- The assignee then requests in writing to the Controller of Patents for addition of his/her name in the register of patents. After the Controller of Patents is confirmed that the interest of the assignee is genuine, the assignment details is then added into their register.
- Along with the application two copies of the deed should also be attached.
- Different individuals are charged differently, and it also differs when charged physically or electronically. First Schedule of the Patent Act mentions a comprehensive division of fees for the process.

Contents of Patent Assignment Agreement:
A patent assignment agreement incorporates the following content:
- Information about the parties to the agreement, i.e., the assignor and the assignee.
- Consideration in lieu of assignment.
- Information about the date of registration, registration number type of patent, etc.

- Obligations and Rights of all the parties that are involved.
- An undertaking of the assignor that they have not assigned or otherwise dealt with patent to create a third-party interest in the patent.
- Termination clause.
- Dispute resolution clauses.
- Indemnity clause that is in favors of the assignee.

Difference between Assignment and Licenses:

Assignment	License
1.It is a term used for transfer of ownership and of the patent to the assignee.	1.A license grants you the permission to use any patented invention, which would otherwise be referred to as infringement.
2.Assignments must be executed in writing.	2.Licenses can be granted without any written documentation.
3.Assignees don't need to pay any royalties to the original owner.	3.Licensees may be expected to pay certain royalties in exchange of using the inventor's product.
4.As you become a proprietor of the patent, it may be a bit expensive to get an assignment.	4.Licenses are much cheaper than assignments as you will also be paying some royalty in exchange of using the patent.

Amendments and Termination:

- **Amending Patent Assignment Agreement**

When an infringement or mutual concession occurs, the parties involved in the assignment may mutually decide to amend some parts of the agreement. Amendments in the patent assignments can be processed in the equitable assignment deed. If the deed requires any amendment, it should be registered with the Controller of Patents, and it cannot be halfway through the process of the assignment.

- **Termination of Patent Assignment Agreement**

The termination of deed is not possible as it is permanent and irrevocable in nature. Transferring the title of a patent through assignment acts as a permanent decision. The termination is possible only when it is a mortgage assignment deed.

Trademark Assignment:

A trademark assignment is a legal process where ownership of a trademark, including its rights and associated goodwill, is transferred from one party (the assignor) to another (the assignee) through a written agreement.

Understanding the term trademark assignment:

The term trademark assignment is defined under section 37 of the Trademark Act, 1999. As per the definition, the trademark assignment means transferring the owner's right, interest, and title in a trademark and a brand mark. In simple words, the process of transferring the right and ownership of the trademark to any other person is known as a trademark assignment. Some of the advantages of the trademark assignment (concerning both the owner and the buyer) are listed hereunder-

> The trademark assignment enables the owner of the trademark to encash the value of his brand.
> With the help of a trademark assignment, the assignee can obtain the rights of an already established brand.
> The assignment of the trademark supports both the assignor and the assignee to expand their respective business.
> In case of any dispute, the trademark assignment agreement would enable the assignor or the assignee to establish the legal right.

Types of trademark assignment:
There are four types of trademark assignments-

> Partial assignment,
> Complete assignment,
> An assignment with Goodwill, and
> An assignment without Goodwill/ Gross assignment.

All the four types of trademark assignments are briefly explained hereunder-

1. Partial assignment-
Under the partial assignment, the assignor transfers only limited ownership with regard to specific products/ services.

2. Complete assignment-
Under the complete assignment, entire rights with respect to the registered trademark are transferred by the assignor to the assignee.

3. An assignment with Goodwill-
Under 'assignment with Goodwill', the assignor of the trademark transfers the rights of the trademark as well as the value of the trademark to the assignee.

4. Gross assignment or Assignment without Goodwill-
Under such type of trademark assignment, while transferring the trademark, the assignor will restrict the buyer's right. The assignor here restricts the buyer from using a brand of the product which is already being used by the assignor. In nutshell, the goodwill attached to the brand is not transferred to the assignee.

Pre-requisites and procedure for trademark assignment:
The list of pre-requisites for the trademark assignment is-
> - The trademark assignment must be in writing.
> - The assignment must have the following two identifying parties-
> - An assignor (owner of the trademark); and
> - An assignee (buyer of the trademark).
> - The assignor must have the intention and consent for the trademark assignment.
> - The trademark assignment must be for proper adequate consideration.
> - Following is the list of documents required for trademark assignment-
> - Trademark assignment agreement,
> - Trademark certificate,
> - NOC from the assignor,
> - Identified documents from the assignor and assignee.

The procedure for applying for a trademark assignment is narrated hereunder-
> - Filing an application for trademark assignment in Form TM-24 or Form TM-23 (in case of joint request). Such an application can be filed by either the assignor or the assignee or both.
> - Filing of Form TM-P.
> - Filing of all the requisite documents relating to trademark assignment with the Registrar of the trademark. The filing needs to be done within a period of six months from the date of acquisition of proprietorship.
> - The registrar of the trademark will specify the advertisement of the trademark assignment.
> - Based on the registrar's specification, the applicant is required to make an advertisement for the trademark assignment.
> - The applicant is required to submit the copy of the advertisement and copy of the registrar's direction in the office of the registrar.

On being satisfied, the registrar will approve the application. Accordingly, the registrar will register the name of the assignee as the proprietor of the trademark.

Copyright Assignment:
Section 18 of the Copyright Act discusses "assignment of copyright." The owner of the copyright in an existing work or the prospective owner of future work has the right to assign to any person the copyright of that work. Since copyright per se is a bundle of rights, assignment of copyright could be:
1. Whole or partial,
2. Subject to certain conditions/limitations,
3. For the whole term of the copyright or any part thereof.
If the work is not yet in existence at the time of assignment (future work), the assignment shall take effect only when the work comes into existence.

<u>Essentials of a Copyright Assignment agreement in India</u>
An assignment agreement shall have the following essentials:
1. It shall be made in writing and identify the work assigned.
2. It shall specify the scope of rights assigned and consideration.
3. It shall mention the duration and territorial extent of such assignment.

It is sufficient if the assignment is made in writing bearing the signature of the author or their authorized agent. Furthermore, in case where the duration of the assignment is not mentioned, as per law, it is deemed to be five years from the date of the assignment and in the case where the territorial extent of such assignment is not mentioned, as per law, it is presumed to extend within India. The assignment shall be exercised within one year from the date of assignment failing which the rights so assigned shall be deemed to have lapsed.

Recordal of Assignment of Copyrights in India with Registrar of Copyrights:
An assignment can be carried out prior to filing the copyright application or even registered copyright can be assigned. This is to be done only if the author/creator of the work is not filing the application and it is being done by a third-party who is now the owner of the work. The formalities in the event of the former have already been dealt with under "<u>Application for Registration of Copyright</u>."
In case of the latter where the assignment is subsequent to registration, a request under <u>Form XV</u> (registration of changes in particulars of copyright) has to be filed with the following documents as attachments:
1. Notarized copy of the Assignment Deed.
2. An affidavit to the effect, attesting that there is no case pending in any court of law relating to the Assignment.
3. A Power of Attorney (POA), in original, if the application is filed through an authorized agent.
4. Attested Copy of the Death Certificate if the original copyright holder is deceased.

Industrial Design Assignment:
Assignment is a legal phrase that refers to the transfer of rights, property, or other benefits from one person to another (the "assignor"). Both contract and property law make use of this term. The term can relate to either the act of transferring or the transferred rights/property/benefits.
Section 30 of the Design Act of 2000(Hereinafter referred to as "Act"), as amended by Rules 32, 33, 34, and 35 of the Design Rules of 2001, recognizes design assignment contracts and establishes a method for their recording. Section 30(1) of the Design Act provides that if a person acquires the copyright in a registered design through assignments, transmission, or other legal means, he may apply to the Controller in the specified form to register his title. According to Section 30(3) of the Design Act of 2000, an assignment must be in writing, and the agreement between the parties must be reduced to the form of an instrument embodying all of the terms and conditions governing their rights and obligations, and the application for registration of title under such instrument must be filed in the prescribed manner with the Controller within the stipulated time-that is, within six months of the execution date. The person registered as the proprietor of the design has the absolute right to assign the design rights, according to Section 30(4) of the Design Act of 2000.
Only if the design's Copyright is statutorily recognized under the requirements of the Designs Act, 2000, is it protected. Similarly, third-party rights obtained through assignments or licenses

are only effective if they are properly registered in accordance with the Act's requirements and the Rules enacted thereunder. Under design law, there is no concept of a common law licence.

Assignment of the Semiconductor Integrated Circuits Layout Design
An electronic circuit made on the surface of semiconductor material is known as a semiconductor integrated circuit. Integrated circuits have transformed the field of electronics by being employed in practically all electronic devices currently in use. The sheer quantity of electronic appliances we use on a daily basis demonstrates the significance of semiconductor integrated circuits or chips in today's environment.

The layout or arrangement of the chip determines its ability to perform a specific function. As a result, a second enactment was required to protect the chip designer's investment. In India, the Semiconductor Integrated Circuits Layouts Design Act of 2000 would provide this protection. This was done in accordance with India's commitments under the TRIPS Agreement.

'An assignment in writing by act of the parties concerned,' according to Section 2(b) of the Semiconductor Integrated Circuits Layout-Design Act, 2000. According to Section 19 of the Act, the registration of the design, as well as all subsequent assignments, will serve as prima facie evidence of its validity.

Assignments and Transmissions are covered in Chapter V of the Semiconductor Integrated Circuits Layouts Design Act, 2000. Section 20 of the Semiconductor Integrated Circuits Layouts Design Act of 2000 gives the owner of a layout design the authority to assign the layout design and to issue effective receipts for any money received in exchange for the assignment. This is subject to the provisions of the aforementioned Act, as well as any rights that appear to be vested in another person based on the register. A registered layout-design is assignable and transmissible with or without the goodwill of the business involved under Section 21 of the Semiconductor Integrated Circuits Layouts Design Act, 2000.According to Section 22 of the Semiconductor Integrated Circuits Layouts Design Act, 2000, when an integrated circuit layout is assigned without goodwill, the assignment will not take effect unless the assignee applies to the Registrar for directions with respect to the assignment not later than six months from the date on which the assignment is made or within such extended period, if any, not exceeding three months in the aggregate, as the Registrar may allow. The assignee must register the title with the registrar, according to Section 23 of the Semiconductor Integrated Circuits Layouts Design Act, 2000.If the matter is still before the registrar or an appeal from an order therefrom is pending, Section 24 of the Semiconductor Integrated Circuits Layouts Design Act, 2000 prohibits the assignee from utilizing the registration as proof of title.

These rights can be assigned with the help of Assignment Agreements
Assignment agreements deal with the transfer of intellectual property rights from one person or Organization to another. An Intellectual Property Agreement (IP Agreement) or an Intellectual Property Assignment Agreement is a documented and enforceable contract that completes and formalizes a purchase and sale of intellectual property rights between two organizations. Copyrights, trademarks, and/or patents are examples of intellectual property that can be purchased. Assignment agreements differ from licence agreements in that an assignment agreement transfers ownership of intellectual property from the assignor to the assignee, whereas a licence agreement merely allows the licensee to use the intellectual property for a certain time.

An assignment agreement cannot be compared to a negotiating document since in a negotiation, the transferee may obtain a superior title than the transferor, which cannot occur in an assignment/transfer.

An assignment agreement may include a complete and exclusive sale of the rights, granting the assignee complete ownership of the intellectual property rights to exploit them in any way, shape, or form it sees fit, subject to any constraints set forth in the agreement. These contracts are governed in India under the Indian Contract Act of 1872 and the Indian Stamp Act of 1899.

Process of Assignment under Designs Act, 2000

- After a design is registered, an application for ownership under Rule 33 of the Design Rules, 2001 must be made to the Controller for the registration of title in the new owner's name.
- The agreement of assignment must be written, and all of the parties' concerns should be provided in the form of the instrument comprising all of the terms and conditions, according to Rule 37 of the Design Rules.
- After all requirements have been completed and the assignment of rights has been registered with the register of designs, the assignment of rights will be enforceable from that date.
- Within six months of the instrument's implementation date, a title registration application must be submitted. This period can be extended for an additional six months.

03-12:IPR LITIGATION

Intellectual property litigation in India plays a pivotal role in safeguarding the rights of innovators and creators. As the landscape of commerce and technology evolves, the need for robust IP rights enforcement in India becomes increasingly critical. This litigation addresses disputes arising from the unauthorized use of intellectual property, including trademarks, patents and copyrights.

Intellectual Property Litigation in India encompasses legal actions taken to resolve conflicts over intellectual property rights. This can involve cases of infringement, disputes over ownership or the validity of IP rights. The primary objective of IP litigation is to protect the rights of IP holders and ensure that their intellectual assets are not unlawfully exploited. This area of law is broad, covering various types of intellectual property, including patents, trademarks, copyrights and designs.

PATENT LITIGATION:

Patent litigation is vital to intellectual property law, particularly in India, where innovation and technological advancements are rapidly increasing. Securing a patent is just the beginning; enforcing these rights through litigation is crucial to prevent infringement and protect the inventor's interests.

The intersection of intellectual property law and technological innovation has become increasingly complex and consequential in recent years. The enforcement of patent rights, particularly within critical sectors like telecommunications, underscores the pivotal role that legal frameworks play in fostering or hindering technological advancements. A recent ruling by the Delhi High Court exemplifies this dynamic, wherein the court adjudicated a high-stakes patent infringement case involving Swedish telecommunications giant Ericsson and the Indian smartphone manufacturer Lava. This case highlights the intricate legal challenges associated with patent enforcement and underscores the role of enforcement and defence strategies regarding patent litigation in India.

UNDERSTANDING PATENT LITIGATION IN INDIA:

Navigating the complexities of patent litigation in India requires a thorough understanding of the legal frameworks and judicial structures that govern intellectual property disputes.

PATENTS ACT, 1970

The Patents Act of 1970[1] serves as the cornerstone of patent law in India, establishing the framework for the protection and enforcement of patent rights. This legislation delineates the substantive criteria for patentability, requiring an invention to be novel, involve an inventive step, and be capable of industrial application. It confers upon patent holders the exclusive rights to manufacture, use, sell, or distribute the patented invention, thus preventing unauthorized third parties from exploiting the patent without permission. The Act also provides for the procedural aspects of patent registration, including application processes, examination, and the maintenance of patents. By offering a structured mechanism for intellectual property protection, the Patents Act is critical in fostering innovation and ensuring that inventors can benefit from their inventions.

SPECIFIC RELIEF ACT, 1963

The Specific Relief Act[2] provides essential remedies for the enforcement of rights under Indian law, including those related to patent infringement. It enables courts to issue injunctions—both temporary and permanent—to prevent ongoing or imminent infringement of patent rights. Additionally, the Act allows for awarding damages to compensate the patent holder for losses incurred due to infringement.

This legal framework ensures that patent holders have effective recourse to protect their intellectual property and seek redress when their rights are violated. The Specific Relief Act underscores the importance of timely and effective enforcement of patent rights by offering equitable remedies.

COMMERCIAL COURTS ACT, 2015

The Commercial Courts Act of 2015[3] was introduced to enhance the efficiency and effectiveness of commercial dispute resolution, including patent litigation. This legislation establishes Commercial Courts and Commercial Divisions within High Courts specifically designed to handle high-value commercial disputes including intellectual property rights relating to trademarks, copyright, patent, design, domain names, geographical indications and semiconductor integrated circuits. Patent Infringement Litigations, over a specified pecuniary value are heard and decided by the Commercial Divisions of High Courts. One of the Act's notable features is its emphasis on expedited procedures and streamlined case management, which aims to reduce delays in the adjudication of complex commercial matters. Additionally, the Act mandates mandatory mediation before proceeding with litigation, thereby encouraging the settlement of disputes outside of court.

This legislative reform significantly impacts patent litigation by providing a specialized and efficient forum for cost-effectively resolving patent disputes, thus improving the overall adjudicative process. It signifies India's intent to align its legal framework with global standards, ensuring the country remains an attractive destination for commerce and investment.

JURISDICTION AND COURT STRUCTURE:

1.DISTRICT COURTS

District Courts in India play a pivotal role in the initial stages of patent litigation. As the first point of adjudication, these courts handle preliminary hearings, assess initial evidence, and address fundamental legal issues related to patent disputes. District Courts are crucial in managing the initial flow of cases and ensuring that preliminary matters are resolved before escalation to higher courts. Their function in the early stages of litigation helps in filtering cases and determining whether they should proceed further in the judicial hierarchy.

2.HIGH COURTS

The High Courts in India, possess significant expertise in handling complex patent cases. These courts are designated to review and revise decisions made by lower courts, including District Courts. The Intellectual Property Divisions within these High Courts are specialized forums that deal with intricate patent matters, providing detailed judicial analysis and authoritative rulings. The Delhi High Court, for instance, is renowned for its extensive experience and expertise in patent litigation, while the Madras High Court similarly has played a vital role in addressing complex patent disputes. The High Courts' proficiency in managing sophisticated patent cases ensures a thorough examination and consistent interpretation of patent law.

3.SUPREME COURT OF INDIA

The Supreme Court of India represents the apex of the judicial hierarchy, serving as the final appellate authority in significant or precedent-setting cases. It has the authority to review decisions from the High Courts and provide binding interpretations on major legal questions, including those related to patent law. The Supreme Court's rulings play a crucial role in shaping the development of patent jurisprudence in India by establishing legal precedents that guide lower courts and influence future litigation. Through its authoritative judgments, the Supreme Court ensures uniformity and consistency in the application of patent law, thereby contributing to the overall stability and predictability of the legal framework governing intellectual property.

STAGES IN IP LITIGATION IN INDIA:
Patent litigation in India typically follows several stages:

1. Filing of the Suit: The patent holder files a complaint in a commercial court, detailing the alleged infringement and seeking remedies such as injunctions or damages.
2. Pre-Litigation Mediation: As mandated by the Commercial Courts Act, the parties engage in mediation to attempt an out-of-court settlement.
3. Interim Relief: The patent holder may seek interim relief, such as a preliminary injunction, to prevent infringement during litigation.
4. Discovery: The court may direct discovery processes, where both parties are required to disclose evidence relevant to the case. Challenges in pre-litigation discovery often necessitate the involvement of expert investigators.
5. Trial: The case proceeds to trial, where both parties present their evidence and arguments. Technical experts may be appointed to assist the court in understanding complex issues.
6. Judgement: After hearing the case, the court delivers its judgement. This may include a permanent injunction against the infringer and an award of damages to the patent holder.
7. Appeal: Either party can appeal the decision to a higher court if they are dissatisfied with the outcome.

PERFORMANCE OF THE INTELLECTUAL PROPERTY DIVISION (IPD)

The establishment of dedicated Intellectual Property Divisions (IPD) within the High Courts have significantly improved the handling of IP disputes. These divisions specialize in intellectual property cases, ensuring they are handled efficiently and effectively. The IPDs have contributed to a reduced backlog and have set benchmarks in adjudicating complex IP matters.

TYPES OF INJUNCTIONS

Injunctions are a critical tool in patent litigation, serving to protect the patent holder's rights during and after the legal proceedings. There are two primary types of injunctions: preliminary and permanent.

A preliminary injunction is a temporary measure granted at the outset of litigation to prevent ongoing or imminent infringement. The criteria for granting a preliminary injunction include establishing a prima facie case of infringement, demonstrating irreparable harm to the patent holder if the injunction is not granted, and showing that the balance of convenience favours the patent holder.

On the other hand, a permanent injunction is issued after a full trial on the merits and permanently prohibits the infringer from engaging in the infringing activities. The granting of a permanent injunction generally follows a finding of patent validity and infringement, and it serves as a final remedy to prevent further violations of the patent holder's rights.

ENFORCEMENT STRATEGIES FOR PATENT OWNERS

FILING A LAWSUIT

To initiate a patent infringement lawsuit in India, patent owners must first gather substantial evidence of infringement. This includes documenting instances where the patented invention is used, manufactured, or sold without authorization. The lawsuit begins with filing a complaint in a competent court, typically where the defendant resides or conducts business. The complaint should detail the patent owner's rights, the alleged infringement, and the relief sought, such as damages or injunctions.

PRELIMINARY INJUNCTIONS

Preliminary injunctions are critical tools for patent owners to prevent ongoing infringement while the case is pending. Seeking an ex parte interim injunction—where the defendant is not present—is particularly effective in halting infringement before it causes significant harm. These injunctions provide immediate relief by stopping the alleged infringer from continuing their activities until the court decides on the merits of the case.

PERMANENT INJUNCTIONS

Permanent injunctions are sought after the court has heard the entire case and ruled in favours of the patent owner. These injunctions offer long-term protection by permanently restraining the infringer from engaging in activities that violate the patent. Obtaining a permanent injunction requires proving the validity of the patent, the occurrence of infringement, and the inadequacy of monetary damages as a remedy.

UTILISING EXPERTS

Expert witnesses are invaluable in patent litigation, providing specialized knowledge on the technical aspects of the patent and the alleged infringement. Their testimony can clarify complex issues for the court, bolster the patent owner's case, and help achieve a favourable outcome.

DÉFENSE STRATEGIES FOR ALLEGED INFRINGERS

CHALLENGING VALIDITY

One effective defence strategy in patent litigation is to challenge the validity of the patent. Alleged infringers can argue that the patent should not have been granted, often based on prior art not considered during the patent's examination. This defence can be raised either as a direct argument in the lawsuit or through a counterclaim seeking to invalidate the patent.

DELAY TACTICS

Delay tactics, such as requesting extensions or filing interlocutory appeals, can be used to prolong proceedings. However, these strategies have limitations and may not always be favourable. Courts often view unjustified delays unfavorably, and such tactics can lead to adverse cost orders or judgments.

RESPONDING TO INJUNCTIONS

When faced with an injunction, alleged infringers can counter by presenting arguments that challenge the necessity or appropriateness of the injunction. This can include demonstrating a lack of irreparable harm or asserting that the balance of convenience favours the defendant.

OPPOSING EX-PARTE INJUNCTIONS

If an ex-parte injunction (granted without the defendant's presence) is issued, the alleged infringer can seek to vacate or modify it. This involves presenting evidence and arguments to the court, highlighting any material facts or legal points that were not considered initially.

MINIMISING DAMAGES

To limit financial liabilities, alleged infringers can negotiate settlements, seek to reduce the scope of damages, or argue that the patent holder's calculation of damages is inflated. These strategies aim to reach a resolution that minimizes the financial impact on the defendant.

ROLE OF THE COURTS AND JUDGES

In India, the judiciary plays a crucial role in adjudicating patent disputes. Judges handling these cases often possess significant expertise in intellectual property law. This specialized knowledge is essential for interpreting complex technical details and legal arguments presented during litigation. Their competence ensures that decisions are well-founded and consistent with the principles of patent law.

TECHNICAL EXPERTS

Technical experts are frequently appointed to assist the court in understanding intricate technical issues related to patents. These experts provide valuable insights and clarify complex technologies, aiding the judge in making informed decisions. Their involvement can significantly impact the outcome of a case, as they offer unbiased and specialized knowledge that may not be readily accessible to the judiciary.

CASE MANAGEMENT

To enhance the efficiency of patent litigation, Indian courts have recently introduced case-management hearings. These hearings help streamline the litigation process by setting clear timelines and guidelines for the proceedings. This approach reduces delays and ensures that both parties are adequately prepared for trial. By fostering a more organised and predictable legal process, case-management hearings contribute to the timely resolution of patent disputes.

COSTS AND TIMELINES

Patent litigation in India can be a significant financial undertaking. The costs include legal fees, which vary depending on the complexity of the case and the expertise of the legal team. Additionally, there are court fees, which are relatively standardized but can still add up. Other costs may include fees for expert witnesses, document preparation, and travel expenses for court appearances. It is crucial for parties to budget for these expenses and consider the potential financial implications of pursuing or defending a patent infringement case.

PRACTICAL TIPS FOR PATENT LITIGATION

> **GATHERING EVIDENCE**
>
> A strong foundation of evidence is essential for success in patent litigation. Parties should compile all relevant documentation, including patent registrations, records of invention, and correspondence that may establish the timeline of the invention and potential infringement. Detailed technical information and expert analyses may also be necessary to demonstrate how the patented technology is unique and how the alleged infringer's actions constitute a violation. Thorough preparation and organisation of evidence can significantly strengthen a party's position in court.

> **PROACTIVE APPROACH**
>
> Taking a proactive stance is vital in patent litigation. This includes promptly responding to legal notices, engaging in settlement discussions if appropriate, and adhering to court deadlines. Being proactive helps to counteract any delay tactics employed by the opposing party, such as unnecessary procedural motions or requests for extensions. Maintaining an active and responsive approach demonstrates a commitment to resolving the dispute efficiently and can be advantageous in the eyes of the court.

> **ENGAGING EXPERTS**
>
> The involvement of qualified and experienced experts can be a critical factor in patent litigation. Experts can provide testimony on technical aspects of the patent, offer opinions on its validity or infringement, and assist in deciphering complex technologies for the court. Their input can significantly influence the outcome of the case, particularly when the issues at stake require specialized knowledge that goes beyond the general understanding of the court.

> **COURT ETIQUETTE**
>
> Adhering to court etiquette and following procedural rules is essential in patent litigation. Parties should ensure that all filings are accurate, complete, and submitted on time. During court proceedings, it is essential to respect the judge and opposing counsel, present arguments clearly and professionally, and avoid unnecessary confrontations. Observing proper court conduct can create a favourable impression and contribute to a positive outcome.

TRADEMARK LITIGATION:

Trademark Litigation is a legal process for resolving disputes related to the Trademark. It covers disputes in which parties oppose the use, registration, or protection of trademarks. The main aim of Trademark Litigation is to obtain legal remedies such as injunctions or damages to safeguard the unique symbols that identify and differentiate goods or services, thus protecting the rights and integrity of trademarks in a competitive economy.

Reasons for Trademark litigation:

Several common issues are covered under Trademark Litigation. Some of them are as follows:

- **Trademark Infringement:** In trademark litigation, the primary concern is infringement, which includes the unlawful use of a similar or identical trademark. This contains many sorts of infringement, such as direct, contributory, and indirect infringement. Establishing a probability of misunderstanding is critical, requiring proof that the defendant's usage might mislead customers about the origin of the products or services. Defence techniques sometimes include claiming a lack of similarity, lack of customer confusion, or fair usage. Navigating the complexities of infringement charges necessitates an in-depth understanding of these factors, as both plaintiffs and defendants seek to establish convincing arguments to either protect or fight infringement claims.

- **Dilution:** In trademark litigation, dilution refers to the progressive loss of a renowned brand's uniqueness as a result of unlawful use by another party. To prove a case of dilution in court, you must first understand the concept of trademark dilution—the loss of a mark's distinctiveness or link with a certain product. This frequently occurs when well-known trademarks, renowned for their widespread awareness, are subjected to unlawful use, which dilutes their value. Legal processes need to establish that unlawful use diminishes the distinctive nature of the recognized trademark, highlighting the importance of a complete approach and persuasive evidence to effectively prove dilution and seek suitable legal remedies.

- **Registration Disputes:** Registration disputes are common in trademark litigation because of competitive trademark applications. This arises when two parties seek registration for identical marks used in connection with similar goods or services. Such disagreements result in opposition and cancellation processes, in which one party opposes the registration of the other or attempts to cancel an existing registration. Resolving these conflicts involves legal processes such as providing evidence, disputing legal points, and negotiating settlements. The purpose is to discover who is the lawful owner of the trademark registration and to verify that it appropriately expresses the distinctiveness of the products or services linked with the mark in issue.

- **Counterfeiting:** Counterfeiting is a major issue in trademark disputes. The identification of counterfeit goods requires a thorough examination of their validity. Filing litigation against counterfeiters requires providing proof indicating the improper use of trademarks. An injunction is commonly used to stop the manufacturing and sale of counterfeit items in counterfeiting cases. Furthermore, monetary damages may be requested to compensate for the injury done. Preventing counterfeiting not only preserves a brand's integrity but also maintains customer faith when purchasing genuine items, stressing the significance of strong legal measures in addressing this common issue.

Process of Trademark Litigation:
The complete process for filing trademark litigation is described in detail. Here's a detailed guide on how to initiate trademark legal proceedings given below:

Stage-1: Pre- Litigation Step: Before filing a lawsuit the trademark holder must take pre-litigation steps that are as follows:- If the Trademark holder faces issues related to Trademark infringement, dilution, opposition or counterfeiting that can harm the brand reputation, can send the Cease & Desist notice to the infringer or opponent. In this notice, the existing TM owner can ask to stop using the trademark and demand its monetary damage. After sending a Cease-and-desist notice, negotiation and mediation come into play. This step permits the parties to engage in conversations and other conflict settlement strategies.

Stage-2: Consult with a professional Lawyer.
The Trademark Litigation process can be a complex task. Therefore, the applicant or Brand holder must consult with a professional lawyer or TM attorney who has a complete understanding of the process and can properly guide you to resolve this dispute.

Stage-3: Filing a Lawsuit
Even after sending the notice, if the infringer does not stop misusing the mark, the TM holder can file a lawsuit in court. In this lawsuit, all the claims must be mentioned, and evidence should be attached to prove the infringement. The TM holder may also request an injunction to prevent further infringement.

Stage-4: Trial in the Court
When the lawsuit has been submitted, your lawyer presents your case in court. Here, you must submit some legal documents and evidence that proves your claim. After this trial, the court will examine all the aspects and conduct a legal argument between both parties. The court will then make a judgement based on the facts and evidence presented. This judgement will be final and binding on both parties.

Stage-5: Final Judgement & Remedies
The trademark litigation procedure includes settling conflicts through legal means. In investigating infringements, remedies and damages are critical. A court-ordered limitation on unlawful trademark usage is known as injunctive relief. Monetary damages compensate for losses and account for financial injury. The winning party may be granted attorney's fees to cover legal expenditures. These elements work together to provide a legal framework for trademark protection, enabling effective enforcement and deterring infringement by providing both preventative measures and compensation for breaches.

Trademark Opposition vs. Litigation
Trademark opposition and litigation serve different purposes and follow distinct legal procedures in trademark law.

Aspect	Trademark Opposition	Trademark Litigation
Purpose	To challenge and prevent the registration of a trademark.	To resolve disputes over trademark infringement post-registration.
Timing	Occurs during the trademark registration process.	It can occur at any time after the trademark has been registered.
Parties Involved	Typically, it is the trademark applicant and the opposing party.	The trademark owner and the alleged infringer.
Forum	Handled by a trademark office or tribunal.	Handled by a court.
Burden of Proof	Generally, the opposing party to prove the trademark should not be registered.	Generally, the trademark owner is to prove infringement.
Outcome	This can result in the refusal or limitation of the trademark application.	It can result in damages, injunctions, or other legal remedies.

COPYRIGHT LITIGATION:

Copyright litigation is the potential result of a copyright infringement upon one or more of the exclusive rights of the copyright owner. These rights include the right to reproduce the work in copies (and sell those copies, if the owner so chooses), create derivative works, and to perform or display the work publicly. Copyright owners also possess the exclusive right to authorize others to exercise those rights. Once an individual creates an "original" work and "fixes" it in a tangible form of expression, that individual is regarded as the author and copyright owner of that work, and the work is protected by copyright.

When copyright litigation Occurs?
Let's say you are the author of numerous original photographs, all registered with the U.S. Copyright Office, and you've identified an unauthorized user who has been persistent in using your works without authorization. You've sent multiple cease-and-desist letters (colloquially known as 'takedown letters'), all with a copy of your registration attached, but the infringement continues. What is your next step? You can decide to file a lawsuit.

<u>The Legal Basis for Copyright Litigation:</u>

Copyright litigation is governed by the Copyright Act of 1976 (17 U.S.C. §§ 101 et seq.), which establishes the framework for protecting original works of authorship. Key sections include:

> ➤ <u>Section 501:</u> Defines copyright infringement and provides the legal basis for pursuing claims.

- ➢ <u>Section 504:</u> Outlines the remedies available, including actual damages, statutory damages, and disgorgement of profits.
- ➢ <u>Section 107:</u> Provides the fair use defense, which allows limited use of copyrighted works under specific circumstances (e.g., criticism, commentary, or education).

<u>**The Copyright Litigation Process:**</u> Copyright litigation typically follows these steps:

1. **Case Evaluation**
   The process begins with a thorough evaluation of the claim. For plaintiffs, this involves determining whether a valid copyright exists and whether infringement has occurred. For defendants, this includes analyzing potential defenses, such as fair use or independent creation.
2. **Filing the Complaint**
   The plaintiff files a lawsuit in federal court, detailing the alleged infringement, the harm caused, and the remedies sought.
3. **Service of Process and Response**
   The defendant is served with the complaint and must file a response, which may include affirmative defenses or counterclaims challenging the validity of the copyright.
4. **Discovery Phase**
   Both parties exchange evidence, including documents, contracts, and expert reports. Discovery may include depositions and interrogatories to gather additional information.
5. **Motions Practice**
   Pre-trial motions may be filed, such as motions to dismiss, motions for summary judgment, or motions to exclude evidence. These motions can resolve the case early or narrow the issues for trial.
6. **Trial**
   If the case proceeds to trial, both sides present evidence and arguments before a judge or jury. The court determines whether infringement occurred and what remedies, if any, are warranted.
7. **Appeal**
   The losing party may appeal the decision to a higher court, challenging legal rulings or procedural issues in the trial.

Common Defenses in Copyright Litigation: Defendants in copyright litigation often raise the following defenses:

- ➢ **Fair Use:** Limited use of a copyrighted work is allowed for purposes such as criticism, commentary, news reporting, teaching, scholarship, or research. Courts assess fair use based on four factors, including the purpose of use and its impact on the market value of the original work.
- ➢ **Independent Creation:** If the alleged infringer independently created the work without copying, there is no infringement.
- ➢ **Invalid Copyright:** The defendant may argue that the work is not copyrightable (e.g., it is a generic idea or fact).
- ➢ **License or Authorization:** If the plaintiff granted permission to use the work, no infringement has occurred.

Remedies in Copyright Litigation:
The Copyright Act provides several remedies for infringement, depending on the circumstances:
1.Injunctive Relief:
Courts may issue an injunction to stop further unauthorized use of the copyrighted work.
2.Monetary Damages:
- ➢ **Actual Damages:** Compensation for the economic harm suffered by the copyright owner.
- ➢ **Statutory Damages:** Set amounts ranging from $750 to $30,000 per work infringed, or up to $150,000 for willful infringement.

3.Disgorgement of Profits:
The infringer may be required to forfeit profits earned from the unauthorized use.
4.Attorney's Fees and Costs:
In some cases, the prevailing party may recover legal fees and litigation costs.

INDUSTRIAL DESIGN LITIGATION:

Industrial design litigation in India is a complex area of law that deals with the protection and enforcement of the rights associated with the aesthetic and ornamental aspects of industrial products. Industrial design refers to the visual features of a product, such as shape, pattern, configuration, ornamentation, or composition of lines and colors, that make the product unique and appealing to the consumer.

<u>Key Aspects of Industrial Design Litigation in India:</u>

1. **Legal Framework**:
   Industrial design protection in India is governed by the **Design Act, 2000**, and the **Design Rules, 2001**. The Act provides the legal framework for the registration, protection, and enforcement of industrial designs. The act also outlines the penalties for infringement.
2. **Registration of Industrial Designs**:
   To claim exclusive rights over an industrial design, it must be registered with the **Office of the Controller General of Patents, Designs, and Trademarks**. Once registered, the owner is granted exclusive rights for 10 years, with a possible extension of another 5 years.
3. **Infringement**:
   If another party uses the registered design without the permission of the owner, it constitutes an infringement. Infringement cases can lead to civil actions in court for the cessation of the infringing activity and for damages. Common causes of action include:
   - o **Unauthorized use of registered designs.**
   - o **Imitation of a design** which may cause confusion among consumers.
4. **Enforcement of Design Rights**:
   If a design is infringed upon, the owner can take the following actions:
   - o **File a suit for infringement** in a civil court or in a district court that has jurisdiction over design cases.
   - o Seek **an injunction** to stop further use of the infringing design.
   - o Claim **damages or compensation** for losses incurred due to the infringement.

5. **Defenses Against Design Infringement**: Defendants can argue several defenses to challenge industrial design infringement:
   o **Lack of originality**: A design that is not original or novel cannot be registered and therefore cannot be infringed.
   o **Public Domain**: The design has already been publicly disclosed or is common in the industry.
   o **Non-Registration**: A design is not registered with the appropriate authorities, so it has no enforceable legal protection.
6. **Case Laws and Precedents**: Indian courts have seen a variety of industrial design disputes. Some key cases highlight important aspects of industrial design protection and infringement. Courts often examine whether the design in question is novel, original, and non-functional.
7. **International Influence**: India is a member of the **World Intellectual Property Organization (WIPO)** and is a signatory to the **Paris Convention for the Protection of Industrial Property**. This means India adheres to certain international standards for industrial design protection, which allows Indian designers to seek protection abroad and foreign designers to seek protection in India.
8. **Recent Trends**: With the growing importance of consumer goods and e-commerce, industrial design litigation has gained prominence. Companies in sectors like fashion, electronics, and furniture are increasingly taking legal action to protect their designs. Additionally, the rise of counterfeiting and copycat products has led to more legal battles concerning design rights.
9. **Role of the Judiciary**:
   The Indian judiciary has played an important role in interpreting the provisions of the Design Act, especially concerning what constitutes an infringement and the extent of protection that a registered design receives. Courts often consider the **overall impression** of a design when adjudicating on infringement matters.

<u>Common Challenges:</u>

- **Determining Novelty**: One of the key issues in design litigation is determining whether the design is truly novel and original, or if it has already been disclosed to the public.
- **Cost and Time of Litigation**: Industrial design litigation can be expensive and time-consuming, often taking several years to resolve, especially if the case goes through multiple levels of the court system.
- **Cross-border Disputes**: Global trade and online retail platforms often lead to cross-border infringement issues, making the enforcement of design rights even more complicated.

SWOT analysis:

A SWOT analysis is a versatile tool used to evaluate the Strengths, Weaknesses, Opportunities, and Threats related to your patent portfolio. This strategic framework helps businesses make informed decisions by providing a clear picture of internal capabilities and external possibilities.

For patent portfolios, a SWOT analysis not only uncovers areas for improvement but also highlights untapped potential and external risks that need to be managed. Grasping the fundamentals of SWOT analysis is essential for maximizing the value of your patents and aligning them with your business objectives.

Strategic Importance of Strengths

The strengths in your patent portfolio are internal attributes that provide a competitive edge. These strengths could be patents that cover groundbreaking technologies, patents with broad claims offering extensive protection, or patents with a strong track record of enforcement.

To leverage these strengths effectively, it's crucial to align them with your business strategy. This alignment ensures that your most valuable patents are used to their full potential, driving innovation, protecting key products, and enhancing your market position.

A practical approach to identifying strengths involves a detailed audit of your patents. Engage with cross-functional teams from R&D, legal, and business development to gather insights into which patents are seen as critical assets.

This collaborative effort can reveal hidden strengths that might not be immediately apparent. By understanding and highlighting these strengths, you can develop strategies to reinforce and expand their impact.

Addressing and Mitigating Weaknesses

Weaknesses are internal factors that can limit the effectiveness of your patent portfolio. Recognizing and addressing these weaknesses is essential for maintaining a robust portfolio. Common weaknesses include patents with narrow claims, those nearing expiration, or patents that have faced significant legal challenges.

To effectively manage these weaknesses, consider conducting regular portfolio reviews. These reviews should focus on identifying patents that are underperforming or at risk of becoming obsolete. Develop action plans for each identified weakness.

For example, patents with narrow claims might be strengthened through continuation applications that broaden their scope. Patents nearing expiration should be evaluated for their continued relevance, and strategies for replacement or renewal should be developed.

Investing in patent landscaping tools can also provide a clearer picture of your portfolio's weaknesses.

These tools offer insights into how your patents stack up against competitors, revealing areas where your portfolio might be lacking. By proactively addressing these weaknesses, you can ensure your patent portfolio remains strong and strategically valuable.

Leveraging Opportunities

Opportunities in a SWOT analysis refer to external factors that your patent portfolio can exploit to generate value. These opportunities often arise from emerging markets, technological advancements, and shifts in industry standards.

To identify opportunities, stay attuned to industry trends and market needs. Engage with industry experts, attend conferences, and participate in technology forums to gain insights into future developments.

Evaluate how your existing patents can be applied to these new areas. For instance, a patent originally intended for one application might find new value in a different, emerging market.

Develop strategic partnerships to maximize these opportunities. Collaborating with other companies, research institutions, or startups can open up new avenues for applying your patents. These partnerships can lead to joint ventures, co-development projects, or licensing agreements that enhance the value of your intellectual property.

Navigating Threats:

Threats are external challenges that could negatively impact the value and effectiveness of your patent portfolio. These can include competitive advancements, changes in patent laws, and market dynamics.

To navigate these threats, conduct regular competitive analysis to monitor what your competitors are doing. This includes tracking new patent filings, technological developments, and strategic moves by your competitors. Understanding their activities allows you to anticipate potential threats and develop countermeasures.

Stay informed about legal and regulatory changes that might affect your patents. Changes in patent law, such as new eligibility criteria or enforcement practices, can have significant implications for your portfolio. Work closely with legal experts to stay updated on these changes and adjust your patent strategy as needed.

Finally, remain agile in response to market changes. Develop a flexible patent strategy that can quickly adapt to shifts in consumer preferences, economic conditions, or technological trends. This adaptability will help ensure your patent portfolio remains relevant and valuable in a changing market landscape.

Analyzing Strengths in Your Patent Portfolio:

Analyzing the strengths in your patent portfolio is a crucial step in a SWOT analysis. This process identifies the internal factors that provide your business with a competitive advantage, ensuring that your patents are not only protecting your innovations but also enhancing your strategic position. By focusing on these strengths, businesses can leverage their patents to drive growth, innovation, and market leadership.

Evaluating Patent Breadth and Scope:

The breadth and scope of your patents are primary indicators of strength. Patents with broad claims provide extensive protection, covering a wide range of applications and potential infringements. These patents are instrumental in preventing competitors from developing similar technologies and entering your market space.

To evaluate the breadth and scope of your patents, conduct a thorough review of the claims and their coverage. Consider how these claims protect your core technologies and products.

Engage with patent attorneys and technical experts to ensure that the claims are as broad as possible without compromising their enforceability. Broad claims that withstand legal scrutiny are powerful assets that significantly strengthen your patent portfolio.

Technological Impact and Innovation:
Patents that represent significant technological advancements or pioneering innovations are key strengths in your portfolio.
These patents often set the foundation for future developments and establish your company as a leader in your industry. The impact of these patents on your technological roadmap and their role in driving future innovations should be closely examined.
Assess the technological relevance of your patents by analyzing their role in current and future product lines. Patents that underpin your most innovative and successful products are particularly valuable. Additionally, consider how these patents contribute to your long-term innovation strategy. Patents that enable new product developments or improvements to existing technologies are crucial for maintaining a competitive edge.

Market Relevance and Commercial Success:
The market relevance and commercial success of your patents are strong indicators of their value. Patents that protect products or technologies with high market demand and significant revenue generation are essential strengths. These patents not only safeguard your current market position but also provide a foundation for future growth.
Evaluate the commercial impact of your patents by analyzing sales data, market share, and customer feedback. Identify which patents are directly linked to your most successful products and services. Consider how these patents have contributed to your market leadership and how they can be leveraged to maintain or expand your market presence. Patents with proven commercial success are valuable assets that enhance the overall strength of your portfolio.

Legal Robustness and Enforceability:
The legal robustness and enforceability of your patents are critical strengths that ensure your intellectual property is well-protected. Patents that have a strong legal standing, with clear and enforceable claims, are less vulnerable to challenges and more effective in deterring infringement. Assess the legal history of your patents, including any challenges, oppositions, or litigation they have faced. Patents that have successfully withstood legal scrutiny are stronger and more reliable. Work with your legal team to ensure that your patents are well-drafted and thoroughly vetted. Regularly review and update your patent filings to address any potential weaknesses and reinforce their enforceability.

Strategic Alignment with Business Goals:
Patents that align closely with your business goals and strategic objectives are significant strengths in your portfolio. These patents support your core business activities, drive innovation, and enhance your competitive positioning.
To identify strategically aligned patents, review your business strategy and technological roadmap. Determine which patents are critical to achieving your business objectives, such as entering new markets, developing new products, or enhancing operational efficiencies. Patents that are integral to your strategic plans should be prioritized and leveraged to support your long-term goals.

Leveraging Strong Patents for Competitive Advantage:
Once you have identified the strengths in your patent portfolio, it's essential to leverage these patents effectively to gain a competitive advantage. Develop strategies to maximize the impact of your strong patents on your business operations and market position.

Consider using your strong patents to block competitors and secure your market space. Patents with broad claims and significant technological impact can be used to deter competitors from entering your market or developing similar technologies.

Additionally, explore opportunities to license your strong patents to other companies. Licensing can generate additional revenue streams and extend the influence of your patents beyond your core business. Engage with your marketing and sales teams to highlight the strengths of your patented technologies. Communicating the value and innovation behind your patents can enhance your brand reputation and attract customers. Highlighting patented features in your products can differentiate them in the market and create a competitive edge.

Enhancing and Expanding Your Strong Patents:

Strengthening and expanding your existing patents can further enhance their value and impact. Regularly review your strong patents to identify opportunities for improvement and extension. This might involve filing continuation applications to broaden the scope of the claims or seeking additional patent protection in new jurisdictions.

Invest in research and development to build on the foundation of your strong patents. Encourage innovation that complements and extends your existing patents, creating a robust portfolio that continuously evolves and adapts to market changes.

By enhancing and expanding your strong patents, you can ensure that your portfolio remains a powerful tool for protecting your innovations and driving business growth.

Identifying Weaknesses in Your Patent Portfolio:

Recognizing weaknesses in your patent portfolio is crucial for mitigating risks and enhancing the overall strength and value of your intellectual property assets.

Weaknesses can undermine the effectiveness of your patents and leave your innovations vulnerable to competition and legal challenges. Addressing these weaknesses strategically ensures that your portfolio remains robust and aligned with your business objectives.

Assessing Narrow Patent Claims:

One common weakness in a patent portfolio is the presence of patents with narrow claims. These patents may offer limited protection, covering only specific aspects of a technology or its application. Narrow claims make it easier for competitors to design around your patents, reducing their strategic value. To address this issue, conduct a thorough review of your patents to identify those with narrow claims. Work with patent attorneys and technical experts to explore options for broadening the claims.

This might involve filing continuation or divisional applications that expand the scope of protection. Broadening your claims can enhance the enforceability of your patents and make it more challenging for competitors to circumvent your intellectual property.

Generate Options for Patents:

To effectively generate options for patents, one needs to start with idea generation, followed by evaluation of feasibility, a patent search, and ultimately, a patent strategy. This process involves exploring potential inventions, assessing their viability, and determining which ones warrant legal protection, such as through provisional or complete patent applications.

1. Idea Generation:
  ➤ Brainstorming:

Gather a group of individuals with expertise in the relevant field to brainstorm potential inventions.

➢ Problem-Solving:

Identify existing problems and develop innovative solutions that could be patentable.

➢ Technical Resources:

Utilize resources like technical journals, research papers, and industry publications to stimulate new ideas.

2. Idea Evaluation:

➢ Feasibility Assessment:

Evaluate the technical feasibility of the idea, considering factors like resource availability, cost, and potential challenges.

➢ Market Demand:

Research the market demand for the invention and its potential for commercial success.

➢ Resource Requirements:

Assess the resources (e.g., time, personnel, equipment) needed to develop and commercialize the invention.

3. Patent Search:

➢ Prior Art:

Conduct a thorough search of existing patents and literature to identify any prior art that could impact the patentability of the invention.

➢ Patent Databases:

Utilize patent databases such as USPTO to search for relevant patents and publications.

➢ Patent Attorneys:

Consult with a patent attorney to assist with the search process and analyze the results.

4. Patent Strategy:

➢ Portfolio Analysis:

Analyze the company's existing patent portfolio to identify areas where new patents could be beneficial.

➢ Patent Application Types:

Determine whether to file provisional applications (which can reserve patent rights for a shorter period) or complete applications.

➢ International Patenting:

Consider whether to file for patents in multiple countries, potentially through the Patent Cooperation Treaty (PCT).

➢ Patent Drafting:

Develop a clear and concise patent application that accurately describes the invention and its claims.

➢ Patent Enforcement:

Develop a strategy for enforcing the patent if granted, including identifying potential infringers and taking legal action.

➢ Patent Licensing:

Explore opportunities to license or monetize the patent once granted.

Evaluate Options for Patents:
Patents, like other forms of Intellectual property (IP), are assets with monetary value, similar to any tangible assets such as real estate. As with any other asset, a patent evaluation must consider countless legal, economic and technological issues. Currently there are four common methods/approaches to evaluating patents. In this article we will briefly discuss each method/approach and how to conduct it.

Significance of Patent Evaluation:
1. **Strategic Insights:** Patent analysis provides invaluable insights into a specific technology domain or industry. By examining patent data, businesses can identify emerging trends, potential competitors, and untapped market opportunities.
2. **Competitive Advantage:** Understanding the patent landscape enables companies to assess their competitive position. It helps identify white spaces in the market and areas where they can innovate without infringing on existing patents.
3. **Risk Mitigation:** Businesses can reduce the risk of patent infringement lawsuits by conducting a thorough patent analysis. It ensures they know existing patents and can design around them when developing new products or technologies.

1.The Cost Method:
In using the "cost method" we will try to establish what would be the cost of replacing the evaluated patent with other solutions for example developing and patenting of a similar technology, in the same countries the evaluated patent is in force.
Establishing the development cost can be very complicated, but patenting costs is more straightforward – A status search of the evaluated patent, gives a clear picture of where and when the patent was filed and granted. Based on that information a patent attorney/agent can give a reasonable estimation of filing and maintenance fee costs.

2.The Market Method:
Through using this method, we will try to answer one main question: What are the prices of comparable and similarly "strong" patents that were recently purchased/sold.
The information regarding sales transactions is often confidential but using business research methods can give in many cases, a good idea of the price range. Getting information regarding the evaluated patents "strength" is much simpler – conducting an Intellectual Property (IP) Due Diligence search.

It is worth mentioning that in the case of a patent that protects a new innovative and revolutionary product/technology there is no way to base a comparison.

3.The Income Method:
The Income method is quite straightforward – Checking the potential future cash income generated from the patent evaluation minus the costs of purchase and maintenance.

This is done by assessing factors such as:
- Direct income (royalties, sales, potential sales increase etc.).
- Indirect income (savings coming from not paying licenses, saving from production costs reductions, blocking competition etc.).
- Costs (buying price, maintenance fees etc.).

Many business practices are used in order to determine these factors (market analysis, sales projections, business intelligence, branding research etc.). As mentioned above patent maintenance fee costs can be easily established based upon a patent status search.

4. The Combined Method which is Not Financially Self Exclusive:
As can be understood from the title, this approach takes into account non-monetary aspects (such as legal status, technological assessment etc.) but it does encompass many of the economical /commercial issues discussed in the previous methods.
Here are some of the main aspects and questions researched using this approach (some of them are nearly identical but assessed from a different angle):

4.1. Legal aspects:
Just like every other asset a patent has clear legal boundaries. When conducting a patent evaluation, it is advisable to first conduct a thorough status search to answer questions such as:
- Whether the patent is in force i.e – it was granted and currently all maintenance fees are fully paid.
- Remaining life of the patent.
- What is the scope of the patient's family and international protection (I.e in which countries it is in-force).

Other important legal issues to check (usually through state of the art, invalidity and freedom to operate searches) are:
- The existence of any litigation, past or present (infringement, validity etc.).
- Future litigation threatening the patent.
- Patent's validity – Prior art that might be used to invalidate it.
- Blocking patents – Any other patent that might hinder the evaluated patent from being realized and commercialized (for example a patent protecting a technology that the evaluated patent is based on).

4.2. Business/commercial/financial aspects:
These aspects include among others –
- Legal costs (maintenance fees, future litigation costs – such as protection from infringement suits, enforcing infringement etc.).
- Development and production costs (prototype and product development etc.).
- Marketing and sales costs.
- Replacement cost (as discussed above in the "cost method" – what would be the cost of development and manufacturing the same product/technology and/or solving the same problems without using or infringing the evaluated patent).
- Current and future income (royalties, sales, licenses etc.).
- Current and future market value (i.e past transactions of the patent, value of similar patents bought/sold in the past and present – as discussed in the market method above etc.).
- Existence of a current and future market for the patent.
- Exclusivity – How unique is the patent i.e how many other related patents exist.
- Business competitors (number, size, market presence, IP portfolios etc.)

The way to establish most of the above lay mainly in the business field (Market analysis, sales projections, business intelligence etc.), however some major questions can be answered only by an Intellectual Property (IP) Due Diligence search and a Patent Landscape Report (PLR).

4.3. Technological aspects

These aspects include among others –

- What is the technology's prominence and influence (novelty, importance, scopes of technical claims, number of citations, number of products and other technology using it etc).
- Technological exclusivity – How unique is the technology protected by the patent.
- Mapping and assessing current and near future alternative technologies (patented and not patented).
- Comparison to those alternative technologies.
- Future technologies that might replace the one protected by the evaluated patent.
- Potential synergies with other technologies (patented and not patented).

SELECT RIGHT OPTIONS FOR PATENT MONETIZATION:

Patent Monetization:

A patent serves as a declaration of a patent holder's ability to benefit from their invention. However, the mere possession of patent rights does not guarantee a steady flow of income. The process of monetizing a patent generates income from an intangible asset – the patent.

Patent monetization is when an inventor or company sells or licenses patents to generate income. IP monetization looks different for each patent and industry. Only market pre-emption and transactions can make a patent valuable.

For certain businesses, patent monetization has emerged as a lucrative revenue stream with the potential to generate large amounts of money in the short or long term. For companies with an extensive portfolio, patent monetization is a standard activity.

Importance of Patent Monetization:

- ➢ A patent enables its owner to convert the invention into a marketable asset by conferring certain legal rights. Businesses frequently re-evaluate and modify their business strategies to continue making money and avoid losses because it creates new revenue sources for the company.
- ➢ Patent monetization is essential in this situation. Moreover, without expert guidance, organizations frequently struggle to select the best monetization approach. Strategic advice from patent practitioners can help these entities choose the best strategy to achieve their business goals.
- ➢ Additionally, the right patent monetization approach can help a business generate income from an idle patent without losing the patent rights (through licensing, enforcement, etc.).
- ➢ Patent monetization may sound like a straightforward concept, but its practical application can be tricky. The next section delves into the various steps involved in patent monetization.

Process of Patent Monetization:

There are numerous ways to monetize patents, but the following are the most common steps involved in the process:

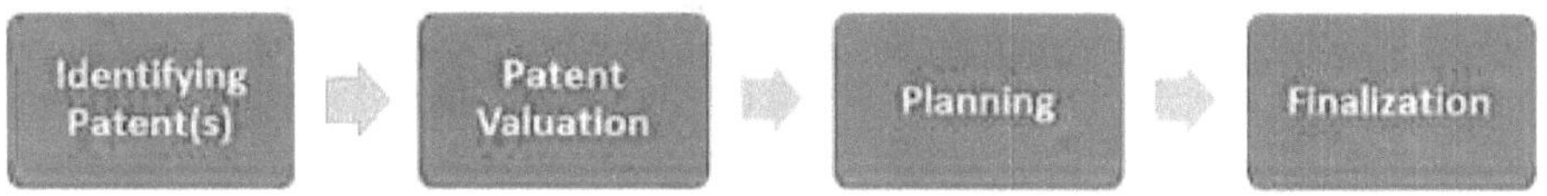

Figure 1: Process of Patent Monetization

1. **Identifying Patents for Monetization:** It is not easy for organizations with extensive patent portfolios to choose the patents that can be sold, licensed, etc., without any complications. Patent monetization begins with identifying the valuable patent assets by studying the market and determining the most significant IP assets as per the business strategy. This is one of the key steps in monetizing patents since it helps the business decide which technologies within a patent portfolio are most likely to have commercial value.

2. **Patent Valuation:** It is the method to determine a patent or patent portfolio's actual market worth. Before monetizing any patent, businesses and inventors must perform patent valuation as it helps them decide whether to proceed with monetization or not.

3. **Planning:** Once the patent(s) for monetization are selected and their approximate market value is ascertained, a team of experts assimilates the information. Afterward, the team works on one or more strategic plans until it selects the best one.

4. **Execution/Finalization:** After selecting a strategy, it is time to implement initiatives. This step can also include government representatives carrying out necessary legal tasks to complete the deal. The following section will go through some of the most popular monetization strategies available for businesses and individual inventors.

Best Patent Monetization Strategies:
Implementing the right patent monetization strategies can open a new gateway for generating cashflows directly from the patent. The four most successful strategies for monetizing patents are as follows:

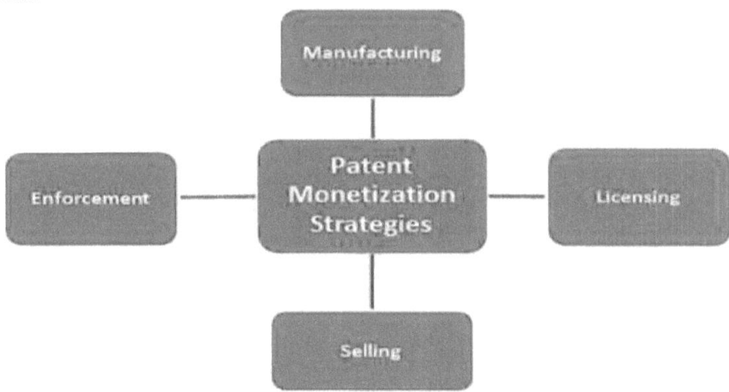

Figure 2: Popular Patent Monetization Strategies

1. Manufacturing:

Before beginning the manufacturing phase, the majority of innovators choose to patent their innovation or concept. Businesses can determine whether to pursue manufacturing by using the aspects mentioned below.

- **Choosing a Manufacturer:** Most start-ups and individual innovators lack manufacturing facilities. Hence, they rely on third parties to produce their products. The signing of non-disclosure agreements is one of the additional complications involved with this. Similarly, unlike giant corporations, start-ups and individual inventors usually do not have the resources or capacity to take calculated risks to build a product. If the patent holder chooses to go into manufacturing through a third party, they should employ a business with proven expertise in manufacturing products in the industry.

- **Quality Assurance:** Using an outside or external manufacturer raises issues with maintaining product quality during manufacturing. To keep its competitive advantage, the patent holder must ensure the maintenance of quality standards.

- **Marketing and Advertising:** Many individual patent owners outsource their marketing efforts to other companies since they might not have the necessary resources or infrastructure to invest in marketing and promotion.

- **Money and Cash Flow:** Due to expensive inventory and logistics, an individual inventor or start-up needs to have enough operating capital and cash flow to engage in product manufacturing as a form of monetization.

2. Licensing:

Due to the higher risks associated with production, businesses, particularly start-ups, prefer to license their patents. It is less risky and more affordable than other ways of generating revenue through patents since the patent holder does not need to worry about marketing or manufacturing. The licensee is usually in control of these business aspects. The following is a list of the factors to take into consideration while licensing a patent:

- **Restricted Transfer of Rights:** The fact that patent owners can transfer their patent rights in a limited manner is one of the most important benefits of non-exclusive licenses. The licensee then uses these limited rights to produce goods with the proprietary technology, giving the patent owner a risk-free way to make money.

- **Cross-licensing:** This method entails the exchange of certain patented technologies between businesses to create a specific product without infringing on each other's IP. Such cross-licensing partnerships are typical in the semiconductor industry, where businesses trade patented technologies to produce their original goods.

- **Patent Pools:** Licensing can also be advantageous in patent pools, where several organizations share their patented technologies related to a specific standard or a well-liked technological field. Due to the decreased likelihood of infringement, all involved companies can earn income off their patents. Additionally, it lowers the transaction costs associated with obtaining licenses from various parties independently.

- **Royalties:** Whenever patent owners grant an exclusive license to a third party, they are entitled to royalties, representing a portion of the licensee's sales revenue from goods utilizing the patented technology. As a result, licensing eliminates all the difficulties associated with manufacturing, allowing the patent owner to reap the rewards of royalty payments without making extra investments.

3. Selling Patents:

This is another option available to patent owners who wish to monetize their innovations. It helps them make a one-time profit from their IP. The original patent owner forfeits all rights to a patent when they sell it to a third party. Therefore, thorough due diligence is vital before taking such a step to determine whether the transaction will be advantageous in the short and long term. Before beginning the patent sale, we advise you to consider the factors listed below:

- **Changing to a New Technological Domain:** A company that holds a patent may adopt newer technology, making a previous patent obsolete in terms of its economic value. In those circumstances, the company needs to sell the older patent at an appropriate price.
- **Competitive Advantage Over a Rival:** Certain older patents can still remain valuable to a competitor, so it is advisable not to sell every old patent. Even if a patent does not bring value to the owner, selling it might cause harm to the business. Therefore, it is essential to know if the patent provides any protective function for the owner against competing enterprises.
- **Patent Valuation:** Before selling any patent, it is necessary to do a patent evaluation to determine the genuine value of the invention. The value of a patent to be sold can be precisely determined using various patent valuation techniques.

4. Enforcement:

The patent's claims that specify the scope of the invention must be carefully examined to ascertain whether there has been a patent infringement in the market. If the infringement exists, then the patent owner can enforce his/her patent rights to generate additional revenue. When infringement is established, the court orders the infringing party to pay royalties based on past use of the patented technology along with other damages to the patent holder. One of the most powerful options for patent monetization, enforcement also comes at a huge cost. If not strong enough, the patent is likely to be overthrown or invalidated, causing the patent owner more harm than good. Therefore, this option should only be considered when you are sure that you have a strong patent that would easily pass the invalidation test.

Before deciding on any patent monetization method, it is advisable to develop the right mindset and understanding since each strategy has its perks and drawbacks. The appropriate strategy can increase the revenue streams needed to grow the company. The section that follows next will go over the practices essential for effective patent monetization.

Best Practices for Patent Monetization:

Developing a thorough, doable, and practical patent monetization plan is critical. Following are a few best practices that you can adopt when opting for patent monetization:

- **Defining Goals:** The first and most crucial step in ensuring effective patent monetization is setting goals. Businesses can have a variety of objectives for monetizing patents, including generating income by selling, licensing or enforcing, or organizing and recovering R&D expenditure to sustain a competitive edge. Without clear goals in mind, it can be tremendously challenging for the in-house or outside counsel to achieve the desired result from patent monetization.

- **Discovering the Right Patents (Core vs non-Core) to Monetize:** The patent monetization process begins with thoroughly analyzing a company's patent portfolio.

It is one of the most significant aspects of the entire patent monetization process as it helps discover which technologies in a patent portfolio are likely to be economically useful. This involves distinguishing non-core patents from core patents and using the former to establish additional cashflows.

- **Using the Right Criteria for Picking Patents to Monetize:** Several factors must be taken into consideration before deciding which patents should be monetized. Each patent monetization service provider may have different standards to satisfy its unique objectives. A business may employ the following standards:
1. How much is the patent worth?
2. How solid are the claims made in the relevant patents?
3. Is there any patent infringement happening in the market?
4. Does the relevant patent cover the client's core or non-core technology?
5. What is the market-based pricing mechanisms for IP?

- **Formulating Strategies for Patent Monetization**: Since there are many strategies for monetizing patents, including direct licensing, enforcement, etc., a business should strive to pick the most suitable strategy. The right choice can help the business maximize revenue generation while sustaining a competitive advantage over other players in the market.

The next section highlights some of the best patent monetization techniques that businesses can utilize to generate revenue.

Techniques for Patent Monetization:
- **Reducing Maintenance Costs of Patents:** It can be challenging for businesses to maintain a sizable patent portfolio since some patents may be outdated or no longer have the same competitive edge over other technologies today. It is preferable to let such IP lapse to avoid the unnecessary strain of paying yearly maintenance costs. Many intellectual property experts recommend companies or inventors revoke any patent that would not increase revenue today or in the near future.

- **Third-party Licensing:** Another successful technique now being employed by businesses to monetize patents is third-party licensing. Here, companies grant licenses to third parties in exchange for the agreed-upon monetary compensation. The license holder has permission to utilize the inventions that the patent holder owns to produce, sell, import, or otherwise use the relevant technology. Apple. IBM, Microsoft, Qualcomm, Nokia, Kodak, Hewlett-Packard, Intellectual Ventures, Acacia, Texas Instruments, Conversant, NTP, and other companies generate billions of dollars every year just by licensing their patent rights to third parties.

- **In-licensing & Out-licensing**: The terms "in-licensing" and "out-licensing" are commonly used in the marketing of drugs. Even though a company might conduct clinical trials to develop a medicine, it might not find it beneficial or feasible to produce and market the drug globally. Therefore, corporations typically out-license these pharmaceuticals to other businesses in a particular region. Usually, the licensees pay the inventor an in-licensing fee in exchange for the commercialization rights.

- **Patent Securitization**: Even in developed countries, borrowing/lending partially or entirely against IP assets is a relatively new practice. However, it is becoming more common to use IP as collateral for commercial loans and bank funding, particularly in the music industry, Internet-based SMEs, and high-tech industries.

- **Acquisitions and Mergers**: Two businesses with complementary patents and technology can pursue acquisitions and mergers to increase their market penetration. This method has also become one of the most effective ways for businesses to monetize patents. For instance, a beer company might decide to acquire a smaller rival brewery, allowing the smaller business to increase production and increase sales to its brand-loyal customers.

- **Donating Patents:** Another significant method of monetizing patents for businesses with sizable patent portfolios is to donate them to universities, research organizations, and other public entities. Donations can result in significant tax benefits and may also allow businesses to improve their connections in early-stage research in universities.

Common Mistakes during Patent Monetization:

For many people, organizations, and corporations, monetizing patents has proven to be the most effective method for generating vast or regular sources of income. However, several errors frequently occur in one way or another and result in a significant loss. Some of the most common mistakes in patent monetization are mentioned below:

- **Wrong Strategy Selection:** There are numerous patent monetization strategies available for inventors and businesses. The patent's technological background and the inventor's expertise play a key role in selecting the right strategy. The decision to use a particular monetization technique, such as licensing, litigation, acquisition, etc. is entirely up to the inventor or owner. Even choosing a monetization strategy needs some form of financial commitment. Many inventors/businesses pick the wrong monetization strategy and end up losing more than they gain.

- **Not Understanding the Right Worth of the Patent:** Before engaging in a license negotiation or legal action, one common mistake is failing to comprehend the value of your patent. If this happens, you could end up licensing a key piece of intellectual property for much less than its market value.

- **Incomplete or Ineffective Analysis of the Market and Industry:** A patent analysis considers comparable patents based on similar market transactions to assess the patent's utility and technological specificity. However, such analysis is not always reliable as all technologies are different, and it is immensely difficult to gauge the impact of technology with certainty. An expert IP professional can provide correct advice at this juncture.

- **Not Consulting an Expert:** It is preferable to seek advice from a competent, experienced, and efficient IP consultant who can assist with complicated procedures like IP valuation, patent litigation, revenue strategies, buyer identification, patent codes, technological knowledge, and patent laws, as well as studying international databases to increase the inventor's work's value and quality simultaneously. Without in-depth market knowledge and technical expertise, monetization cannot proceed profitably.

- **Impatience:** This is quite common while monetizing patents. The monetization process is highly sluggish and must be done carefully. Otherwise, this error could cost the patent holder a lot of money. Therefore, by avoiding these typical errors, patent owners can increase their income significantly and enable their property to realize its full financial potential.

- **Systematic IP Valuation**: Patent owners frequently skip performing an IP valuation, which can be greatly helpful in determining the worth of your patent. When calculating a patent's current value, the nature of the innovation and competition analysis must be considered. IP valuation can be used to determine the best price for your patent. You can get paid less if you do not know how much your patent is now worth. It includes extensive market knowledge, which is essential for the patent's fundamental operation in relation to the market.

- **Partnering with the Right Company:** It is not easy to traverse the path of patent monetization on your own because it encompasses many technical and non-technical components and calls for idea brainstorming. To monetize your patents, the proper firm must have a comprehensive understanding and practical experience. Choosing the correct organization to partner with can assist you in achieving the highest ROI.

04-14:INNOVATION LIFE CYCLE

Innovations are challenging with uncertainty, risk, and complexity. Developing structured processes and phases is crucial for successful new product development, ensuring creativity and focus while avoiding mistakes and maximizing innovation performance.

Innovation is the key to success in any industry, but it's not just about coming up with a great idea. It's about taking that idea and turning it into a reality. That's where the four phases of successful innovation come in: inspiration, ideation, implementation, and iteration.

Innovations are challenges, characterized by uncertainty, risk and complexity. This makes it all the more important to develop a structure, system and methodology for the development, development and implementation of new products. This also includes a practical innovation process according to different phases, which on the one hand leaves enough space for creativity, but also leads to the goal in a focused manner.

The 4 phases of innovation

The phases of an innovation, ie an innovation process, can be divided into four main steps:

1.   **Idea**: collection of innovation potentials, derivation of ideas, evaluation and release of ideas.

2.   **Concept**: Extensive analysis and derivation of concepts for the solution, implementation and marketing.

3.   **Solution**: Development and testing of the solutions to the finished product.

4.   **Market**: Arouse and fulfill a customer's needs by implementing in procurement, production and logistics as well as marketing and sales.

The development of the individual phases depends very much on the individual requirements of a company. For example, larger companies have a more intensive assessment with several decision-making stages in the idea phase. Or technology-intensive organizations with complex products will have a more comprehensive production implementation. And service providers have different requirements.

Phase 1: Ideas:

An innovation process always starts with the search for and finding innovative potentials and the derivation of ideas, which are subsequently evaluated.

An innovation potential is a newly discovered opportunity for innovation. This can be:

- An unfulfilled customer requirement
- A problem with the customer
- A possible new market
- A new technical solution.

There are countless possibilities for tracking down innovation potentials. There are essentially two different approaches:

- **Targeted search**: The search for potentials is based on the innovation strategy and the derived search fields. Various methods are used to collect ideas internally and externally e.g. creativity workshops, lead user workshops, idea competitions.

- **Random Finding**: One encounters randomly discovering impulses for potentials. For example, one finds a new technology in searches. However, employees can also generate impetus via the company's suggestion or on the basis of customer feedback.

An idea emerges from the potential for innovation, a thought-like construct, such as the new solution in the sense of a new product or a new service. In practice, it can merge into a one-pager with a description and sketch. In the case of a first description of the ideas, the reason why the idea is relevant to the company, the potential and the usefulness of the idea is important. The conclusion of the first phase makes the idea assessment. On the basis of defined criteria, the potential benefits and the feasibility of the company are evaluated. Based on this, the idea is given a priority and the release for the next phase is decided where the objectives and expectations are also concretized.

Phase 2: Concept:
From Phase 1 comes a concrete and released idea with goals and expectations. This is followed by an intensive analysis phase in order to gather as much information as possible about the idea and its further processing:
- Market and customer requirements
- Market potential, e.g. Market size, market attractiveness
- Chances, e.g., Differentiation possibilities for the competition
- Risks and feasibility, e.g. Technical feasibility, market entry barriers
- Framework conditions, e.g. Laws, standards, patents

The most intensive and important analysis is that of the customer requirements, for example:
- What are the needs of customers?
- Are there any unfulfilled or unconscious customer needs?
- Which customer problems are there and should be resolved?
- What is the importance of needs?

Here, a systematic approach with professional methods such as customer interviews, focus groups, lead user workshops or customer observations is recommended in order to gain the greatest possible insight. Especially Lead Users are a very valuable source, because they have many experiences and many own ideas and solutions as advanced users.

On the basis of the analyzes, first concepts are developed with regard to the
- Solution
- Implementation
- Marketing

The solution first includes the requirements for the new product, the specification. Furthermore, there are first solution concepts in the form of descriptions, sketches or models.
For a successful and feasible implementation, first thoughts have to be gathered for an implementation concept. It covers procurement, production and logistics.
Marketing is also very important. The best solution is not successful if it is not marketed well. This includes the product strategy, which defines the positioning, the USP, target markets, possible sales channels, the pricing strategy, etc. This strategy is the basis for marketing and distribution throughout the product life cycle.

In order to release the idea or concept for the next phase, a concept evaluation is necessary. It analyzes the requirements for solution, implementation and marketing thoroughly. Particular attention is paid to the solution concept, which is best evaluated with future customers and users.

The optimal approach is iterative, where initial raw concepts are evaluated and continuously developed in continuous feedback loops until a coherent, first-class concept is established.

Depending on the scope of the concept phase, an innovation project can already be started here in order to work with the tools of the project management.

Phase 3: Solution

The aim of Phase 3 is to develop a ready-to-use solution that can be brought to the market. Solutions are being developed, prototypes built and tests carried out. In addition to concept and lab tests, the tests also include market tests under real conditions in order to gain comprehensive feedback. Once the solution has reached maturity, it will be released for implementation and marketing. At the same time, the concepts for implementation and marketing are further developed and adapted. Outputs of this phase are usually technical specifications, CADs and know-how for application and production.

Phase 4: Market

The last phase is about bringing the product to the potential customers. On the one hand, this requires the physical availability of the product. These include procurement, production and logistics based on defined concepts.

On the other hand, the customer is aroused and then fulfilled. All marketing and sales channels are activated. As a basis, internal sales must be convinced and trained in order to bring the products to the customers in the main step. All these activities can be summarized as innovation marketing. At the end of the innovation phases, the new product is transferred to product lifecycle management in the responsibility of product management. On the basis of the continuous evaluation and analysis of the product on the market by, for example, customer feedback or quantitative market analyzes, measures are taken to increase sales, margins and customer satisfaction.

Process models

Various process models are available for the management of the innovation phases. The most popular in practice are the

- Stage gate process,
- Design Thinking,
- Lean start-up and
- Scrum.

Regardless of the chosen process model, the content and sequence of the phases are always the same. Only the structure and type of settlement are different.

Conclusion: 4 phases of innovation

Innovative processes after phases are indispensable. This is because they create structure and systematicity to avoid mistakes and to increase the innovative performance. This ensures that all important steps are completed in a timely and correct manner. If there were no processes and phases, one would orientate without orientation constantly back and forth rather than focused on the goal.

<u>**Scaling Up the Product:**</u>

Scaling up a product patent involves several stages, from initial development to commercialization. Once you've secured your intellectual property (IP) through a patent, the next major step is bringing your invention to market. This requires careful planning in terms of production, manufacturing, and distribution. Here's a breakdown of the key steps involved in scaling up a product patent:

1. Prototype Testing and Refinement

- **Test the prototype**: After you have a working prototype, it's essential to conduct extensive testing to ensure the product performs as intended. This may include stress tests, user experience testing, and market validation.
- **Iterate based on feedback**: Based on test results, refine the design or functionality. The patent should already cover the key design or technology, but small refinements might be necessary for the final version.

2. Manufacturing & Production Planning

- **Pilot production runs**: Conduct a pilot run of your product to identify issues in the manufacturing process. It's important to work with a manufacturer that can scale production when the time comes. During this stage, evaluate the costs, time efficiency, and quality control measures.
- **Supply chain management**: Establish a reliable supply chain for sourcing materials and components. Be prepared for potential disruptions or shortages.
- **Manufacturing partnerships**: If you're not manufacturing in-house, identify a reputable manufacturer who can handle the scale you need and adhere to quality standards. This might involve negotiating contracts with factories or scaling up your own facilities.

3. Regulatory Compliance

- **Industry-specific certifications**: Depending on your product's industry, you may need to acquire certifications or approvals (e.g., CE marking for European markets, FDA approval for health products).
- **Quality control and testing**: Compliance with regulatory standards means ensuring that your product is safe, effective, and high-quality. This could involve various certifications, like ISO for manufacturing processes, or specific industry certifications (e.g., UL for electrical products).

4. Funding and Investment

- **Secure capital**: Scaling production often requires significant capital investment. You might seek venture capital, angel investors, or loans to fund the scaling process. This will also include financial projections and demonstrating the product's potential return on investment.
- **Cost optimization**: As you scale, you'll need to find ways to reduce production costs. This might involve negotiating better deals with suppliers, increasing production volume, or automating parts of the manufacturing process.

5. Marketing & Branding

- **Create a marketing strategy**: For a patented product, brand identity is crucial. Establish a clear marketing plan that explains what makes your patented technology or design unique and why it provides value over competitors. This could include digital marketing, influencer partnerships, trade shows, and product demos.
- **Build a website and e-commerce platform**: Having a strong online presence is critical. You can leverage e-commerce platforms or your own website to generate direct sales or lead generation.
- **Launch strategy**: Plan a product launch that captures media attention and sets up the foundation for ongoing marketing efforts.

6. Intellectual Property Management

- **Patent enforcement**: With your patent secured, it's important to monitor the market for infringement. If competitors attempt to copy your design or technology, you can enforce your patent rights, potentially leading to legal action.
- **Expand IP portfolio**: Consider filing additional patents to protect variations or improvements on your initial product. Broadening your IP portfolio can help prevent competitors from encroaching on your market.

7. Distribution and Sales Channels

- **Retail partnerships**: If you plan to sell through traditional retail channels, begin establishing relationships with retailers or distributors who can get your product onto store shelves.
- **Direct-to-consumer sales**: Many companies now scale by selling directly to consumers through online platforms. This could mean setting up an e-commerce platform or using existing platforms like Amazon.
- **International expansion**: Once you're established in your home market, scaling internationally can offer new revenue streams. This involves understanding local regulations, customs, and distribution networks.

8. Customer Support and Feedback Loop

- **Customer support**: A strong customer support system is essential for long-term success. Offering warranties, easy returns, and troubleshooting resources can build customer trust.
- **Continuous feedback**: As your product sales, customer feedback becomes invaluable. Use reviews, surveys, and direct outreach to continually refine and improve your product.

9. Sustainability & Scalability

- **Eco-friendly practices**: Consider implementing sustainable practices in your production process to reduce your carbon footprint. Many consumers today are drawn to companies with strong sustainability credentials.
- **Scalable operations**: Make sure that your systems—whether in production, customer service, or sales—are designed for scalability. This way, you can grow smoothly without a massive increase in operational costs.

Distribution- patent Product Development:

In product development, patents play a crucial role in safeguarding inventions and ensuring exclusive rights for the patent holder. They protect novel products and methods, granting the inventor the right to make, use, or sell the invention for a specific period. Patents incentivize innovation and provide legal protection for inventions, impacting distribution strategies.

Retirement-End of Patent Lifecycle

The **end of the patent lifecycle** typically coincides with the **retirement** of a patented product or technology. Here's an overview of what that process looks like, along with the factors that impact the end of a patent lifecycle:

1. Patent Expiry

Patents generally last for **20 years** from the filing date of the application (this can vary in some jurisdictions). Once the patent expires, the protected technology or innovation enters the **public domain**, and anyone can use or produce it without facing legal repercussions. The end of this term marks the official "retirement" of the patent's exclusivity.

- **Utility Patents** (for inventions) last **20 years**.
- **Design Patents** (for ornamental designs) typically last **15 years** from grant.
- **Plant Patents** (for new plant varieties) also last **20 years**.

After the expiration, the owner no longer has exclusive rights and cannot prevent others from using the technology.

2. Market Dynamics

The end of the patent lifecycle doesn't always align with the exact expiration date because factors like **market competition**, **product development**, and **consumer demand** might influence a company's decision to phase out a product even before the patent expires.

- **Generic competition**: Once the patent expires, generic versions (if applicable) of a drug or technology can enter the market, leading to increased competition and price drops.
- **Product obsolescence**: As newer technologies emerge, a product may become outdated, even before the patent expires.

3. Post-Patent Period (Generic or Follow-On Products)

After the patent expires, a number of things can happen:

- **Generics/Knockoffs**: Especially in pharmaceuticals, generic manufacturers can produce a cheaper version of a drug that is no longer patent-protected, typically leading to a drop in price for the original patented product.
- **Patent Evergreening**: Companies sometimes make minor modifications to a patented technology or product to extend patent protection. This can involve creating new patents for improvements to the original product.
- **Brand loyalty and differentiation**: In some cases, companies may use branding strategies, superior quality, or product enhancements to keep customers even when competitors can legally produce similar products.

4. Retirement Strategies

When the patent is nearing expiration or when market conditions dictate, companies may develop a **retirement strategy** for their products:

- **Phase-out**: Gradually winding down production of the patented product, especially if the market becomes too competitive or the technology is outdated.
- **Reinvestment**: The Company may reinvest in innovation, possibly developing newer technologies or products that extend beyond the scope of the expired patent.
- **Licensing or Sale**: Some companies opt to license their expired patents or sell them to other parties, often in different markets, to continue generating revenue.

5. Considerations for IP Strategy

Even as a patent expires, companies must decide what to do with the **intellectual property (IP)** that surrounds the product:

- **Trademarks:** While the patent expires, companies often maintain trademarks on product names, designs, and branding, which continue to offer legal protection.

- **Trade Secrets**: Certain confidential business information or manufacturing processes may still be kept as trade secrets to maintain a competitive edge even after a patent expires.

6. Example: Pharmaceuticals

The pharmaceutical industry offers one of the clearest examples of patent expiry and product retirement:

- When a blockbuster drug's patent expires, generic manufacturers can produce cheaper versions, significantly lowering the price of the drug.
- The original manufacturer may attempt to shift to a new formulation, a combination therapy, or a different version of the drug to extend market exclusivity.
- Once the patent for a particular drug expires, it's often "retired" from the brand's flagship lineup, while the focus shifts to newer products or improved versions.

04-15:IPR VALUATION

Intellectual Property Rights (IPR) valuation is the process of determining the monetary worth of intangible assets like patents, trademarks, copyrights, and trade secrets. This valuation is crucial for various business decisions, including mergers and acquisitions, licensing agreements, financial reporting, and legal disputes.

Prerequisites for IPR Valuation :
To be able to value an IP asset, the asset should meet the following conditions:

- It must be separately identifiable (subject to specific identification and with a recognizable description)
- There should be tangible evidence of the existence of the asset (e.g., a contract, a license, a registration document, record in financial statements, etc.)
- It should have been created at an identifiable point in time.
- It should be capable of being legally enforced and transferred.
- Its income stream should be separately identifiable and isolated from those of other business assets.
- It should be able to be sold independently of other business assets.
- It should be subject to destruction or termination at an identifiable point in time.

Why is IPR Valuation Important?
- **Transactions:**

Determining the fair market value of IP is essential for selling, licensing, or entering into commercial arrangements based on the IP.

- **Financial Reporting:**

IPR valuation is necessary for accurate financial statements and reporting.

- **Legal Disputes:**

In litigation, establishing the value of IP is crucial for determining damages and other legal outcomes.

- **Internal Management:**

IPR valuation can help manage and optimize IP assets within an organization.

- **Taxation:**

Understanding the value of IP is important for tax planning and compliance.

- **Investment Decisions:**

It helps investors assess the value of a company's intangible assets.

- **Licensing and Partnerships:**

IPR valuation facilitates negotiations for licensing agreements and partnerships, ensuring fair terms.

PATENT VALUATION:

It is very important for businesses to account for a patent's value in their books. This value is especially important to businesses in transactions involving mergers and acquisitions, business dissolution, bankruptcy, and infringement analysis. A key part of valuing a patent is to obtain a value of the invention in question. It does not make good business sense to obtain a patent on an invention that will not result in a suitable return for the inventor. Because patents are intangible assets, it is often difficult to assign a monetary value to them. The most common patent-valuation method is the economic-analysis method.

The Economic Analysis Method:
The economic analysis valuation method has three approaches: cost, income, and market.

a)Market Approach : In case a reason for valuation calls for a valuation which draws on market prices, this is generally only possible if and to the extent the market prices concern sufficiently comparable assets. In addition, the market concerned must be active. A market is active if all the following conditions are fulfilled: a) the goods in the market are homogenous; b) purchasers and sellers willing to enter into agreement can generally be found at any time; and c) prices are publicly known. Since intangible assets are generally not traded in active markets, it must be determined whether comparable.

Transactions can be drawn upon for the valuation of an intangible asset. By means of analogies a comparison between the observable price for a comparable object and the value sought for the (to be valuated) intangible asset can be made. Since adequate data from comparable transactions are very rarely accessible, it is necessary to provide a detailed background and reasoning for the choice of comparable transactions and the key indicators deducted therefrom.

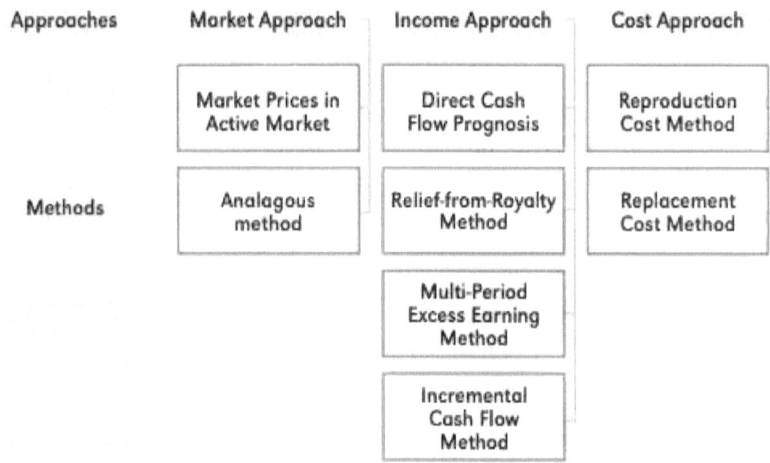

Advantages:
- relatively straightforward evaluation method
- useful to check the validity of other approaches.

Disadvantages:
- limited formal markets for IP.
- relevant pricing information not usually public
- uniqueness of IP makes direct comparison difficult.

b) Income Approach :
The income approach assumes that the value of an intangible asset results from the future success which will be generated by the asset in the form of cash flows. The value of an asset is

considered to be the sum of the present value of the future cash flows that can be generated as of the day of valuation (Discounted Cash Flow) from the use of the intangible asset within the expected economic useful life and possibly its divesture/disposal. The central tasks within a valuation are therefore the prognosis of the cash flows relevant for the valuation and the determination of the capitalization interest rate/capitalization cost rate depicting the risk of the concerned intangible asset. A major task in connection with the valuation of single assets is isolating the specific cash flows that can be credited to the asset to be evaluated. These cash flows are a type of added value to the cash flows that could be generated without the specific asset. The planning period for the cash flows is to be based on the economical useful life of the intangible asset or its remaining useful life.

The useful life of intangible assets is usually limited wherefore a valuation may not consider revenues in perpetuity from such an asset. In exceptional cases, revenues in perpetuity may be considered in case the useful life of the asset is sufficiently long so that it becomes irrelevant whether the present value of a limited series of cash flows is considered or whether the present value of cash flows in perpetuity is considered. The income approach allows valuations from different perspectives. Aside from standardized concepts of value, e.g., the fair value, which are relevant for company external objectives, it is possible to include individual and subjective components and thereby reach strategically relevant decision values. This is relevant in cases in which the valuation is carried out not only for tax or accounting purposes, but for example shall be used for a purchase price finding or shall facilitate other decision-making processes. There are basically four different methods to evaluate intangible assets based on an income approach each of which allows for a different way of isolating the specific cash flow for the relevant intangible asset. These methods are generally equivalent. In individual cases, one method or the other may be better suited than another due to the importance of the specific intangible asset for a company or the fact that the information required for the application of one specific method may be difficult to come by.

Within the income approach, the following methods are applicable:

- Direct Cash Flow Prognosis Method,
- Relief-from-Royalty Method,
- Incremental Cash Flow Method and
- Multi-Period Excess Earnings Method

Advantages:
- relatively simple
- likely availability of required inputs from company's financial statements and market information - may be possible to identify/forecast cash flows.

Disadvantages:
- can be an uncertain method and subject to subjective assumptions.
- both uncertain and distant cash flows and the discount rate have to be estimated

c) Cost Approach:

The third approach for the evaluation of intangible assets consists of the Reproduction Cost Method and the Replacement Cost Method. However, this approach has a major conceptual weakness since it is not use driven and since the data used always refers to the past. For these reasons, the cost approach for the valuation of intangible assets can generally only be used to verify plausibility or to determine minimum price thresholds, e.g. in purchase price negotiations. In applying the cost approach, the costs.

Advantages:
- ➢ patents become visible in the company's books and patent awareness is increased.
- ➢ useful indicator of patent value in the case of patents whose future benefit is not yet evident.

Disadvantages:
- no direct correlation between cost of development and the future revenue of patents
- future revenue from patents is not considered.
- the cost method can encourage overspending.

TRADEMARK VALUATION:

Once a trademark is registered, it becomes a company's intangible asset. It can then be sold, licensed, pledged, and even royalty can be earned on it. The worth of a trademark can be used to determine the overall value of a company in the event of a merger or purchase. **Analyzing a brand's value** through its Intellectual Property is a wonderful technique for filtering and deciding on numerous investment opportunities and developing fresh and distinctive marketing strategies that will help further increase the brand's image. Companies must comprehend the worth of this asset at this point.

Importance of Trademark Valuation:
Trademark valuation plays a critical role in several business scenarios beyond mergers and acquisitions. Some of the key reasons to assess trademark value include:
- **Licensing and Royalty Agreements:** Companies monetize trademarks through licensing. Accurate valuation ensures fair royalty rates and compliance with transfer pricing regulations.
- **Litigation and Disputes:** In legal contexts such as trademark infringement or bankruptcy, valuation helps determine damages or settlement figures.
- **Financial Reporting and Compliance:** Valuations may be required for accounting purposes, especially under GAAP or IFRS standards where trademarks are considered intangible assets.
- **Tax Planning:** For estate planning or intercompany transfers, a reliable valuation is essential to avoid disputes with tax authorities.
- **Internal Strategy:** Valuation supports investment decisions, brand portfolio management, and internal performance assessments.

Methods of Valuation of Trademark:
The **valuation of trademarks** is an important practice, especially given the growing number of cases in which intangible assets such as intellectual property are valued higher than tangible assets. To create pricing and contract terms for transactions such as a purchase or sale, a license, or a contribution to a partnership such as a joint venture or co-branding campaign. To assist in creating and implementing particular corporate or individual tax strategies or ensuring compliance with tax legislation relating to intercompany transactions (i.e., transfer pricing), corporate reorganizations, and trust and estate issues.
Valuation analysts use three widely accepted valuation methodologies to determine the worth of intangible property, such as trademarks. The following are some of the most often used ways to value intangible assets:

- **Cost approach** – The cost technique is less frequent than the other ways of estimating trademark value. Because a trademark gives the owner exclusive rights, it provides economic benefits that aren't always represented at the expense of creating and developing the property. As a result, the cost technique is not always appropriate for a trademark valuation analysis.

- **Income approach** – In trademark valuation, income approach strategies are frequently employed. In practice, numerous income methodologies and valuation methods are applied. Calculate the present value of future income streams estimated to be produced by the use of the trademark during its remaining useful life to determine the worth of a trademark (RUL). In general, the procedures for determining those income sources vary.

- **Market approach** – Trademark sales are less prevalent than trademark licensing since trademarks are connected with certain items and enterprises. As a result, there is a good amount of publicly available information about trademark licensing, which is frequently gleaned from financial reports filed with the Securities and Exchange Commission. This data enables the researcher to create trademark comparison units, most notably a royalty rate.

- **Relief from royalty method** – The commonly used model implies that if a company possesses a trademark, it is exempt from paying a royalty, allowing for the estimation of a hypothetical royalty payment. This analysis is also classified as a market approach.

- **Intercompany transfer price method** – The Internal Revenue Code and related rules govern transfer pricing procedures, which are a specialist area of valuation. The Section 482 regulations compel the transfer price analyst to use the "best method" rule to allocate taxable revenue between related parties in certain transactions.

COPYRIGHT VALUATION:

Copyright valuation determines the monetary worth of a copyrighted work, considering factors like future income potential, comparable market transactions, and the cost of recreating the work. It's a crucial process for licensing deals, mergers, acquisitions, litigation, and tax purposes.

Importance of copyright valuation:

- **Licensing:** Determining fair royalty rates for allowing others to use a copyrighted work.

- **Mergers & Acquisitions:** Identifying the value of a company's copyright portfolio during M&A transactions.

- **Litigation:** Establishing damages in copyright infringement cases.

- **Tax Compliance:** Determining the fair market value for tax purposes.

- **Financing:** Securing loans or other financial instruments using copyright assets as collateral.

Widely adopted copyright valuation approaches:

When carrying out a copyright valuation Intangible Business adopts widely accepted approaches based on a combination of the income, market and cost approaches.

1. The income approach: It uses estimates of future estimated economic benefits or cash flows and discounts them, for the associated time and risks involved, to a present value. Each type of copyright has key sensitivities to consider such as the duration of the copyright and the expected lifetime of its creator. Another key consideration during copyright valuation is what drives the value of the copyright. The Income method values the IP asset based on the amount of economic income that the IP asset – Copyright is expected to generate, adjusted to its present-day value.

To determine the Economic Income

• Project the revenue flow or cost savings generated by the Copyright over the remaining useful life (RUL) of the asset.

• Offset those revenues/savings by costs related directly to the Copyright. Here, Costs could comprise labour, materials, required capital investment and any appropriate economic rents or capital charges.

• Take account of the risk to discount the amount of income to a present-day value by using the discount rate or the capitalization rate.

The Various Income Approach Methods typically involve some form of the following types of Analysis.

1. Incremental Income Analysis: This is the estimation of the difference between the amount of income that the owner/operator would generate with the use of the subject copyright and the amount of income the same owner/operator would generate without the use of the subject copyright.

2. Profit Split Income Analysis: The estimation of the total income that the owner/operator would generate from the use of the copyright where the total income estimate is split between the copyright and all of the other tangible and intangible assets that contribute to the generation of the owner/operator total income estimate.

3. Residual or excess Income Analysis: The estimation of the residual owner/operator income with the ownership/operation of the copyright. This residual income analysis is accomplished by first estimating the total owner/operator income. The analyst then identifies and values all of the owner/operator tangible and intangible assets. A fair rate of return, which represents a capital charge or an economic rent, is then assigned to each category of the tangible and intangible assets. The analyst would then subtract the capital charge on contributory assets from the total owner/operator income estimate. Finally, the residual or excess income is assigned to the copyright.

2. The market approach: It uses market-based indicators of value. For copyright this can be transactions involving selling, buying, franchising or licensing copyright and related IP rights, which are often in practice bundled together. The Market Method is based on comparison with the actual price paid for a similar IP asset under comparable circumstances. Market approach methods are commonly used in a copyright valuation analysis.

3. The cost approach: This method is based on the intention of establishing the value of an IP asset by calculating the cost of developing same or identical IP asset either internally or externally.

Note: The Cost Method is generally the least used method as, in most cases, it is considered suitable only as a supplement to the income method. Both creation cost and re-creation cost methods may be used with regard to copyright valuation analysis. In all cost approach valuation analyses of copyrights, the analyst should consider as cost components both, the developer's profit and the entrepreneurial incentive – both of which often represent the largest components of value.

INDUSTRIAL DESIGN VALUATION:

Industrial design valuation involves assessing the worth of design work, considering factors like its impact on brand, market value, and potential for future innovation. It's a multifaceted process that goes beyond aesthetics, encompassing functionality, manufacturability, and user experience.

Importance of Industrial Design Valuation:

1. **IP Protection & Licensing:**
   - Industrial designs are a form of **intellectual property (IP)**.
   - Valuation is essential for licensing deals, IP sales, or franchising.
   - Helps determine **royalty rates** or lump-sum payments.
2. **Business Strategy & Branding:**
   - Well-designed products often drive **brand recognition** and customer loyalty.
   - Valuing the design helps in **strategic decisions** about pricing, marketing, and investment in design innovation.
3. **Mergers, Acquisitions, & Investment:**
   - During M&A or funding rounds, investors need to know the **true value of a company's design assets**.
   - A strong portfolio of well-valued designs can significantly boost a company's market worth.
4. **Litigation & Dispute Resolution:**
   - In cases of IP infringement, a proper valuation helps courts **quantify damages**.
   - It strengthens legal claims by demonstrating the **economic value** of the design.
5. **Financial Reporting & Taxation:**
   - For companies that capitalize IP, design valuation plays a role in **balance sheet reporting**.
   - It also affects **taxation strategies** when dealing with amortization or IP asset transfers.
6. **Insurance:**
   - Businesses can insure valuable industrial designs—valuation is necessary to determine **coverage amounts and premiums**.

Methods : Valuing industrial design involves assessing the worth of a product's design elements—such as form, function, aesthetics, and user experience—in financial, strategic, and legal terms. This can be important for mergers, acquisitions, IP licensing, litigation, or investment decisions. Here are the primary **industrial design valuation methods**:

1. Cost-Based Methods:
Estimate value based on the costs incurred in developing the design.

- **Historical Cost Method**: Adds up all design-related costs (e.g. R&D, prototyping, testing, designer salaries).
- **Replacement Cost Method**: Estimates how much it would cost to recreate the design from scratch.
- **Reproduction Cost Method**: Focuses on replicating the original design exactly, often used in legal disputes.

Pros: Easy to calculate if records are available
Cons: Doesn't reflect market demand or competitive advantage

2. Market-Based Methods:
Value is determined based on comparable market transactions.
- **Comparable Transactions**: Looks at recent sales, licenses, or royalties of similar designs or products.
- **Industry Benchmarks**: Uses standard industry metrics (e.g., royalty rates in the sector, valuation multiples).

Pros: Reflects real-world data
Cons: Good comparable are often hard to find, especially for unique designs

3. Income-Based Methods:
Estimates the future economic benefits generated by the design.
- **Relief from Royalty**: Estimates what the company would pay to license the design if it didn't own it.
- **Incremental Income Method**: Values the extra income/profit attributable specifically to the design, beyond the base product.
- **Discounted Cash Flow (DCF)**: Projects design-driven cash flows and discounts them to present value.

Pros: Captures actual value contributed by design
Cons: Requires many assumptions and future forecasts

4. Option-Based Methods
Used when design-related decisions involve uncertainty or flexibility.
- **Real Options Valuation**: Values the flexibility that a design offers (e.g., ability to adapt or be extended to new products).
- Rarely used unless the design is part of a complex or evolving business model (e.g., platform products, modular systems).

04-16:BUSINESS CASES: IPR

The different landmark Judgements on IPR Law in India are as follows:

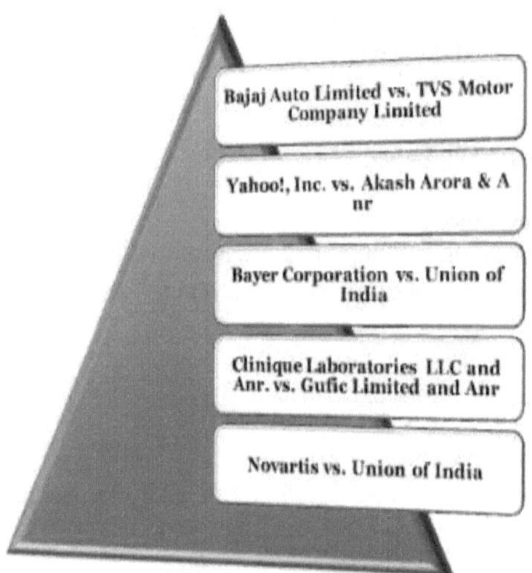

1.Bajaj Auto Ltd vs. TVS Motor Company Limited [JT 2009 (12) SC 103]
In this case of the IPR Law is related to a Dispute over Patent for the Usage of a Twin-Spark Plug Engine Technology. The Supreme Court (SC) of India, in this one of the Landmark Judgments on IPR Law in India, has directed all the Indian courts for the speedy trial and disposal of Intellectual Property (IP) related case laws in the courts of India.
In this case, a 2-year-old dispute which involved two big companies, which were locked in a Patent dispute over the usage of twin-spark-plug engine technology. The Supreme Court (SC) of India observed that the case laws relating to the matters of Trademarks, Patents, and Copyrights that are pending for several years and litigations are mainly fought between the parties about the temporary injunction.
The Supreme Court has directed that the hearing in the matters of Intellectual Property in India should be proceeded on a day-to-day basis, and the final judgment related to a case should be given generally within 4 months from the date on which the suit was filed. The Supreme Court (SC) of India further directed all the tribunals and courts in the territory of the country to faithfully and punctually carry out the orders, as mentioned above.

2.Yahoo!, Inc. vs. Akash Arora & Anr [1999 (19) PTC 201 (Del)]
This is one of the first Landmark Judgements on IPR Law in India that is related to the protection of Intellectual Property Rights on the Internet. The Delhi High Court (HC), in this case, that is known till date as one of the Landmark Judgments on IPR Law related to cyber-squatting held that the domain name of a product serves the same function as of a Trademark and hence, a domain name is entitled to equal protection.
In this case, the domain names of the plaintiff 'Yahoo!' and the domain name of the defendant 'Yahoo India!', were nearly phonetically similar and identical. In such a case, there was a very strong possibility that the users of the internet using the domain name of the plaintiff will get

confused and deceived into believing that both the domain names of the defendant and plaintiff have some common source or connection.

The Delhi High Court also observed in this case that the disclaimer used by the defendants was not sufficient because the Internet nature is such that the use of a similar or identical domain name cannot be remedied by a disclaimer, and that also it did not matter that the domain name 'yahoo' is a dictionary word. The name 'Yahoo' had acquired distinctiveness and uniqueness when it was associated with the plaintiff. The Bombay High Court (HC), in the case of *Rediff Communication vs. Cyber booth & Anr [2000 PTC 209]*, also observed that the importance and value of a domain name are as a corporate advantage to a company.

3. Bayer Corporation vs. Union of India [162(2009) DLT 371]

In the case of *Bayer Corporation vs. Union of India*, in the place of filing an Infringement suit, an inventive writ petition can be filed in the Delhi High Court (HC) desiring that since the applications of Cipla "SORANIB" allegedly infringed the plaintiff's Patent, Cipla's approval of marketing application under the Drugs Act should not be entertained or processed. It was for the first time that an attempt was made to link the approval of a drug to Patent Infringement in India. However, the Delhi High Court (HC), disagreeing with the injunction, levied a substantial cost of Rs. 6.75 Lakh to prevent any such future attempts.

Bayer Corporation depended on the argument that a combined reading of *Section 2* of the *Drugs and Cosmetic Act*, with *Section 48* of the *Indian Patent Act, 1970* establishes a Mechanism Patent Linkage under which no approval from the market for a drug can be granted if there is a Patent existing over that same drug. The Bayer Corporation also claimed that CIPLA's "SORANIB" is a "Spurious Drug" as well-defined under the Drugs Act, 1940, for which market approval cannot be approved.

The Hon'ble Delhi High Court (HC) of India held that there is no such Drug- Patent Linkage mechanism in the territory of India as the objectives of both the Acts are different. Under both the Acts, the authority to determine the Patent standards, is under the exclusive domain of the Controller of Patent under the Patent Act, 1970.

Furthermore, the Patent linkage will have an objectionable effect on the Policy of Public Health of India. The Delhi High Court further held that the market approval of any drug does not amount to Patent Infringement. Therefore, the Infringement of Patent cannot be presumed; it is required to be established in the court of law. Such an adjudication is beyond the limits and jurisdiction of the Drug Authorities.

On the issue of Cipla's "SORANIB" being a spurious drug, the Delhi High Court held that Cipla's "SORANIB" drug does not come under the category of spurious goods as there is not any element of Passing-Off like imitation or deception present in this drug of CIPLA.

4. Clinique Laboratories LLC and Another vs. Gufic Limited and Anr [MANU/DE/0797/2009]

In this case, a suit for infringement has been filed by a registered Trademark owner against a registered Trademark Holder. The present dispute, in this case, was between the registered Trademark of the plaintiff and the defendant. It is very interesting to note that before the filing of the suit of Infringement, the plaintiff Clinique had filed a petition of Cancellation before the Trademarks Registrar of India, against the defendant Gufic Limited for the Cancellation of Trademark of the defendant "CLINIQ."

Under the provisions of *Section 124(1) (ii) of the Trademarks Act, 1999*, any suit is liable to be stayed till the petition of Cancelation of Trademark is finally decided by the competent authority of Trademarks. However, under the provisions of *Section 124(5) of the Trademarks Act, 1999*, the court has the authority to pass an interlocutory order, including the orders of granting interim injunction, appointment of receiver, keeping of account, or attachment of any property.

In the case, the court held that an Infringement suit of a registered Trademark is maintainable against another registered owner of an identical or similar trademark. This case is considered to be one of the Landmark Judgements on IPR Law in India.

It was further held that in this case that in such an Infringement suit, while staying the proceedings of the suit and there is any decision pending the decision on Rectification or Cancellation petition, the court is allowed to pass an interim injunction for restraining the usage of the registered Trademark by the defendant, considering the condition that the court is convinced prima facie of the invalidity of the **registration of Trademark** of the defendant. In this case, an interim injunction was granted in the favor of the plaintiff till the disposal of the petition of Cancellation by the competent authority.

5. Novartis vs. Union of India [CIVIL APPEAL No. 2706-2716 OF 2013 (ARISING OUT OF SLP(C) Nos. 20539-20549 OF 2009]

This is one of the Landmark Judgements on IPR Law in India. The case is related to the rejection of a Patent for a Drug that was not 'inventive' or had any superior'efficacy.' **The Company** Novartis filed a registration of Patent application for one of its drugs called as Gleevec by covering the drug under the word invention mentioned and provided under *Section 3 of the Patent Act, 1970*[1]. The Supreme Court (SC) of India rejected the application of Novartis after a period of 7 years-long battle. *The reasons cited by the Supreme Court (SC) were:*

- There was no invention of any new drug, a mere discovery of an already existing drug will not amount to an invention under the *Patent Act, 1970.*

- Supreme Court of India supported the view that under the **Patent Act, 1970**, for the grant of pharmaceutical **Patents in India**, apart from proving the traditional tests of inventive step, novelty, and application, there is a new test of improved therapeutic efficacy for claims that cover some incremental changes to already existing drugs which the Novartis's drug also did not qualify.

This case became one of the Landmark Judgments on IPR Law in India because the Supreme Court (SC) looked beyond the procedures and into the fact that the attempt of all such companies to 'evergreen' their respective Patents and make them unreachable at some nominal rates.

Conclusion:

Intellectual Property Rights play a very important role in each sector and have also become the basis for vital decisions of investment. Intellectual Property Rights are exclusive rights provided to the owner of Intellectual Property, and therefore there is a challenge always to maintain a balance between the interests of the society and the innovators. Another important aspect is to have a proper legal framework for the protection of the interests of the innovators and encourage confidence among them that their Intellectual Property will be protected, in turn generating further innovation.

www.ingramcontent.com/pod-product-compliance
Lightning Source LLC
Chambersburg PA
CBHW051233130726
47988CB00001B/331